Grandmothers

Writing American Women
Carol A. Kolmerten, *Series Editor*

Grandmothers

Granddaughters Remember

EDITED BY

Marguerite Guzman Bouvard

SYRACUSE UNIVERSITY PRESS

First Edition 1998
98 99 00 01 02 03   6 5 4 3 2 1

The paper used in this publication meets the minimum requirements of
American National Standard for Information Sciences—Permanence of
Paper for Printed Library Materials, ANSI Z39.48-1984. ∞™

Library of Congress Cataloging-in-Publication Data
Grandmothers : granddaughters remember / edited by Marguerite Guzman
Bouvard. — 1st ed.
     p.   cm. — (Writing American women)
     ISBN 0-8156-0534-X (cloth : alk. paper)
     1. Grandmothers—Biography.   2. Women—Family relationships.
3. Intergenerational relations.   I. Bouvard, Marguerite Guzman,
1937– . II. Series.
HQ759.9.G7245 1998
306.874'5—dc21   98-24246

Manufactured in the United States of America

Contents

The Rub of Love

Searching for a Grandmother

Grandmother Histories

Illustrations

ix

Acknowledgments

I WISH TO THANK the following sources for use of materials in this book: Naomi Shihab Nye for permission to reprint "One Village" from *Never in a Hurry: Essays on People and Places* (Columbia: University of South Carolina Press, 1996); Robin Becker for use of the photo of Laura Weiner; Michael Nye for use of the photo of Sitte Khadra; to Jacques for his computer expertise; and to Jean Gould for her perceptive and unwavering support.

Introduction

MANY PEOPLE ARE SURPRISED at the intense lives of older women, as if they were supposed to become faint embers, rather than flaring up in all their colors, as if our lifespans could be segmented and categorized rather than representing a continuum that gathers force and meaning through time. But in this collection, grandmothers claim their rightful place; taking part in historical events, weaving public and private spaces as they tell us stories and revealing their own rich experiences.

What makes these stories so compelling is that they are also a journey into different ways of being. We travel to a small village in the West Bank with poet and essayist naomi Shihab Nye, inhaling lentil soup and orange blossoms, and experiencing the Arab-Israeli conflict first hand as we listen to her Sitti's stories. We sit at Padma Hejmadi's grandmother's knee as she recounts tales told by her own grandmother, accounts of social injustice nested in the joy of a family reunion at the confluence of a jungle and a holy waterfall. With Patricia Traxler, we listen to her Irish grandmother recite Shelley's poetry. As Americans we live in many worlds: *Grandmothers: Granddaughters Remember*, seeks to celebrate the differences that help create our uniqueness.

The grandmothers in this collection represent a wide spectrum of cultures. They are Palestinian, Lebanese, American Indian, Irish, Austro-Hungarian and Italian, Chinese, Cuban, German, English, African American, and Indian and Jewish. Like Aimee Liu's grandmother and Paula Gunn Allen's, they defy social taboos and marry into another culture, creating a kaleidoscope of future generations that experience the thirst for self-discovery. The voices that we claim as *American* are woven from strands that stretch to the four corners of the world.

We enter confluence of private and public space and learn important lessons from our grandmothers' stories, as they are busy preparing dinner, performing household chores, or just sitting down with us. Their stories move through our days with their own force and become part of us as we grow up. One of their most important aspects lies in their repetition. They are like a leitmotif through our years and also a certainty we are able to tap in a very unpredictable world. Through them we learn of our place in the world, of geography and of our connections in time and space. Sometimes we learn through the disconnections we witness as a grandmother moves between the culture she has left and the one she adopts in varying degrees. As we listen to our grandmothers speak, we absorb languages, idioms, viewpoints that are a foil against which we grow, that we either rebel against or accept but always, in the long run, incorporate into the persons we become.

Relieved from the daily work of child rearing or the pressures of combining work with bringing up children, grandmothers do not fade into oblivion. They come into their own, adding to our lives the depth and perspective they have acquired through their experiences. In our highly mobile and fragmented society, the present bears down on our consciousness, leaving little room for either world history or our own family histories. We are made of both, however, and when we ignore them, we lose important perspectives and paths to self-knowledge.

For grandmothers are both living testimonies of their times and players in the whirlwind of historical events. Their stories illuminate larger historical dramas. Many of them have lived through searing times, but rather than being brought down by wars, racial and class prejudices, they have often overcome them, becoming their own person, mingling the sorrows of daily life with a joyous determination. The grandmothers in this collection endured the Nazi occupation of their city with defiance and strength, the political turmoil in Shanghai, the Blitz of London, and the violence and oppression of racism, anti-semitism, and poverty. They demonstrate that injustice is not an abstract concept, but is often a wounded yet triumphant life.

While history books often deny the complexity of the truth, glossing over the injustices visited by the dominant cultural group over minority peoples and women, the histories our grandmothers tell us represent the voices of people who experienced dramatic events first hand or suffered their consequences through migration and loss. Noted author Mary Helen Washington unmasks the words "freedpeople" and "emancipation" to reveal the widespread aggression against suppos-edly freed slaves. Researching her grandmother's life, she uncovered a reality that has remained hidden because it conflicts with our country's vision of its past. Beryl Minkle's Bubba tells us a tale of cultural and re-ligious injustice that also includes the suppression of women's free-dom, a strand of history which has been neglected in the accounts of the oppression of Jews.

Grandmothers' tales are not only oral histories of family but may also serve as models, guiding us and opening up the way for our own becoming. Much as some of us may admire our parents, we do not al-ways wish to emulate them simply because of their proximity and be-cause we wish to chart our own paths. Often, we seem to find an understanding of our dreams and of our struggles for self-knowledge from our grandmothers, whether they guide us as literary or political mentors, or simply as free spirits whose examples sink into our uncon-scious as we grow up. Marilou Awiakta's Grandmother Corn is a spiri-tual guide who honors the balance of genders and illuminates the prominent space due older women that is in stark contrast to the view of women defined by Western culture. The Grandmother called Selu weaves the stages of a woman's life with a spirituality that is immanent rather than remote and abstract.

Even if we take issue with our grandmothers' world views, we gain from them the parameters of our own maps, born out of the spark of contention and the resulting self-awareness. Prizewinning poet Robin Becker's loving conflicts with her grandmother sharpen their respec-tive identities and teach her forbearance, and Christina Chiu's misun-derstandings with her grandmother ultimately lead her to bridge the distances of time and culture that separate them.

In a society that values individualism, the absence of a grandmother is a greater void than we have been willing to admit. Self-knowledge is cultural and generational. When we have not experienced a grand-mother's presence, we may feel dissatisfied as we face the lifetime task of understanding our identities. Martha Collins reflects that she has had to turn to literature for guidance, and Anna Kimmage expresses her yearning for the comfort and sense of belonging a grandmother im-parts. The role of a grandmother in our lives is so important that if we have not known them, we often re-create them in our imaginations or spend our lives wondering who they really were.

Yet our family identity is often a very complex one bringing together different nationalities that may conflict. Paula Gunn Allen, a noted American Indian writer, pursues the elusive trail of a Lebanese great-grandmother for whom she was named. During her journey, she reflects upon the different cultural streams that she carries, finding little resolution and encountering disappointments as well as reflecting upon the injustices of her Sitte's life.

Depending upon our generation or our nationalities, we women may wear our father's name, or our husband's if we are married. However, we also wear the imprint of our grandmother's journey in this world and often her voyage has been a lesson in humanity that runs deeper through our lives than our formal education. A grandmother walks before us as we enter the various phases of life, yet our Western culture rarely celebrates the gifts of older women. The women in this collection reveal what it is to endure, to live well, and to confront the boundaries established by society.

Despite differences in culture, nationality, and personal history, none of the extraordinary women in this book fit into the stereotypes of grandmothers or of older women. They are at once defiant and tradition bound, loving and stubbornly dogmatic, achieving triumphs so at odds with their times that those accomplishments have remained unspoken. Reading these stories and memoirs someone might imagine that any of these women could have had a "brilliant career." But the point is that they were strong and effective presences in their times, while anticipating the future status of women. As our grandmothers taught us, we did not suddenly become, we always were.

Wellesley, Massachusetts   Marguerite G. Bouvard
October 1997

Grandmothers as Mentors

The Day My Grandmother's Eyes Turned to Glass

Patricia Traxler

I'LL ALWAYS REMEMBER THE DAY my grandmother's eyes turned to glass. It was just one moment of one day during the year when I was four, and yet all my life it has haunted me.

It was a quiet autumn afternoon in the small East San Diego house of my childhood. Gran was sitting in her old platform rocker, looking on while my brother Donnie and I colored and cut out the pictures my mother was drawing for us; pictures of flowers, butterflies, beach balls, dogs, cats, ice cream cones, and birds. I was perched on the window seat near Gran's chair, and Mom and Donnie were seated at the coffee table across the living room. We were half listening to a scratchy old Inkspots recording, one of my mother's Salvation Army finds. "I'll get by," the voices crooned, and I'd never heard anything like the way they twined and floated together in the air; the sound was smooth, silky smooth, and sad in a way that seemed to enjoy itself.

I had stopped my cutting for a moment, scissors poised, to watch the way my grandmother's thin hands fit exactly over the carved wood claw at the end of each chair arm. My eyes moved then from Gran's hands to her face, and that was when I saw it: my grandmother's eyes had turned into broken glass, pale, polished blue glass, shattered and sparkling in the light from the window behind me. I couldn't pull my eyes away from her eyes, which were not looking back at mine but were gazing off into what seemed to be nowhere. I wondered how she had done that with her eyes.

Then she spoke, her voice quieter than I'd ever heard it, but emerging from her lips rough and ragged, in a kind of soft croak.

"I'm old," she said.

Somehow then I realized that Gran's eyes hadn't turned into broken glass at all—they were crying; she was crying. I'd never seen my grandmother cry, in fact I'd not seen any adult cry, nor had it occurred to me that such a thing was within the realm of possibility. Crying was something kids did, something Donnie and I might do when we fell down or got punished for misbehaving. Our crying was noisy, though, and this crying was silent, which made it seem more serious, something more than just regular crying. And *Gran*, of all people—it didn't make sense to me. I knew her as smart, loving, funny, cranky, holy, opinionated—she was many things, but I'd never known she was sad.

"You're not old, Gran," Donnie said, looking up from the bluebird he was cutting out, and I admired the way my brother was able to speak words of comfort to an adult while I sat on the window seat, paralyzed by shyness and fear in the face of grown-up tears. Donnie was five and a half, nearly two years older than I, and he seemed to possess a familiarity with the larger world that I hadn't yet learned. He'd even begun going away from our house each morning to kindergarten, and he didn't come home till lunch time. I adored and envied him.

I looked at Gran again, and then I scrambled down from the window seat to take one of her hands from the wooden claw of the chair.

"You're not old, Gran," I echoed, unable to come up with my own language of comfort. I looked at her withered hand then—saw the spots, the veins, the bones. Something was definitely wrong with my grandmother's hands. I looked up into her face, felt my voice falter. ". . . are you?"

"Oh, Mother," my own mother said brusquely, "you're not old." The way she said it made the mere idea of getting old seem foolish.

"I'm old," Gran said again, as if none of us had spoken, and although I would always remember that moment, it was only in my adult years that I would fully understand. I witnessed the moment of a harsh realization for my grandmother—the sudden knowledge that she had passed the age of expectation.

As a four-year-old, though, I only knew I'd seen my grandmother crying, and I wanted to understand why. From that day on I watched her, trying to learn how life had let her down. And I often studied the large hand tinted portrait of her that sat on a bookcase in our living room in an ornate gold oval frame, the glass over it convex, rounded outward like a bubble. The picture, taken in Cork when she was around nineteen, shows the well-dressed, prosperous young woman she'd been in Ireland: Nora Dunne, convent-educated, a fresh-faced young woman with upswept auburn hair, a full bust and the wasp waist fashionable at the time, a small corsage of rosebuds below the left shoulder of her pale green-and-ivory striped taffeta dress. What a contrast that image made in a child's mind, when compared with the tiny, brittle-boned, flat-chested old woman I knew as Gran! I would study the portrait for hours and in the wide blue eyes, the rounded planes of her young face, the serene smile, I'd look for clues. Then, when I thought she wasn't looking, I'd search her old face for some hint of the young Nora Dunne whose optimistic smile had not yet been compromised by hard experience.

What had she hoped for in her life? I've often tried to imagine her dreams, and I know that one of them might well have been to have a book of her poetry published. She had published her poems in magazines and newspapers during her teens and early twenties in Ireland. When she came to the United States they began appearing in U.S. publications as well. They were lyrical poems, deeply felt—odes to nature or poems about Ireland written in a spirit that might be called romantic nationalism, as in this poem published in her late teens in the *Cork Weekly Examiner* and reprinted in the Dublin Independent around the time she left for the United States in 1911:

Sing a song of April—sunny gleam and shower,
Hill and vale and wildwood bursting into flower.
Nature's hand overthrowing sullen Winter's pall,
Sing a song of April—the sweetest month of all.
Sing a song of Maytime—child of mood more staid,
Hawthorn garbs the roadside, bluebells throng the glade,
Thrush and blackbird making soft and mellow call—
Sing a song of Maytime—the fairest month of all.
Sing a song of Summer—roses hanging low,
Weighted with their fragrance, pale and crimson glow.
Like young hopes that leave us, will their dead leaves fall—
Sing a song of Summer—the happiest time of all.
Sing a song of Ireland—hills of mist-clad height,

Scenes of rugged grandeur with deep peace unite.
Rivers tell their story—chant it as they fall—
Land of love and glory—dearest land of all.
Sing a song of Freedom—sing a song of Hope,
Of men who died for Ireland—faced the steel and rope.
Defenders of our Sireland, ye gloried so to fall—
Sing a song of hero hearts—the truest hearts of all.
A song, a song of Ireland—tho Winters darksome reign
Is on Her now, bright dawn shall break and Spring come back again.
For Hopes bright flowers are waking and Freedoms voice shall call—
Then Ireland be the grandest song, the sweetest song of all.

However it changed in style and mood as years went by, my grandmother's poetry was always a force in our house. It was there without announcing itself and we could feel it, though she was intensely private about what she wrote. Gran worked at her poetry in the quiet hours when she wasn't busy helping Mama with the meals, the dishes, and the babies. As soon as I was old enough, I would read those few poems she showed the family, thrilled by words like *rill*, and *throng*, and *darksome*, always reading them for clues to the mysterious woman who lived in our midst. I'm certain she must have dreamed of having her work between the covers of a book.

What else did she hope for? Surely to go home again to the village of Whitegate in County Cork, Ireland. There she had relatives she'd not seen since she left home in her early twenties with her widowed mother, Mary, and her elder brother John, who had been stricken with tuberculosis, to seek Arizona's fabled cure of sun and a dry climate. Years later she would describe it as a grueling journey: tuberculosis patients were not allowed on the ship because of the danger of contagion, so Mary stayed below in the hold with John throughout the trip, hoping to hide his condition. TB was rampant at that time, and many of the other passengers in the hold were ailing from it and trying to lie low, for fear that they would be refused entry into the United States where they hoped to find a cure. Mary cautioned Nora to stay above where she could breathe fresh air, and thus Nora was apart from her family for most of the three-week journey.

I've often imagined my grandmother as a young woman alone on that ship at night for weeks, daydreaming about love, writing her poems, counting off the beads of her rosary, and maybe reading tea leaves in a cup, a ritual she would observe nearly every day of her life, even as a very old woman. Little did she dream that within months of their arrival in Tucson, her brother John would be dead and her mother would lie dying of tuberculosis contracted while caring for him.

And there was Nora, alone in America. Without the money to pay for return passage to Ireland, she didn't know what to do. In what may well have been a decision born of desperation and loneliness, she soon married Liver Foltz, a local merchant more than twice her age and an alcoholic who became violent when he drank. After a few years and many frightening scenes, Nora left him, moving with their two small children to California where she took a job as a cleaning woman in a downtown San Diego hotel. It was there that eventually she met Frank Hanes—an artist who told her he'd lived alone since his wife had died in Oklahoma a few years earlier. Mr. Hanes was a quiet, handsome man of Cherokee Indian ancestry. He worked somewhat irregularly, occasionally earning a few dollars painting a mural in one of San Diego's downtown movie theaters, and supplementing his income with gambling. Nora was attracted to the artist in him. He became her second husband, my mother's father.

I never set eyes on Frank Hanes, though he was my grandfather, but I learned a lot about him early in my childhood by eavesdropping—a habit I fell into after I saw my grandmother's eyes turn to glass and began to realize that adults had complicated secrets. My mother and her sisters, Jane and Marjorie, liked to gossip over a pot of tea when they got together. The gossip was sometimes about Gran—not unkind gossip, just speculation and observations about the woman who was such a vital and often cryptic presence in our lives.

On their afternoons alone, Gran and Mama would read tea leaves at the kitchen table. Always I listened in: "This is your present . . . . This is your future . . . ." There was a lot to overhear, and when I was still small enough I hid between the landlord's old piano and the wall, where they wouldn't see me. "You'll meet a dark and handsome stranger. . . . You'll have earthly riches and a fine house on a hill someday. . . . you'll take a trip across the sea to the old country. . . . None of the fortune-telling ever seemed to come true, but I kept eavesdropping on it, and on the gossip. The gossip was far more fruitful.

It was in this way that I learned about my grandfather's gambling, and that he had beaten my grandmother on numerous occasions in front of my mother and Marjorie. I was shocked that a man who was my grandfather would do such a thing, but never having met him, it was hard to imagine him at all. The more I heard of him, the harder to fathom he became. Most shocking was the revelation that Mr. Hanes had lied to Gran about his marital status; his first wife was not dead after all, but was locked in the mental institution to which he'd committed her before he gave their twin sons up for adoption and headed to San Diego for a fresh start. Even when the first Mrs. Hanes was pronounced ready for release, he refused to sign the necessary papers taking responsibility for her welfare, and she would live out her life in the asylum to which he'd committed her. After Nora discovered what Frank Hanes had done to his first family she could hardly look him in the face.

In the wake of Nora's discoveries, her husband's violence accelerated, as did his gambling, and eventually Nora got wind of his plans for *her:* Mr. Hanes, apparently wishing to start fresh in his life yet again, had decided to make good on his longtime threats to have Nora committed—threats that now had the ring of truth about them—and he'd also begun making arrangements to give two-year-old Orville away. Her baby. Nora surreptitiously packed what meager belongings she and the five children could carry, set her bags and boxes outside through a bedroom window, and told Frank Hanes she was taking the children to the birthday party of a neighbor child. She walked out the front door with her children, collected their belongings at the rear window, and never returned.

Soon after Nora left Mr. Hanes—during the Depression years of the early thirties—the unthinkable happened: money became so scarce that she couldn't pay rent on the East San Diego house she'd moved to, couldn't afford to feed her family. Nora put the children into Nazareth House Catholic orphanage while she worked as a live-in housekeeper in East San Diego, determined to earn enough money to make a home again for herself and her children. She went to see them every Saturday morning when she had time off from work.

Though she did manage to bring her four children home from the orphanage after a year or so, there would never be money for more than bare essentials. During those years Nora worked as a cleaning woman during the week, and on the weekends she mended parachutes for the WPA.

Through it all she kept her humor—a wickedly funny, often acerbic, humor. And she never stopped writing her poems, which began to appear with regularity in the old *San Diego Sun,* sometimes under a rather bizarre and startling nom de plume: Angelina Roar. Perhaps this name sounded brave and fearless to Nora, a name to get her through hard times. Maybe it even sounded American to her—a name more befitting her new poems. Certainly the poems of these years were different from the hopeful and romantic poems of her teens and early twenties before she left home. In America Nora's poetry became inward and lonely, a poetry of loss and isolation, poems of the city as seen through the eyes of a grieving and disillusioned young Irish woman:

> Strange cities chill me—the unfamiliar streets,
> The frozen look on every face one meets.
> And even the lofty buildings do look down
> And to my lonely fancy seem to frown . . .
> Aloof—alone—with that strange homesick ache
> For well-loved scenes my heart cannot forsake.
> I would go back from all this symmetry
> Of architecture splendid just to see
> A sloping roof beneath the summer rain,
> The way a branch leaned by my windowpane—
> I would go back—my truant fancy clings
> To the sweet comradeship of familiar things . . .

All her life my grandmother would speak nostalgically of "the Old Country," where, as she would tell us, "things were always green," as opposed to the landscape in San Diego where for much of the year everything was sun-dried a parched yellow. I've no doubt she held onto the hope of seeing home again one day.

Perhaps my grandmother also held onto a dream of romance—the idea that she might finally meet a man who would love her, laugh at her jokes, read her poems, tell her stories of his own childhood, touch her with tenderness, come home every night. (On several occasions I'd heard whispers about a secret love who had come into Gran's life after Mr. Hanes—someone my mother and aunts called the Redhaired Man—but it was clear I wasn't going to be told about it and I wasn't, not until I was grown.) Of course I can't say with certainty what Nora continued to hope for after she hit hard times in America. I only know that the day my grandmother's eyes turned to glass in our living room she was in her sixties. She died at eighty-eight, more than twenty years beyond the realization that her life was all it would ever be; only what it was, and nothing more.

Not having a home of her own, for several years Gran lived with our family—my mother and father and their brood of eight children. In our small domestic world of the '50s and early '60s, my grandmother was a large presence—funny, cranky, and irritating, spouting "Thanatopsis" or "To a Skylark" at the breakfast table while I poured my Wheaties; making corny puns upon every occasion. She whispered fervent prayers at night in her iron bed in the small room we shared, always open to the possibility of a holy apparition or a miracle. Her necessity was my good fortune, for it kept her near me and she was a powerful and enduring influence in my life.

Throughout my childhood, I found my grandmother's room an unfailingly magical place to visit. Against the backdrop of our quotidian household, her room was a riot of mysticism, religion, intellect, and color, yet also a haven of quiet and solitude, an escape from an increasingly crowded house of baby cries, television, and bickering siblings. Gran's room was filled with an array of treasures: rocks and shells, old photos, odd lengths of lace and fine cloth from secondhand stores, miraculous medals, rosary beads and scapulars, assortments of Woolworth glass cups, saucers, and bowls, mismatched china and costume jewelry from the Salvation Army, horehound candy and mints, as well as the occasional Irish chocolate sent from Cork by her sister Ellie. She possessed relics of the saints (God knows where she got them), dolls with tiny waists and beestung lips modelling wondrous and often elaborate crocheted dresses my grandmother had fashioned (these well-dressed dolls seemed to compensate for the lack of finery in Gran's own life), and books—hundreds of books: novels, biographies, and books of poetry, books about medical problems and cures, lives of the saints, UFO's, out-of-body travel. There was always the intriguing smell of old books in Gran's room. As a child I thought of it as the smell of poetry.

I was never bored in my grandmother's universe. I would spend hours in that quiet and eventful space with her, learning to crochet or reading poetry aloud, all the while surreptitiously moving my eyes across the walls to examine the pictures she'd hung there, most of them shadowy paintings of landscapes unpopulated by humans (though sometimes there was a sheep or two), and in each picture there would be a path, narrow and winding or straight and broad, but always a path which seemed to invite the rhythm of human footfall, and which seemed to promise fulfillment when followed bravely and faithfully to one's destination.

During our hours together in her room, my grandmother often recited her favorite poem for me, Shelley's "To a Skylark," a poem which excited me with its transcendent optimism, its sense of eternal possibility:

> Hail to thee, blithe spirit!
>   Bird thou never wert—
> That from Heav'n or near it
>   Pourest thy full heart
> In profuse strains of unpremeditated art.
> Higher still and higher
>   From the earth thou springest,
> Like a cloud of fire;
>   The blue deep thou wingest,
> And singing still dost soar, and soaring ever singest.

These opening stanzas of Shelley's long poem were thrilling to both of us, and she would speak them to me in a sort of urgent rush, as if imparting dire instructions to a grandchild before it was too late. I watched her mouth around the words, took them to heart. As she spoke them, her fingers moved rapidly through the crochet she was teaching me and somehow I learned both, crochet and poetry, though the latter would shape my life, would become my own vocation. I didn't realize then just how fortunate I was to have art beside me, around me all the time at home. With a child's smug sense of entitlement, I expected it as I did food, television, a new baby in the house, my comfortable bed at night.

One thing I was desperately curious about in those days was the poster-sized, black-and-white photo, faded to greys, of a baby laughing in a washtub—a cracked cardboard blowup my grandmother kept in her closet wherever she happened to live, but which she never hung on the wall and never spoke about. Even after I learned that this was supposedly a photo of Gran's son Orville who had died somehow in his childhood, I had questions—for example, how did a woman who'd probably never even owned a camera come into possession of such a big picture of one of her children? And what had happened to Orville, anyway?

But somehow I knew I wasn't to ask Gran these questions. As a child I often wondered if this was what had made my grandmother so sad, so secretly sad, on the day I saw her eyes turn to broken glass.

As I got older I eavesdropped less (not so much from a burgeoning sense of honor as from the simple fact that I'd become too large to se-

crete myself away in small places while the grown-ups talked nearby).
It was then I began quizzing my mother, and the things I most wanted
to know were: What had happened to Orville? Was that really him
in the big picture in Gran's closet? And who was the Redhaired Man,
anyway?

Though eventually my mother would recount to me the sad story of
Orville's death, it was only years later when I was an adult that she
would see fit to tell me the story of the Redhaired Man and how the
two griefs were wound together as one ineluctable sadness in my
grandmother's life.

It seems that when Nora was alone with her children after she'd left
Mr. Hanes and after she'd managed to bring her children home from
the orphanage, she'd fallen in love with someone her daughters called
the Redhaired Man, a gentleman who had a grocery store in their East
San Diego neighborhood. A *married* man. He would come over to the
house and read poetry with Gran out on the stoop; they would go on
Sunday drives in his late-model automobile. He was a handsome man
with curly red hair, a sturdily built and courtly man who was kind to
the children. Gran blossomed, became a new person in the eyes of her
watchful children, happy and full, funnier than ever. She was in love. I
don't know if the following poem refers to the Redhaired Man, but
knowing Nora's life before and after him, it seems likely that it does:

> I wandered by the brookside, I wandered by the mill,
> I could not hear the brook flow, the noisy wheel was still;
> There was no burr of grasshopper, no chirp of any bird,
> But the beating of my own heart was all the sound I heard.
> He came not, no he came not, the night came on alone,
> The little stars sat one by one, each on his golden throne;
> The evening wind passed by my cheek, the leaves above were stirred;
> But the beating of my own heart was all the sound I heard.
> And then I heard a footfall the branches swayed behind,
> A hand was on my shoulder, I knew its touch was kind;
> It drew me nearer, nearer, we did not speak one word
> For the beating of our own hearts was all the sound we heard.

It was during this time that Orville, by then seven years old, fell ill
with fever and violent abdominal pain. Nora, still working for low
wages as a housemaid, took him to the charity ward of San Diego's
County Hospital. There Orville languished for days, misdiagnosed as a

flu case until his appendix burst. He died there, as much a victim of poverty as of anything else. But as Nora saw it, she alone was responsible for her son's death, for she believed it was her punishment for having fallen in love with a married man. By that reasoning, she believed she had *caused* her child's death, and she feared for the lives of her remaining children. She broke off her relationship with the Redhaired Man, and lived out her grief for a lost child in the sudden absence of the man who had come to be her mainstay and companion.

As to the fading poster in Nora's room—the photo of a laughing baby in a tub, his plump skin wet and shiny, covered with suds—my mother told me that Gran had spotted it in the window of a Rexall drugstore as she walked up University Avenue in East San Diego during the year after Orville died, and she'd been struck dumb when she saw it, so certain was she that this was a photo of Orville when he was a baby.

Nora walked into the Rexall with a characteristic determination I can easily imagine, a set to her jaw. That was a photo of her son in the window, she told the proprietor urgently, her son who was dead now, and she had to have it. Without asking a single question the man gave it to her, and she would keep it with her for the rest of her life, propped against a wall of her closet, visible to her from her bedroom but private, her own to look at.

And despite the fact that Nora kept to her resolve not to see the Redhaired Man, she never forgot him, never stopped loving him. Through the years as he became more and more prominent in San Diego society, Gran would clip his name from the newspaper and save it, whether it was an article about one of his business ventures or some brief mention in the society pages about a fancy dress ball he and his wife had attended. These clippings yellowed and then browned and curled with the years, but still she held onto them, kept them between the pages of her poetry notebooks or in desk drawers with her prayer books and treasured belongings. She never had a gentleman caller again.

Throughout her later years Gran could occasionally be heard to mutter, "God forgive me for the things I've done." To her daughters it always seemed obvious that the Redhaired Man was the sinful secret, the wrong which Nora muttered about and feared would earn God's wrath in the afterlife. Though we didn't realize it for years, there was another secret, one which Gran kept to herself for all her life—a secret uncovered many years later by my mother when she herself was in her sixties and checking out family documents in a geneological search. My grandmother and Frank Hanes were never legally married. Despite all that the family had heard about my grandfather, no one in the family ever realized that the woman he'd committed to the asylum for life remained his legal wife—no divorce had ever been filed.

Now when I think back over all the years when my grandmother lived a quiet and celibate life in a room of one daughter's house or another, when she attended early morning mass, said rosary after rosary, wore miraculous medals and scapulars close to her skin beneath her many layers of clothes, it's painful to consider the power and weight of the unspoken in her life. It was a burden she carried alone through the years, always fearful that her children might one day uncover her shameful secrets, certain God had punished her by taking her child away, doubting that she would ever enter Heaven now.

But whatever she suffered, she raised her children well, and she continued to write her poems and to publish them, though the poems became sadder, darker, more private and mysterious. In some of them it's impossible to tell whether she's writing to her lost child or to the Red-haired Man—or both:

> I did not know how dear you were to me
> Till you were gone.
> I did not know how drear the world could be
> Without your footstep treading near;
> Without your face, your form to look upon;
> Sweetheart, I did not know till you were gone . . .

I often think of the moment my grandmother's eyes turned to glass, because I know that for the two of us it had distinctly different meanings. In my mind, it's the day when I began to try to know her. I'll never be sure whether the closeness that developed between the two of us as years went on was attributable to the fact that I was to be a poet too—or if perhaps I grew into poetry as a result of our closeness. I can say with certainty that my grandmother helped me to see the necessity of art to the human soul, the necessity of poetry in particular, and she made me understand, as well, that poetry is best and most enduring when it's lived with, when it's simply an ordinary part of each day on the earth, like food or air.

For my grandmother, the day her eyes turned to glass was the day when she began to live with death's inevitability, or more exactly, it was when death came to live with her, and thus with the rest of us, a hovering presence. She took it with her wherever she lived from that day forward, from daughter's house to daughter's house, and ultimately to the one-room converted garage apartment where she lived out her final years behind my parents'' house.

There in her last real room, a room in which somehow she'd reconstructed the magical universe of her earlier quarters, Nora often slept in her old flowered chair at night, as if to be ready when death called on her. She sat in the chair, her hands on the mahogany claws at the ends of the arms, just as she'd sat the day her eyes turned to glass in our living room on Wightman Street. Only now she was openly watching for death, and sat there, ready to fight or run if it arrived in darkness, unannounced.

Late one night in my grandmother's last year when I was visiting my parents' house, my mother and I found Gran wandering in the driveway on her way out to the street in her flannel gown, hair askew and panic in her eyes; she was looking for little Orville, the son who had died some fifty years before in the county hospital.

"He's just a little boy," she was saying, "and it's so dark for him all alone out there." She might have been describing eternity.

The two of us led her to her iron bed and tucked her in, hoping that would keep her from getting up again in her sleep. I watched my mother kiss Nora—*her* mother—something I was pretty sure she hadn't done in years, as I had not (in my experience, the Irish are not physically demonstrative). I imagined how the skin of Nora's face must feel—thin as tissue—beneath my mother's lips.

"Orville's home now, Mama," my mother whispered close to Gran's face. "He's home. Everything's fine." And we watched as Nora's eyes slowly accepted sleep, closing against the American night and everything in it she'd always feared and desired.

Soon after that night the family was forced to accept the idea that Nora needed to be where she could get twenty-four-hour care. She'd been falling a lot, couldn't take herself to the toilet, and continued to wander away from her room in the night and out into the street, looking for Orville. My mother was exhausted all the time from caring for her handicapped youngest son and raising a houseful of teenagers. It was a painful decision because Nora was so private, and she was a person who'd always harbored fears and suspicions of the World Out

There; she was a woman who only wanted to be "at home, in my own four walls." Despite the fact that it didn't seem we had a choice, and despite the fact that we all promised to go and visit her often, and most of us did, still it felt like a betrayal to us, our collective failure of faith.

Not long after my grandmother was moved to the nursing home, my mother went there one day to pick up Gran's laundry and she told me later, her voice unsteady, that she'd found a note in her mother's robe pocket. She handed me the note to read, I suppose because it would have been too painful to hear the words spoken aloud. The note was in Nora's familiar elaborate script, now gone a bit shaky. It read: "Please help me. I am being held prisoner here. If you contact my mother at Whitegate, in Cork, she will give you a sum of money."

It was over twenty years ago that I last sat on the side of Nora's bed in that nursing home, taking turns with her reciting stanzas of her favorite poem aloud for the last time. She was eighty-eight and had been there for nearly a year. She couldn't remember a lot of things, even some family names. But she'd not forgotten a word of that poem. Now each time I visited, this was the ritual that supplanted conversation, Nora having gone rather quiet these days unless the talk was of poetry or the distant past in Ireland, the two things that had never let her down—unlike America and her family, both of which she may well have felt had forsaken her.

I remember watching her mouth forming the words of the final stanza, how I looked away as I heard the lines, too cowardly to watch those particular words coming from my grandmother's lips now, in this place.

> Teach me half the gladness
> That thy brain must know;
> Such harmonious madness
> From my lips would flow,
> The world should listen then, as I am listening now.

Although I didn't know it yet as I sat with my grandmother trading stanzas of Shelley's poem, the following Sunday she would lie dying, her false teeth removed by the nurses, her spectacles off.

I entered the room quietly and looked around for her, at first not recognizing the sunken, expressionless face as that of my grandmother. I wondered if they might have moved Gran to another room. The nurse came in then and nodded at the bed, telling me that Nora was not doing well today, that my mother and father had been in to see her this morning and were coming back later. She said that Nora had not recognized them, nor had she responded to anything at all. And indeed, there was no recognition in her face now, at the sound of my voice in the room. I knew she was dying, though it had never seemed quite possible to me that she would do such a thing.

I didn't sit on the side of her bed this time—it seemed an intimacy bordering on disrespect as she prepared to take leave of her earthly body. Instead, I came and stood beside her at the head of the bed and leaned forward until my lips nearly touched her ear. I could smell my grandmother's long-familiar scent then, in her white hair and on her neck, beneath the rest home smell. I wasn't sure if I had a right, but I whispered in her ear the words she'd taught me as a child:

> Hail to thee, Blithe Spirit!
> Bird thou never wert—
> That from Heaven or near it
> Pourest thy full heart
> In profuse strains of unpremeditated art.

And my grandmother's eyelids startled and fluttered at those words as they had to nothing else, her lips working to continue the poem, trying to take her turn. I could barely hear her whispered beginning "Higher still and higher" and faltering, she continued to move her lips, but no sound issued from them. I picked up the verse then, a little shakily, letting my own whispers give sound to the movement of my grandmother's lips

> From the earth thou springest,
> Like a cloud of fire;
> The blue deep thou wingest,
> And singing still dost soar, and soaring ever singest.

And those would be the last words of my Irish grandmother.

A few days after Gran's death I went to her room with my mother for the first time since she'd gone to the rest home. We had to sort through her things, a job which we both knew would be painful. But I also felt a kind of sad anticipation, for I knew that I would finally see the whole body of her work, the poems she'd kept to herself through the years.

The room still held the familiar jumble of possessions that represented Nora's lifetime, and though it was strangely still without her there to animate it, I found that even now it smelled like poetry. The faded black and white poster was there—now badly waterstained from a roof leak—of the baby laughing in the wash tub. We'd been warned by the administrators of the nursing home not to bring anything irreplaceable along with Gran when she was admitted, because some of the old people there tended to steal from one another. If anything had been irreplaceable to Nora it was that photo, and somehow, I suppose, we'd all imagined it possible that she would overcome what ailed her and return home again eventually. That was the power and presence of my grandmother—that an entire family of otherwise rational beings thought it possible she might outfox death somehow.

Around the room we found recipes and health articles she'd clipped through the years—I recall an article about the mysteries of the human spleen. In her top drawer I found a voter registration slip, only a couple of years old, on which she'd written on the line for occupation, Housewife. Housewife, though she had no house, hadn't been a wife in more than fifty years. I wish she'd known that she'd earned the right to declare herself a Poet instead.

And yes, we found the clippings about the Redhaired Man, most of them now brown and crisp with age, countless clippings representing many years of longing—the most recent one dated less than two years before her death at the age of eighty-eight. My mother told me then, as we sat on the floor in my grandmother's room sifting through scraps of paper that had dried and turned color like autumn leaves, that one day a year or two before Gran went into the nursing home she'd confided, "He was the only man I ever truly loved." I thought of Mr. Foltz, of Mr. Hanes. And then I couldn't help thinking of the day when her eyes had turned to glass in our living room on Wightman Street, and of all the years she'd lived beyond that day.

Of course we found her poems everywhere we looked—in drawers, on tabletops, tucked into books—each one of them carefully written out again and again in her graceful hand in ledgers and on scraps of paper, as if in the hours when her spirit had wearied too much to compose, she'd taken comfort in moving her hand along the lines of an older poem on the page, watching it take form again before her eyes, and in that way reexperiencing the moment of its creation.

When I'd put all the poems together in a stack, I discovered that there were only twenty-one—all of them poems I'd seen through the years. I was astounded. Where were all the poems that had constituted her life, that had made her the model I took for myself of a working poet? Was it possible that these were all she'd ever written—or had she destroyed other poems too personally revealing to leave behind? I'll never know, and I've come to accept the idea that either way it doesn't matter. Whatever she left behind of herself is what she wanted us to have of her in her absence. But in that moment, as I sat in her stilled universe holding in one hand the poems that represented her entire existence on the earth, I was angry—angry at the circumstances in her life that had militated against whatever she held dear and necessary.

The day my grandmother's eyes turned to glass was the day when I began to really look at her, to wonder what she knew and felt. It was as if a window had broken open and I couldn't stop looking through it to see what lay beyond ordinary view. And though she kept her secrets to herself, she chose to pass along to me what was of most value to her; she gave me poetry. Now when I remember the moment her eyes turned to glass, I think of her life whole and entire, as perhaps she did in that moment herself. I see my grandmother, Nora Dunne, who came to America from Ireland on a crowded ship to make a future she couldn't have dreamed of; who wrote poems all her life, sometimes as the California woman Angelina Roar; who told jokes and made bad puns, kept a Kleenex up her sleeve and scapulars next to the skin above her heart, went to Mass faithfully and said uncountable rosaries in the night, understood Fear of the Lord; who believed in miracles, leprechauns, tea leaves, privacy, extra-terrestrial life, saints, ghosts, and out-of-body travel; who carried a weighty secret to her grave not knowing that secrets are often exhumed; who never forgot the Redhaired Man who almost loved her once; who kept faith in the power of poetry to transform all manner of earthly disillusionments by giving voice to what is unknowable, indefinable, and eternally possible in the human heart.

The Color of Anguish

Ana Alomá Velilla

EARLY EVENINGS IN OCTOBER are especially delightful in Havana. The summer heat begins to subside and the luminous skies over the intensely blue sea form an unforgettable palette.

One late afternoon in October I left my classes a little worried. With a six-course program I felt I was not going to have enough time to give to Classical Greek II that seemed to become more difficult with each session. I left the building where this class was held and set out for Plaza Cadenas on my way to the monumental flight of stairs leading to the avenue below. There I would take the bus that would leave me two blocks away from my grandparent's house where I stayed while I was at the university.

Among the four university buildings framing Plaza Cadenas is the Faculty of Natural Sciences whose classical Corinthian columns enclose an airy patio. The Teatro Clásico Universitario used to perform the tragedies of classical Greek Theater on the front steps. That particular evening some students were beginning to rehearse *Electra*. Lights and other props were being installed in the plaza.

After observing the beginning of the rehearsal in a reverie I woke up to reality and hurried home. My petite and genteel grandmother was sitting and reading when I arrived. Still overcome by what I had seen, I told her everything and how it affected me.

My grandmother listened attentively and looking into my eyes asked me, "Do you really like the theater?"

"I love it!" I exclaimed, still under the magical spell of what I had seen.

"Then," she replied, "study drama and join a classical company."

"But grandmother," I interrupted, "Father would not like . . ."

"It's your life," she said, and I perceived a certain sadness in her voice. "If you don't do it now it's going to be too late."

I realized at that moment that she was speaking for herself, for her truncated dreams, for her life shaped by her class and the time in which she lived in that made no concessions to her dreams. My grandmother was born in 1873 in a well-to-do family with extensive land holdings. At that moment, the Ten Year War (1868–1878) was at its peak. Cuba, a small country with a population of no more than a million people, was fighting for her independence from Spain against an army of over 100,000 seasoned soldiers. After losing South America, Spain had concentrated her veteran forces in Cuba, an army larger and more experienced than that ever faced by Bolívar, San Martín, or Washington. My deeply patriotic family contributed money to the Cuban army by selling the family jewels.

Cuba lost that war, but among the conditions Cuba demanded for surrender was granting freedom to the slaves who had fought in the Cuban Army. Always yearning for freedom, Cuba went to war again in 1895 after several attempts to mount an uprising.

By 1878, my grandmother's uncle had to leave the Island because of his involvement in several conspiracies to free Cuba. His wife and small daughter were left with considerably reduced circumstances but with their patriotic spirit intact.

When my grandmother married in 1896, she retained the love of Cuba ingrained by her family. My grandparents started a family and eventually had six children. They settled in a small provincial town where my grandmother confronted domestic life with very little enthusiasm. She left the supervising of domestic matters to a trusted servant and used to say, "The house will always be there, but I will not always be here."

When the time came for me to begin studying at the University of Havana, my grandparents had already been living in Havana for some time. Since I had always been interested in literature, history, and philosophy, I was very happy with my courses. From the very beginning my grandmother shared my interests. She even learned the Greek alphabet and later on would pass me notes written in Spanish but using Greek characters, which lent a delicious secrecy to our exchanges.

When I began studying literature, she started reading all my assignments. Although she had a marvelous sense of humor and enjoyed comedies, her heart was in drama. She always identified with the protagonist and experienced all the emotions playwrights sought to arouse in the reader and spectators. On reading *Agamemnon* she was fascinated by Clytemnestra and, as she came to the passage where the watchman speaks about her "male strength of heart," she paused.

"Why male strength," she exclaimed, rather upset. "Is it that we cannot have it, too? I tell you Ana," she continued, "I have seen women as strong, maybe stronger than any male."

"Amen!" I concurred laughing.

We went through most of my assignments in this way. Her opinions, which she was never shy about expressing, her clear feminism, long before the concept was even conceived of, helped me to see aspects of a play that might have eluded me had I been struggling alone.

I delighted in her ideas and her grounds for preferring different characters. In the *Iliad* she liked Diomedes. As for the Trojans, she preferred Hector although with reservation. When I asked her why, she replied, "Because of his deep concern for his reputation."

Often I marveled at the way in which a woman who was brought up to acquire only social graces could see aspects of life that eluded me, all because of her intense love of the theater. When we read and discussed the *Odyssey* she told me it was her favorite because "the ideas of love, devotion and family loyalty were so important."

Reading, exchanging ideas, sometimes arguing, we went through the classics and came to modern literature, where Nora, the protagonist of Ibsen's *A Doll's House* became her favorite. She would frequently read the final dialogue between Hjalmer and Nora. When Hjalmer mentions Nora's "most sacred duties, her husband and children," Nora's fiery retort seemed to fascinate my grandmother. Nora reminds her husband that she also has other equally sacred duties, duties to herself. This answer seemed to be a revelation for my grandmother, one that coincided with her own doubts about the constricting role of religion in a woman's life.

Sometimes I would fall behind in my assignments because of extracurricular activities. My friends and I were publishing a newspaper *Redención* and between writing my column, usually criticizing the government, and going to the printers on the other side of Havana, I found myself short of time and falling behind on my assignments. I remember sitting at the dining room table with all my papers, notes, and books and with the comforting presence of my grandmother, who would be sitting in her favorite rocking chair reading, always reading. The fan-shaped stained glass arches that topped the wide doors opening onto the patio filtered the sunlight and colored whatever happened to be in its luminous way. Fascinated as I have always been by color, the light sometimes distracted me. I would see my grandmother's beautiful white hair turning blue, red, or whatever hue the light was painting her.

One day my grandmother made a comment that years later I would hear from a Cuban novelist of my generation. She told me that Cuban literature was, for the most part, literature in exile. "Notice," she said, "that most of our greatest writers have been outside of Cuba for political reasons when they wrote their best pieces." She mentioned Martí, Heredia, and Gómez de Avellaneda among others. Many years later, Reynaldo Arenas, the well known novelist, expressed the same observation during a lecture on Cuban literature in the United States. I marveled at my grandmother's insights, especially because they were her own and not the result of contacts with literary groups or friends.

She was fascinated by other subjects. I saw her reading texts on Theosophy, books on and by H.P. Blavatsky, Annie Besant, and others. She loved Krishnamurti. The theory of karma and reincarnating seemed to clarify many of her questions about the destiny of human beings.

I joined her in these pursuits, as attracted as she was by the mysteries of our personal destinies, by the differences among persons born in the same family, the unfairness of class and racial differences. We would have long conversations about these subjects, expressing our doubts as well as our views.

My grandmother and I not only shared our love of literature, but we also had the same taste in music. During the concert season, the Havana Philharmonic Orchestra offered Sunday morning concerts attended by students, children, and people of modest means. Monday nights the same program was repeated for patrons of the orchestra and a more elegant crowd. Although my grandparents had a subscription to the Monday night concerts, my grandmother, who enjoyed the company of young people, would accompany me as well as attending the Monday night performances with my grandfather.

My grandmother's legacy was not only her love for the arts. Cuba and her destiny were always prominent subjects of our conversations. She bitterly resented the imposition of the Platt Amendment to our constitution that gave the Americans the right to intervene in Cuba when they considered it necessary, ignoring the fact that Cuba had been fighting for her independence from Spain for years. Cuba's strategic position at the entrance of the Gulf of Mexico was a temptation for the expansionist drive so much a part of United States foreign policy at the time.

The explosion of the battleship *Maine* in the port of Havana gave the United States government the excuse it needed to declare war on Spain even though it could never be proven that Spain had anything to do with it. Talking about these events was painful for my grandmother.

"We were at the end of our resources, Ana. We needed weapons not men."

She was also upset that Dr. Carlos J. Finlay, a Cuban doctor who discovered that yellow fever was transmitted by a particular kind of mosquito, had been ignored and the credit given to Dr. Walter Reed, the United States doctor who tested the theory. Delving into Cuban history, she explained to me that the famous capture of the San Juan Hill during the so-called Spanish American War was only possible because a Cuban military man, General Calixto García, developed a strategy for Theodore Roosevelt because his approach was costing so many American lives.

"It was the battalion of Cuban soldiers who opened the way for the American Rough Riders to advance," she added.

The imposition of the Platt Amendment giving the United States the right to occupy the Island when the American government deemed it necessary to protect the United States' interests was a thorn in the side of all Cubans who were unceasing in their efforts to annul the infamous amendment. When the Platt Amendment was finally abolished in the Panamerican Conference in Montevideo in 1932, my grandmother had a big party, toasting our newly liberated country.

My grandmother's patriotism took root in my life as a newly-married young college graduate. By 1950, many of my former classmates and I had joined the Orthodox Party, whose leadership included many of my professors. One of them, Dr. Roberto Agramonte was running for the presidency. Others were running for the Senate. My professor of Latin was head of the Committee for Women and Children which I joined. I also asked the party leaders to let me work in the Committee for Peasants and, once a member, petitioned the committee to study the rate of deforestation in Cuba, a subject that was one of my greatest concerns.

At the time Fidel Castro, who must have been around twenty-five years old, was running for the House. His reputation was tarnished, however, because of his alleged involvement in the Bogotazo Incident in Colombia, riots that resulted in the murder of a presidential candidate and included criminal elements with which Castro was said to be associated.

All of us were hard working and idealistic in our political efforts, blindly believing that Cuba had finally achieved the political stability we had all hoped for because we had enjoyed a democratic system for the past ten years. Little did we know that in the shadows a man with an insatiable appetite for power was ready to strike a blow to our dreams. During the night of March 10, 1952, Fulgencio Batista and a small group of military men captured the barracks of the Columbia Headquarters and issued an ultimatum to the President, ordering him to leave the country. Colonel Martín Elena, trying to stop the military coup, disconnected communications between Havana and the neighboring province of Matanzas where he was commander, and the rest of the Island. The small Cuban military fleet sailed to the high seas to avoid obeying orders from the leaders of the insurrection. Members of the University Students Organization were in the Presidential Palace begging the President not to give up. Claiming that he did not want a bloodbath on the Island, President Prío Socarrás left the country with his family, leaving Cuba in the hands of the hated military. Years later, while living in exile in Miami, Dr. Prío Socarrás, the last freely elected president of Cuba, committed suicide.

Because I had lived with my grandmother's stories of the sacrifices of the Cuban people in our never ending quest for liberation, there was not a moment's hesitation in my mind as to what I should do. After our initial shock and sense of disorientation had passed, my friends and I decided that we would fight by whatever means necessary to overthrow the tyrant Batista and restore democracy to Cuba. That very same morning, a group of friends stopped at our house. They were as confused as my husband and I were, but also decided to work toward the return of our constitutional government.

Havana was eerily quiet. The streets were crawling with military men. Behind closed doors, however, was a group of idealistic and inexperienced young people arguing how to proceed, whom to call, what to do. We knew that in many other places, similar groups were being formed. It was difficult to formulate a clear and sensible plan at such short notice and in our state of mind.

The Federation of University Students called upon people to pledge their allegiance to the Constitution of 1940, boldly defying the new government that had abolished it. They set up a table on the steps of the university with certificates for people to sign, declaring their loyalty to democratic ideals. An impressive crowd covered the length of the steps and kept filing before the table to take the oath. Meanwhile police cars were cruising up and down the street in a futile attempt to intimidate those who not only pledged their support but shouted, "Long Live Free Cuba."

Taking the oath was a very emotional experience for me. Although my grandmother died four months before the coup, I felt so close to her it seemed that she was right there smiling her approval and urging me to fight for my ideals. I know she would have done the same as I did.

During the first few years of the Batista regime, several groups sought to overthrow the government, often acting without the support of any national organization. There were many instances of groups organizing quixotic attempts on military headquarters or the Presidential Palace, only to be tortured and killed.

On July 26th, 1954, a group of young people prepared to attack the Moncada Military Headquarters in Santiago de Cuba, the second largest city in the country, and capital of Oriente, the easternmost province of Cuba. They left in two trucks intending to meet at their point of attack. One of them arrived at Moncada only to engage in a most unequal battle during which the best of the rebels were either killed or imprisoned and mercilessly tortured. Curiously, the truck Fidel Castro was riding in never reached military headquarters. Fidel claimed that they had been lost, a difficult excuse to accept since he was born and raised in that city.

When the news of the failed attack reached him, Fidel fled to the mountains where he was captured a few days later. The intervention of the Bishop of Santiago de Cuba saved his life because although he was taken prisoner, he was well treated. After a year Fidel was granted amnesty and left Cuba to organize the 26th of July Movement, the group that would ultimately carry him to power.

While Fidel was outside the country organizing the exiles, my husband and I were working in the underground. At this point, the 26th of

July Movement was the most active organization, and we had decided to help in every possible way. We worked in a cell whose main purpose was fund-raising for the movement. On December 7, 1955, we took the ferry that used to make the daily round trip between Havana and Key West, Florida, to meet Fidel and work on the Second Manifesto to the Cuban People.

Fidel was living in a boarding house while preparing to leave for Mexico. I had known him from our student years and also as a member of the Orthodox Party. For more than four hours, he, my husband, and I worked on the Second Manifesto which I still have with me. All through that afternoon, he was courteous, charming, and very interested in our efforts. When we were finished, he gave us his address in Mexico. The name of the person he would be staying with turned out to be Hilda Gadea, Che Guevara's first wife. We returned to Cuba that evening with a sense of accomplishment.

At that time, Batista was so sure of himself that he had relaxed his vigilance. We were neither searched on our way to Key West nor upon our return. How fortunate, since we were carrying the Second Manifesto with us.

In December 1956, Fidel Castro landed in Cuba. Some of my friends and former classmates were in the landing party. One of them, whom we affectionately called Ñico Siete Pisos (Ñico seven floors) because he was so tall, lost his way, and ended up in a part of the Oriente Province that is like a desert. He died of hunger and thirst. However, the main group managed to reach the mountains.

As soon as Fidel established himself in Oriente Province, the situation in Cuba changed, and government security was tightened. In the cities police began conducting house-to-house searches, arresting and torturing innocent people.

In the meantime, we continued our work in Havana. There were five of us in the cell. I still remember Armando Hart, who became Minister of Education under Fidel and who spent the night at our home hiding from the police. I remember translating an interview that Herbert Mathews had with Fidel Castro in the mountains and that was published in the *New York Times*. I remember sleeping in a friend's house because we thought we too were being watched.

I also remember Haydee Santamaría and Vilma Espín, two women who had participated in the assault on the Moncada Military Headquarters, visiting our house. In the early sixties, Haydee would marry

Armando Hart, and Vilma Espín became Raul Castro's wife. On July 26, 1979, Haydee committed suicide, presumably disenchanted with the Castro regime.

Meanwhile, the situation in Havana was becoming progressively more dangerous. If a member of our movement was thought to be in danger of being caught by the police, he or she was ordered to join Fidel in the mountains, which was considered safer than the city.

In early May of 1957, two members of our group were captured by the Batista police. Not realizing what had happened, I called one of them. A strange voice answered and asked me who I was. We never asked such a question in our cell. Suspecting the worst, I immediately hung up. From that moment on, we knew not only that we were in danger but that we were also endangering our other contacts. By June of that year, the leaders of the movement advised us to leave Cuba.

For the first time, I would feel the pain of being away from my own country, unable to return. I felt what it was like to be surrounded by well-meaning people who were unable to understand my homesickness. Yes, we were grateful to be in a free society, but we also needed to help the country that gave us our identity, our language, and our pride.

My husband found a job with Gillette and we moved to Boston. With the few Cubans living in the area we organized a group to collect money for the Revolution.

After two years of our exile, the rebel forces triumphed in Cuba. Our country was—or so we thought—free of the hated military dictatorship. The overthrow of Batista and the coming to power of the 26th of July Movement was joyously celebrated. In April 1959, Fidel Castro came to the United States and was invited to address the public at Harvard University. In his group was Manolo Ray, Minister of Public Works and a close friend of ours. He came to our apartment to have coffee with us while Fidel was giving his address in Cambridge. During this visit, he told us that Fidel had forbidden the ministers that had accompanied him to accept any offer of help from the United States. We were extremely surprised, but not alarmed. We were not yet able to see the implications of that order.

In October my husband and I returned to Cuba. I remember the exhilaration of being on Cuban soil again and believing that I had returned for good to participate in a new society. I was not aware that under orders from Fidel Castro, nightly executions were carried out by the military in the moats of La Cabaña, the old Spanish fortress. People were being rounded up like cattle and thirty or forty prisoners were herded into cells built for three or four people. I learned about this from my teenage cousin who had been rounded up and imprisoned on flimsy charges. He told me that he and his cell mates could tell how many people were executed every night by counting the final shots.

It was not long before a deep fear began to permeate all levels of our society. One by one our best newspapers were being shut down. My husband, who had a high position in the Ministry of Foreign Affairs, saw what was happening. I argued with him that what he was trying to tell me simply wasn't possible. But soon I had to recognize that something was terribly wrong and that by the time the Cuban people would come to realize it, it would be too late.

Broken-hearted, we decided to leave. By June.1960, it had become once again very difficult to leave the country. Even though we were associated with the 26th of July Movement, we had to have an excuse, and so we claimed that we needed to go to Canada, birthplace of our adopted children, to finalize some papers. We left with just the clothes on our backs, pretending to be going for a brief visit. We thought the government suspected nothing, but later friends told us that only half an hour after we had left, the police came to our home.

And so I began my second exile, one which turned out to be a very long one. I often wondered what my grandmother would have done in my circumstances. But I think I knew the answer because I feel that I knew her better than any other member of our family did. Her words still resonate in me today, her admonition when I returned home so moved by the rehearsals for *Electra,* "Do what you feel you must."

The years have passed. Time has erased the lines between my memories, so that they often announce themselves out of sequence. However, I feel that there are invisible threads joining the generations, that although my grandmother and I seemed to be facing different problems, we were both driven to work for our country.

I still see so clearly with my heart, with my whole being, the drama of the years we shared and all the light and colors of my childhood. "We knew, didn't we, grandmother, the color of our sky, and the sea, the flowers and the trees? But grandmother, what is the color of anguish?"

The Grandmothers Speak Forever

COMMUNING WITH THE ANCESTORS

Marilou Awiakta

MY CHEROKEE GRANDMOTHERS are powerful communers. I invite you to share an experience I had with them.

One source of the Grandmothers' power is our homeland. Our mountains are very old. When the Rockies birthed bare and sharp against the sky, the Great Smokies were already mellowed down, shawled in forests, steeped in mist, like ancients deep in thought: the Oldest Grandmothers have always shaped the people who dwell among them, as human grandmothers, in turn, shape their families.

So it was that through many centuries, the Cherokee evolved into seven matrilineal clans. Women were the center of the family and had a central voice in government as well. In the Council, people sat according to their clans. Each clan was represented by a Clan Mother—usually a woman of grandmother age—who was chosen for her wisdom and strength. The Beloved Woman spoke for the seven. The War Chief and Peace Chief were men. People of both genders attended the Council and participated in deliberations.

In the vast Cherokee nation, each town was autonomous, governing through its own Council. My ancestors (and much later my birth family) lived in the foothills of the Great Smokies known as the "Overhill." In the mid–1700s, Henry Timberlake, a young colonial officer from Virginia, visited here and attended Council meetings, probably at the town of Chota. Observing the proceedings through the eyes of his own patriarchal culture, he was amazed and wrote in his *Memoirs* that the reader would be surprised to find "the story of the Amazons not so great a fable as we imagined, many of the Cherokee women being as famous in war, they are as powerful in the Council."

In truth, he had encountered the Grandmothers. Are the spirits of these women accessible to us today? Yes! According to Albert Einstein, there is a dimension beyond time and space where time stands still—past, present, and future are one. American Indians have always known this dimension as "the time immemorial," a spiritual place we enter into to commune intimately with all that is, a place abidingly real. Going there now, I return to my native mountains in East Tennessee and walk with the strong Cherokee Grandmothers Timberlake met on his journey more than two centuries ago.

"Where are your women?"

The speaker is Attakullakulla, a Cherokee chief renowned for his shrewd and effective diplomacy. He has come to negotiate a treaty with the whites. Among his delegation are women "as famous in war, as they are powerful in the Council." Their presence also has ceremonial significance: it is meant to show honor to the other delegation. But that delegation is composed of males only. To them the absence of women is irrelevant, a trivial consideration.

To the Cherokee, however, reverence for women/Mother Earth/ life/spirit is interconnected. Irreverence for one is likely to mean irreverence for all. Implicit in their chief's question, "Where are your women?" the Cherokee hear, "Where is your balance? What is your intent?" They see that balance is absent and are wary of the white men's motives. They intuit the mentality of destruction.

I turn to my own time. I look at the Congress, the Joint Chiefs of Staff, the Nuclear Regulatory Commission . . . at the hierarchies of my church, my university, my city, my children's school. "Where are your women?" I ask.

Wary and fearful, I call aside one of Attakullakulla's delegation. I choose her for the gray streak of experience in her hair, for her staunch hips and for the lively light in her eyes that indicates an alert, indomitable spirit. "Grandmother, I need your courage. Sing to me about your life."

Her voice has the clear, honing timbre of the mountains.

SONG OF THE GRANDMOTHERS

I am Cherokee.
My people believe in the Spirit that unites all things.

I am woman. I am life force. My word has great value.
The man reveres me as he reveres Mother Earth and his own spirit.
The Beloved Woman is one of our principal leaders.
Through her the Spirit often speaks to the people. In the Great
Council at the capital, she is a powerful voice.
Concerning the fate of hostages, her word is absolute.

Women share in all of life. We lead sacred dances. In
the Council we debate freely with men until an
agreement is reached. When the nation considers war,
we have a say, for we bear the warriors.
Sometimes I go into battle. I also plant and harvest.

I carry my own name and the name of my clan. If I
accept a mate, he and our children take the name of my
clan. If there is deep trouble between us, I am as free to
tell him to go as he is to leave. Our children and our
dwelling stay with me. As long as I am treated with
dignity, I am steadfast.

> I love and work and sing.
> I listen to the Spirit.
> In all things I speak my mind.
> I walk without fear.
> I am Cherokee.

I feel the Grandmother's power. She sings of harmony, not domi-
nance. And her song rises from a culture that repeats the wise balance
of nature: the gender capable of bearing life is not separated from the
power to sustain it. A simple principle. Yet in spite—or perhaps because—of our vast progress in science and technology, the American
culture where I live has not grasped this principle. In my county alone
there are twenty-six hundred men who refuse to pay child support,
leaving their women and children with a hollow name, bereft of eco-
nomic means and sometimes even of a safe dwelling. On the national
level, the U.S. Constitution still does not include equal rights for
women.

The Grandmother can see this dimension of time and space as well as I—its imbalance, its irreverence, its sparse presence of women in positions of influence. And she can hear the brave women who sing for harmony and for transforming power. "My own voice is small, Grandmother, and I'm afraid. You live in a culture that believes in your song. How can you understand what women of my time have to cope with?"

Grasping my chin gently, the Grandmother turns my face back toward the treaty council. "Listen to Attakullakulla's question again. When he says, 'Where are your women?' look into the eyes of the white delegation and you will see what I saw."

On the surface, hardness—the hardness of mind split from spirit, the eyes of conquerors. Beyond the surface, stretching future decades deep, are crumpled treaties. Rich farms laid waste. And finally the Cherokee, goaded by soldiers along a snowbound trail toward Oklahoma—a seemingly endless line of women, men, and children, wrapped in coats and blankets, their backs bowed against the cold. In the only gesture of disdain left to them, they refuse to look their captors in the face.

Putting my arms around the Grandmother, I lay my head on her shoulder. Through touch we exchange sorrow, despair that anything really changes. I'm ashamed I've shown so little courage. She is sympathetic. But from the pressure of her arms I also feel the stern, beautiful power that flows from all the Grandmothers, as it flows from our mountains themselves. It says, "Dry your tears. Get up. Do for yourself or do without. Work for the day to come. Be joyful."

"Joyful, Grandmother?" I draw away. "Sorrow, yes. Work, yes. We must work . . . up to the end. But such a hardness is bearing down on my people. Already soldiers are gathering. Snow has begun to fall. This time we will walk the Trail for Fire. With the power of the atom, they can make the world's people walk it. How can you speak of joy?"

"Because for those who die, death is death. A Trail of Tears for the Cherokee, a Trail of Fire for all—it is the same. But without joy, there is no hope. Without hope, the People have no chance to survive. Women know how to keep hope alive . . . at least *some* women do."

The reproach stings and angers me . . . because she is right. My joy, my hope, *are* lost. I don't know how to find them again. Silently, my thoughts flow toward her. Hers flow back to me, strong, without anger.

"Come," she says.

"Where?"

"To Chota—the capital—to see the Beloved Woman."

I've heard of her—Nanyehi—"Whom many call a spirit person, immortal, or 'the Path.'" Nanyehi whom the whites call Nancy Ward and hold in great respect . . . the Beloved Woman whose advice and counsel are revered through the Cherokee nation. She is said to have a "queenly and commanding presence," as well as remarkable beauty, with skin the color and texture of the wild rose.

Not ready . . . I'm not ready for this. Following the Grandmother along the forest trail, I sometimes walk close, sometimes lag behind. Puny—that's who I am. Puny, puny, puny—the worst charge that can be levelled at any mountain woman, red, white, or black. It carries pity, contempt, reproach. When we meet, the Beloved Woman will see straight into my spirit. I dread to feel the word in her look.

I know about her courage. She works ceaselessly for harmony with white settlers, interpreting the ways of each people to the other. From her uncle and mentor, Attakullakulla, she has learned diplomacy and the realities of power. She understands that the Cherokee will ultimately be outnumbered and that war will bring sure extinction. She counsels them to channel their energies from fighting into more effective government and better food production. To avoid bloodshed, she often risks censure and misunderstanding to warn either side of an impending attack, then urges resolution by arbitration. In the councils she speaks powerfully on two major themes: "Work for peace. Do not sell your land."

All the while, she knows the odds.

As the Grandmother and I pass through my hometown of Oak Ridge, I look at the nest of nuclear reactors there and weigh the odds of survival—for all people. The odds are small. But not impossible. My own song for harmony with, and reverence with the atom is a small breath. But it may combine with others to make a warm and mighty wind, powerful enough to transform the hardness and cold into life. It is not impossible.

I walk closer to the Grandmother. In this timeless dimension, we could move more rapidly, but she paces my spirit, holding it to a thoughtful rhythm as we cross several ridges and go down into the Tellico Valley. We walk beside the quiet, swift waters of the Little Tennessee River. Chota is not far off.

What time and space will the Grandmother choose for me to meet the Beloved Woman? I imagine a collage of possibilities:

1755 . . . Nanyehi fights beside her husband in a battle against the Creeks. When he is killed, she takes his rifle and leads the Cherokee to victory. Afterward, warriors sing of her deeds at Chota and the women and men of the Great Council award her the high office she will hold for more than half a century. She is seventeen, the mother of a son and daughter.

1776 . . . Having captured the white woman, Mrs. Lydia Bean, Cherokee warriors tie her to the stake. Just as they light the fire, Nanyehi arrives on the scene crying, "No woman will be burned at the stake while I am Beloved Woman!" Her word is absolute. Mrs. Bean goes free. She teaches dairying to Nanyehi, who in turn teaches it to the Cherokee.

1781 . . . At the Long Island Treaty Council, Nanyehi is the featured speaker. "Our cry is for peace; let it continue. This peace must last forever. Let your women's sons be ours; our sons be yours. Let your women hear our words." (Note: No white women are present.)

Colonel William Christian responds to her, "Mother, we have listened well to your talk. . . . No man can hear it without being moved by it. . . . Our women shall hear your words. . . . We will not meddle with your people if they will be still and quiet at home and let us live in peace."[1]

Although the majority of Cherokee and whites hold the peace, violence and bloodshed continue among dissenting factions.

1785 . . . The Hopewell Treaty Council convenes in South Carolina. Attending the council are four commissioners appointed by Congress, thirty-six chiefs, and about a thousand Cherokee delegates. Again the Beloved Woman speaks eloquently. Knowing full well the pattern of strife that precedes this Council, she bases her talk on positive developments. "I take you by the hand in real friendship. I look on you and the red people as my children. Your having determined on peace is most pleasant to me, for I have seen much trouble during the late war. . . . We are now under the protection of Congress and shall have no more disturbance. The talk I have given you is from the young warriors I have raised in my town, as well as myself. They rejoice that we have peace, and hope the chain of friendship will nevermore be broken."[2]

Hope—that quality so necessary for survival. The Beloved Woman never loses hope. Perhaps I will learn the source of her strength by

1. Ilene J. Cornwell, "Nancy Ward," in *Heroes of Tennessee* (Memphis, Tenn.: Memphis State University Press, 1979), 41.
2. Pat Alderman, *Nancy Ward* (Johnson City, Tenn.: Overmountain Press, 1978), 69.

sharing her private moments: I may see her bend in joy over her new-born second daughter (fathered by a white trader, Bryant Ward, to whom she is briefly married in the 1750s) or hear her laugh among her grandchildren and the many orphans to whom she gives a home. Or I may stand beside her in 1817 as she composes her last message to her people. Too ill at age seventy-nine to attend the Council, she sends the last message by her son. Twenty years before it begins, she sees the Trail of Tears looming ahead and her words have one theme: "My children, do not part with any more of our lands . . . it would be like destroying your mothers."

The Grandmother's hand on my arm halts my imaginings. We stand at the edge of a secluded clearing, rimmed with tall pines. In the center is a large log house, and around it women—many women—move through sun and shadow. Some walk in the clearing.

Others cluster on the porch, talking quietly, or sit at the edge of the forest in meditation. Not far from us, a women who is combing another's hair leans forward to whisper, and their laughter rises into the soughing pines.

A great weaving is going on here, a deep bonding.

"This is the menstrual lodge," says Grandmother. "When our power sign is with us we come here. It is a sacred time—a time for rest and meditation. No one is allowed to disturb our harmony. No warrior may even cross our path. In the menstrual lodge many things are known, many plans are made."

"And the Beloved Woman?"

"She is here."

"What year is this, Grandmother?"

"It is not a year; it is a *season*. You and the Beloved Woman are meeting when each of you is in her forty-seventh season." From the expression on my face the Grandmother knows I appreciate the wisdom of her choice: four and seven are the sacred numbers of the Cherokee, four symbolizing the balance of the four directions, seven signifying the seven mother clans and the wholeness of the People and of the universe. It is the season when no women can afford to be puny. The Grandmother nods. Motioning me to wait, she goes toward the lodge, threading her way through the women with a smile of recognition here, the touch of outstretched fingers there.

With my hands behind my hips, I lean against the stout, wiry-haired trunk of a pine. Its resinous scent clears my mind. These women are not the Amazons of the Greek fables. According to Greek legend, the Amazons hated men, using them only at random for procreation and killing or making servants of their sons. But did the Greek patriarchy tell the truth? If Attakullakulla had asked them, "Where are your women?" they would have answered with a shrug. I'm wary of Greeks bearing fables. Although there is little proof that they described the Amazons accurately, ample evidence suggests that they encountered—and resented—strong women like my Grandmothers, and characterized them as heinous in order to justify destroying them (a strategy modern patriarchy also uses).

In any case, I have the spirits of the Grandmothers, whose roots are struck deep in my native soil and whose strength is as tangible and tenacious as the amber-pitched pine at my back.

Like the husk of a seed, my Western education and conditioning split, and my spirit sends up a green shoot. With it comes a long-buried memory: I am twelve years old. Mother has told me that soon I will be capable of bearing life. "Think of it, Marilou. It's a sacred power, a great responsibility." I think . . . and wait for the power sign. It comes. Mother announces to my father, "Our little girl is a woman now."

He smiles, "Well . . . mighty fine."

In the evening we have a dinner in my honor. Steam from corn on the cob, fried chicken, green beans, and corn bread mingle in my mind with the private odor, warm and pungent, that Mother describes as "fresh" (the rural term for mammals in season). I feel wholesome, proud, in harmony with the natural order.

I am now ready to meet the Beloved Woman.

"What was it like," you ask, "to be in her presence?"

"Come. I will show you." It is midnight, June, the full moon. Behind a farmhouse near the Kentucky border, you and I walk barefoot through the coarse grass. Crickets and treefrogs are drowsy. Birds are quiet. And we are enveloped in a powerful, sweet odor that transforms the night. Too pungent to be honeysuckle. Too fecund for roses. It recalls a baby's breath just after nursing, along with the memory of something warm and private that lingers at the edge of the mind. . . .

Sniffing the air, we seek the source—and find it. The cornfield in bloom. Row on row of sturdy stalks, with their tassels held up to the moon. Silently, in slow rhythm, we make our way into the field. The faint rustle of growing plants flows around and through us; until we stop by a tall stalk, there seems no division between flesh and green. We rub the smooth, sinewy leaves on our cheeks and touch a nubile ear, where each grain of pollen that falls from the tassel will make a kernel, strong and turgid with milk. Linking arms around the stalk, we lift our faces to the drifting pollen and breathe in the spirit of the Corn-Mother—the powerful, joyous, nurturing odor of one complete in herself.

As Selu guided the Grandmothers of old, so do her traditional teachings guide me.

In the Beginning
the Creator made our Mother Earth.
Then came Selu, Grandmother Corn.
She lives in the blue-veiled mountains
with Kanati, The Lucky Hunter
her partner in life and wisdom—
eternal companions, like the deer and corn,
and Selu taught the People saying
   "This thing you call corn is I.
   I will be the Corn-Mother.
   The Law of Respect is in the seed.
   When you take, always give back
   and there will be plenty for everyone.
   Remember."

As it was then, so it is now.
When the People work together, plant with care,
they learn the Corn-Mother's wisdom and the Law.
Adapting her form to mountain or desert,
to cold or heat, Selu remains herself,
putting down roots deep and wide—a heritage
to hold her tall, strong, balanced.
As the People tend Selu they see
the male tassel grow in beauty,
the female silks grow in beauty.
Pollen sweetens the air
as it joins silks to make a tiny ear,
cradled in the curving leaf
as in the arm of its mother.
The rustle of the fields is an ancient voice,
"This thing you call corn is I."
To bring in the harvest, Selu again
requires the People to work together.
And when her silk plume turns brown,

Selu walks from the stalk
as the People should walk,
   in strength,
   in balance,
   in beauty.

The Corn-Mother's body is her sweet heart,
speaking unity in diversity, her great wisdom.
In the colors of her People
the kernels circle round and round—
red, white, black, yellow, brown
each respecting the space of the other
no one first or last,
each one different
each one good,
living together like a family
like a community
like a nation.
In harmony. In democracy.
And there is plenty for everyone in the world.

The Grandmothers speak forever.

The Essence of You

Michelle V. Cloonan

LA WALLY, VALERIA, VALERIE, Schlegel von Gottlieben, Guzman, Galembert, Grandma. Your essence was distilled from all of these names, spanning all your countries, and all of your languages. For me, your sweet redolence was captured in your New York City apartment. Seventeen stories up, parquet floors covered by old family Persian rugs, African violets, avocados, rosemary, ivy, paintings by Italian masters, books in French, Italian, German, and English, Angel records, and you: lightness, learning, and love.

I remember you most vividly there, for you moved back to New York when I was just four. You explained life to me in your polyglotted accent. But sometimes you fell back on your other languages; counting in German, ordering meat in Italian, speaking French in certain restaurants, and using the Yiddish you picked up—"Where did you get that *shmatta* (rag)?" a question you asked me frequently during my hippie years. First you would look at me with mock disapproval, and then you would smile and tell me some story about your own youthful rebelliousness. "*Eviva*" you always said just before you drank your mysterious bedtime potion and went to sleep.

You showed me the world from your living-room windows. We watched the East River turn into the Atlantic, the Adriatic, the Alps, Warsaw, Paris— real places, imagined places, places of the heart and of the mind. You were my navigator, my port, and after you died, I drifted; as perhaps you once did, before the war, before you fled, before New York.

Memories of you float back to me in phrases and little episodes. Experiences from twenty, thirty, almost forty years ago.

Red shoes: how I desired them. But how to get them? I know! "Grandma, my feet hurt!"

"What's wrong with them *darleeng?*"

"I don't know. It must be my shoes. They're so *tight!*"

And with that, Grandma did a u-turn in her capacious white Oldsmobile, leaving in the dust our previous destination. Away we went to a shoe store, where miraculously there were beautiful red shoes to fit a three-year-old's feet.

And that is when I discovered that Grandma could be counted on to make anything possible.

I wish that I could remember this experience: little me sans shoes, having my feet washed, or whatever they do to you during a baptism. I will have to improvise the facts.

Grandma comes over one Saturday afternoon to baby-sit me. As usual, we take off on an adventure. This time, she takes me to church, the first church that I have ever been to. (My father was an agnostic, my mother a Baha'i.) The others are waiting for us. Van, one of my grandmother's best friends, becomes my godfather. After Grandma has had this "dirty" little deed performed, she takes me home and tells my parents. They are furious.

"At least you're covered," Grandma chuckled when relating her side of the story many years later, "and you never know." She was an agnostic who described herself as a "cultural Catholic." The Church was "a necessary evil," and though she strongly disagreed with most Catholic dogma, she told me that she never considered converting to another religion. She could not understand why my mother became a Baha'i.

A postscript to the story. My Aunt Guita and I always assumed that I had been baptized as a Methodist because Grandma briefly dated a Methodist minister during that period. But Guita discovered my baptismal certificate after Grandma's death, and I was christened a Catholic. Both of my names were misspelled on the certificate, probably by the priest who knew me for only about five minutes. How Grandma arranged for a Catholic baptism to be performed in the 1950s, without my parents present, and with a gay man as my godfather, is a secret that died with her. A miracle, I suppose.

Then Grandma was gone. Her work took her to St. Louis, Mississippi, and then back to New York where she, my mother, and my aunt had lived when they first came to this country. Auntie Guita left for Harvard and my great-grandmother returned to Italy. I was painfully alone with a mother who could never be interrupted, and a father who worked all day and spent all evening in school. Even my German shepherd Kimmy was gone. "She's too wild," my mother explained after she took Kimmy away while I was at school.

My loneliness would soon be relieved by the birth of my little sister. But something went wrong, and my mother spent a long time in the hospital. Then came my four grandparents whom I had never seen together; both sets having been divorced long before I was born. I remembered feeling so anxious; whose lap should I sit on?

Finally my mother returned home with Christine, the tiniest of babies. She was born more than a month prematurely.

The next Christmas, the four of us went to visit Grandma in New York for the first time. Grandma's apartment was small compared to her houses in Wilmette and St. Louis. But once again, as all her dwellings, it was magical. She found novel ways to hang her paintings and display her beautiful objects. And she always had interesting things, like wondrous papers, toys, or buttons tucked away in secret places. I loved her wrapping paper box and all the ribbons, strings, and exotic papers that it contained. That particular Christmas, Grandma bought a miniature tree that fit on top of her coffee table. Instead of her usual ornaments, she covered this tree with Italian chocolates wrapped in brightly colored foils. Edible ornaments!

"Don't take away my blankie. PLEASE!!!"

"But it's filthy, my love."

"But Grandma, it's my BLANKIE!!!

"I'll get you another one. A nice new *clean* one."

"Grandma, POLEASE!!!"

No use. I followed Grandma down the hall in desperation as she walked to the incinerator. Down seventeen stories it fell. I could hear the flames at the bottom, smell the burning ashes as my beloved blankie was engulfed. Grandma shut the incinerator's malevolent mouth. And I cried all night.

The next day, Grandma presented me with three new blankets, but she sensed my agony, and I sensed that she understood. I never forgot it, nor did she. And in that moment of pathos our relationship changed, for I now fully shared her deep recess of pain.

After Grandma left the Chicago area, we saw her only once or twice a year, either in New York or Chicago. I always preferred seeing her in New York where we went to the Central Park Zoo, or had hot chocolate and strawberries at the Plaza. She took me to work with her in the garment district. I would sit on the floor playing with buttons while she ordered hundreds of thousands of yards of fabric for her next fall or spring fashion line. And of course there were Saturday afternoon puppet shows at F.A.O. Schwartz.

On one visit to F.A.O., I saw a life-size log cabin and stepped inside. I immediately began to fantasize about life out West with dogs and horses and cows roaming somewhere nearby. Grandma must have shared my fantasies for she got the attention of a salesman.

"Would it be possible for you to have this shipped to the Chicago area?"

"I don't know, madam." Grandma must have graced him with *her look*, which I can't possibly describe. But there was a quality to it that made people want to do anything possible for her. I often noticed the phenomenon in stores, taxis, or restaurants. Her glance must have expressed utter determination coupled with genuine kindness, for everyone loved Grandma. She took care of so many people—her two daughters, her mother, her employees, friends, or strangers in need—that somehow, when there was something that she wanted, other people became eager to help. "But then again, I'm sure that we can arrange to have it shipped wherever you would like, Madam."

"Why, that would be absolutely *mahrvelous*, don't you think so, Meecky?" But I was already out on the range riding my horse while she was graciously thanking the salesman.

Several weeks later, back in Northfield, Illinois, the log cabin arrived, with a construction crew. The cabin was my retreat from my mother and the setting of many Wild West adventures. But by a sad coincidence, the log cabin met with the same fate as my blanket. One summer it became infested with termites, and the older kids on the block tore off some of the bark. So my father burned it down as I stood behind him. This time I felt none of the hysteria that I had experienced years earlier upon losing my blanket. At a young age, I had already learned resignation.

My mother walked out on us shortly before my thirteenth birthday. She met a French sailor, Pierre, and the two of them went to France and later to Mexico where they waited for my mother's divorce to become finalized. Then they got married and returned to Chicago. Grandma had apparently tried to dissuade my mother from leaving, but to no avail.

The first and only time I ever saw Grandma act unkindly toward someone was when she met Pierre. Grandma happened to be in town for a visit when Pierre came to our house for the first time. My mother was taking a nap and Grandma answered the door. Pierre didn't speak much English, and when he spoke to my grandmother in French, she responded in English, "I'm sorry, but I don't remember any French."

I remember thinking what an odd thing it was for Grandma to say because I had heard her speak French so many times. But then, I didn't have an inkling of what was going on. My mother had a wealth of friends who came over, and I didn't know that Pierre was a different kind of friend. And of course, I didn't know what Grandma knew. Not long after that meeting, mother and Pierre went off.

A few months after mother returned to Chicago, she decided that she wanted custody of me and my two younger sisters, and she sued my father. My sisters and I all wanted to stay with Dad. For my mother had always been emotionally absent anyway, and her physical absence was actually a relief.

In Illinois, a child could not legally decide where to live until the age of fourteen. Dad was able to get a trial date set for just a few days after my fourteenth birthday. My sisters were only eight and nine, however, so the judge would have to make the decision for them. My father's attorney was worried that my mother would win the suit because, at that time, the courts generally preferred to grant custody to the mother. My father needed to have effective witnesses. Our only hope was for my grandmother and Aunt Guita to testify on his behalf.

My sisters and I didn't have to sit through the trial. We were summoned only to the judge's chambers, where he interviewed the three of us together. To this day I have no idea what happened in the courtroom. It was one of the only things I never asked Grandma about.

As I look back on it now, I realize that it must have been one of the saddest days of Grandma's life. She testified for her granddaughters more than for my father, and she did the right thing. My father was able to retain custody of us, but of course it was the end of her relationship with my mother. (My mother's decision, not Grandma's.) I don't think that Grandma ever forgave herself for doing something for which she had no choice.

Grandma had always wanted to go to Japan, but as vice-president of a clothing design and manufacturing firm, she hardly ever took any time off. Then a wonderful opportunity presented itself. A Japanese woman who worked for Grandma learned about a charter flight and tour of Expo '70 in Osaka that was being organized by a Japanese electronics firm. Grandma decided to go, but thought that the trip would be much more fun if her friends Marge and George and I went too. My father decided that it was okay for me to miss a month of high school, and I knew instinctively that a month-long trip with Grandma would be far more exciting and educational than all four years of high school put together.

My only reservation about the trip was having Marge and George with us. Of all of Grandma's many interesting friends, they were the only ones I didn't like. They were relentlessly midwestern: big, broad, meat-and-potato, Republican, small town, conservative. They were in every way the opposite of Grandma, who was slim, soignée, urbane, and liberal. But Grandma loved them, and as it turned out, they were her most constant friends. Marge later became the inspiration for a line of clothing which Grandma designed for larger women. Marge always dressed beautifully, but because of her size, she had to have her clothing custom-made. Thanks to Grandma and Marge, large women are no longer condemned to a life of wearing tent dresses in dark colors.

So the four of us went to Japan and I was careful not to share my views on the Vietnam conflict with them. As it turned out, Marge and George, both of whom seemed larger than Japan itself, and who always had to bend down to go through doors since they were each over six feet tall, were good travelers.

I did not keep a diary of the trip and my impressions now must be expressed with broad strokes rather than fine details. So it was with excitement and curiosity that I read Grandma's travel diary. Guita found a fragment of it in her attic and it covers only about half of the trip. But reading even those scattered pages brought me right back to Japan and the view of the world that was Grandma's. Her writing is full of exuberance: everything about Japan interested her from the garbage bags that were included in our boxed lunches, to the moss gardens in Kyoto; from the layout of farms, to quality control on the assembly lines at the Panasonic factory. A few brief examples illustrate both Grandma's "lexicon" and her charming observations.

Upon seeing the Imperial Plaza Grandma observed that "Buckingham Palace is the ice follies compared to this venerable institution." A few days later, when we were in Kyoto, she described the Golden Pavilion as a "lacy structure with gables in four directions mirroring itself in a pond. We were lucky to have a ray of sunshine on it."

She loved Nara and included a vivid description of its shrine where "Buddha is in the middle and his two assistants are on each side!" She also mentions the sacred deer there. But then there is a curious omission of an event which I remember well: my elegant grandmother being bucked by a deer. As I recall, she cursed the deer in polite but firm French.

Of the subway she wrote that "sardines are loosely packed compared to this." And throughout the diary some of Grandma's characteristic phrases are repeated: "This is something else" (a phrase of wonderment and delight for Grandma), "ghastly" (used to describe some of the displays in the Ginza) and, "wow!"

The Panasonic plant received three full pages of treatment. Grandma could not stop marveling about the quality control and efficiency there. I must confess that I skipped out on that tour choosing instead to go to an anti-Vietnam rally in Osaka. When I was nearly fifteen, factories held little interest for me. However, Grandma's "factory gene" must have been dominant because over the years I have dragged countless students to paper mills and library binderies.

When it was time for me to consider colleges, Grandma and Guita made arrangements for my college tours. Although I considered going to Berkeley, I wanted to be closer to them, so I wound up at Bennington. Upon my arrival, there were large boxes from Grandma waiting for me in my dorm room. These were like all of Grandma's boxes: compact and neat. She would use new boxes and wrap them mummy-style with the kind of big brown tape that requires a sponge and water for adhesion. It always seemed to take an hour to open them. These boxes were filled with towels, pillows, and basic tools. Among the tools were beautiful scissors accompanied with strict instructions: one pair was for cloth and one for paper and I must never use either for the wrong task. Grandma had wanted to be an engineer when she was growing up but her mother sent her to art school instead. Her innate engineering skills were readily apparent when she packed boxes, organized her tools, or assembled her spring and fall fashion lines. Grandma was always organized, organized, organized.

One of my greatest pleasures while I was in college was bringing friends to New York City for a weekend with Grandma. I especially enjoyed bringing friends who had never been to New York so that they could see it à la Grandma. One such friend was Christopher, who was from Los Angeles. In my senior year he introduced me to southern California, then the two of us drove to New York. Grandma loved lemons, so we picked a bag's worth from Christopher's back yard and hand-delivered them to her. She was as excited to receive such a gift as Christopher was in getting to know her. He fell so in love with New York after Grandma's introduction to it that he later moved there. And Grandma, unbeknownst to me at the time, gave him some rather personal advice about life in the city.

Grandma inadvertently set me on the path to my eventual career while I was at Bennington. I decided to study bookbinding and she immediately offered to pay for my lessons. She felt that everyone should learn a craft. I became so intrigued by the world of the book that I abandoned plans to go to law school. I suppose that this seed was planted not only by my grandmother's love of books, but by the fact that the Morgan Library was right across the street from her apartment and we went to many exhibitions there. The Morgan was my intellectual playground, but I also think of it as part of Grandma's classroom. Given different circumstances, she might have created such a library herself.

Nearly half of my life has been lived in the absence of you. Twenty years, but not a day without some thought of you. You're alive in the jewelry of yours that I wear, the rugs in my house, a whiff of my Chanel, the fine herbs that I use in cooking. I think of you whenever I hear Mahler's First Symphony, Spanish guitar, or P.D.Q. Bach, or when I see early Knopf books. When I need to trim back my herbs, I can hear you in the background saying, "It's time to give *these* plants a haircut." And of course I am always very careful to use the correct type of scissors for the task at hand.

I think of your advice, more of which I should have taken. In retrospect, almost everything you told me about relationships, careers, and finances was sage and practical. Without you I have stumbled, and I have missed your counsel. But because of you, and your unshakable confidence in me, I have managed to survive.

I think of your laugh, your enthusiasm, your ability to rise above disasters so quickly. Once, while I was visiting you, there was a telephone call in the middle of the night. Your entire spring line had been stolen from your office with just weeks to go before the shows. Somehow you worked around the clock to reassemble it.

Yes, I think about your strength, but I also remember your vulnerability. After your first heart attack, your doctor told you to lose weight, cut out salt, and exercise more. I could hardly believe it; you who were already so slender and weighed 115 pounds at most, you who walked everywhere and had taken Mom and Guita for walks across the George Washington Bridge every week when they were girls. You who ate yoghurt, Rye Crisps, and Swiss granola before it was fashionable. But you trusted your doctor and followed his recommendations as though they were marching orders. Out went the salt, and down went your weight.

The last time I saw you was just before I left for a conservation internship in Dublin. I hugged you goodbye, and I couldn't believe how thin you had become. It was as though you were wasting away in my arms.

Just two months later you did waste away. After your Saturday routine of the hairdresser followed by the Metropolitan Opera, you must have gone home and written a number of letters and then posted them. That night you went to bed and read, as usual. You probably never even had your *Eviva* drink because you died with the book in your hands. You were sixty-seven.

I flew to New York from Dublin, my mother came from Paris, and Guita from Boston. Pressed for time, we divided among us, gave away, or sold all of your possessions too quickly. Even now I dream that you have returned to your apartment, but it is empty. Or, conversely, that I have returned to your apartment and it still looks lived in, but you are not there and I cannot find you.

Once back in Dublin, one of your familiar tangerine-colored envelopes was waiting for me. I have never read your last letter to me in its entirety. I opened the envelope, pulled out the letter to read it, but my eyes first fell on the last sentence, "I can't wait for the spring which will bring my Mickey back."

My Adopted English Gran

Laurence B. Calver

I'VE JUST MET my boyfriend's grandmother, Maud, for the first time. Meeting The Family is always a significant step in any relationship, and I think I've been introduced to the entire clan now. Typically English, they've been ever so polite, but wince at my American frankness and purse their mouths over my European roots. After living in Britain for more than five years I still feel foreign, out of sync with this tightly traditional island society which regards multinationals like myself with puzzlement and suspicion. Gran, though, as Neil calls her, feels different from anyone I've encountered so far. Upon introduction, she hugged me with her grandson's warmth, genuinely pleased to be included in his life, accepting him utterly and thus accepting me. Her openness set the tone for the visit as she ushered us into her life for the afternoon.

Gran's warmth and directness were just the first of many surprises. Despite being fairly deaf, nearly eighty, and wearing a pacemaker, she leads a happily independent life. I was amazed at her apartment. She lives on the fourteenth floor of a rather dubious tower block, with watery flourescent lighting in the hallways and menacing graffitti on the walls; but once you step inside, it is as cosy as a cottage. It is her domain, and with her husband long dead, she rules it contentedly. The miniature sitting room is a monument to her several grandchildren, whose toothless school photos jostle for position with more adult poses—one in a wedding dress, another in university robes, a third in a spotless policeman's uniform. The whole place speaks Granny, and has a certain timelessness found only in grandparents' homes. I can tell Neil likes to come here to grasp the cord connecting him to his past; he showed me the hall where he and his cousin used to kick a ball, and the disposal that would chew up any garbage, much to their intense delight. We perched on the sofa that oozed around our behinds, working valiantly on dry salad and leaden "kwich," as Gran calls the eggy pies she gets from Marks and Spencers specially. It was apparently a favorite of Neil's when he was little. Apparently. We naturally washed this all down with oceans of tea; vast quantities of that amber liquid so near and dear to the British soul. I loathe the stuff, particularly since they sully it with milk, but I make the occasional exception. Goodness knows what Maud thinks of me, this strange dark-haired foreign girl who chokes on the national drink and is prone to Public Displays of Affection. Still, I was fascinated by her narrations of family life and the photographs she produced of places and people that fill in the outlines of Neil's background. By the time we left, my head was whirling with Dotties and Flossies and Gavins, trying to keep straight who was related to whom. We gave her some silk from the Far East that she will make into a dress, and hugged her goodbye at the door.

I mentioned to Neil afterwards that she didn't have much difficulty understanding me despite her hearing impairment, and that I felt rather pleased at the fact. He merely chuckled and said that she hates to admit when she can't follow the conversational flow, so she just nods and agrees. I'm impressed at her artfulness in preserving her dignity; I was completely fooled. Oh well. I'll just have to project a bit more next time. I'll write her a little thank-you note tomorrow.

As of tonight, Neil and I are engaged. I guess that means I'll be in England for a little while longer.

We've been to see Neil's Gran again today. She's terribly excited about the wedding, and has sewn up the silk we brought her into a new dress for the occasion. Her pure delight is refreshing in the face of all the other hassles we've been dealing with regarding invitations and mixed religions and who has the right to marry whom where and when. While the various officials furrow their brows and invited guests lead us through the guessing game of whether or not they are going to come, Gran is merely looking forward to the pleasure of being involved in our big day. She's simply happy for us, and doesn't mind too much that I'm foreign, an unusual attitude in this culture. Maud is more at peace with herself and her surroundings than most people I know, and thus she is more concerned with the fact that Neil appears happy. Every time I touch him, whether I stroke his cheek or hold hands, she crows delightedly that I can't keep my hands off of him. I realize that such blatant affection is not in the national character, so it must quite startle her, but to her credit she seems to be revelling in this obvious proof of our affection for each other.

It makes me wonder about her own marriage and how a strong-minded woman like her coped with the stern silent man who was her husband. I know that the marriage lasted until the day he died of heart trouble about ten years ago, and that she grieved painfully for him. After his death, Maud moved next door to her younger daughter's place, but was so unhappy with the change that she went back to the Council Office in tears asking to return to her little flat where she had lived with Neil's granddad, and where she remains today. And yet, when she casually mentions details of their life together, I'm outraged at how she fetched and carried for him, while he laid down the law as to how the household should be run. When he was away fighting during World War II, she single-handedly took care of her two small girls, not easy when the house was destroyed in the Blitz. Still, she seems to take all of this in her stride. Wish I could be as patient with the various imbeciles whom I must hurdle over to make it down the aisle on my wedding day.

Well, it was an amazing honeymoon; a whole month out of the country, time to rest after the stress and whirlwind of the wedding. We've returned refreshed, ready to start married life with the autumn. With the proud self-consciousness of the newly married, we went to visit Gran today, to show her our photos and bring her more Thai silk. While we've been away, the British summer sunshine, rare as an Anglo-Saxon emotional outburst, has been working its magic on the country's greenery, and we were treated to a viewing of Maud's own little garden. She is an avid horticulturalist and her balcony a wonder to behold. No bigger than an open air walk-in closet with a view across London, it is a secret kingdom where she reigns supreme. If it's not the season for her favorite flowering plants, she supplements her display with vivid plastic imitations and fills in gaps with cheery figurines. On the wall are ceramic reminders of the places she visited with her husband, plaques of

Lago di Como and the West Country. It is no trivial pastime, though. Like most Brits, cultivating vegetation is firmly printed in her DNA, and she tends her flora with the seriousness and skill of an artist. With the satisfaction of a mechanic leaning over a purring engine, Maud talks us through her designs, what problems she has solved, which invading insects she has vanquished. Though she speaks to both of us, I know that the knowledge she imparts is meant for Neil, in whom her abilities are already beginning to show. I accept that I am outside of this cultural connection; my lack of Anglo-Saxon blood has long been obvious in my indifference to growing things and small animals, a fact of which I am perversely proud. However, watching Gran talk through her garden with Neil, I have a momentary respect for the gift that runs in both their blood.

The three of us went to Kew Gardens not long ago, to see the new blooms of the season. (In Britain, springtime comes in June.) Gran was in her element, taking photographs, pointing out rare plants by name, exclaiming over the exotica in the greenhouse like long lost friends. Kew is one of the few parks in London with an entrance fee, which covers the upkeep of this living botanical museum. It has its own police force as well, for reasons that became apparent halfway into our visit. As we approached a particularly lovely flowering tree, Maud got a gleam in her eye. Marshalling Neil over under pretext of smelling the blooms, she used her grandson as a cover and quickly snapped a few sprigs into her handbag. Rosy with innocence, she retreated with her booty. By the time we left the park that afternoon, waving cheerily at the guards on the entrance gate, she had several hundred dollars worth of clippings, enough for both her garden and ours, all tucked away under her tissues and extra film in her purse. Now the purloined flora are thriving happily in glass jars on her balcony. Needless to say, our own snippets have given up the ghost, rotting reproachfully despite Neil's ministrations.

Neil has just gone to drive his Gran home after a merry afternoon over at our place for tea. She was in excellent form; I wish I could remember everything she tells us. Always a great raconteuse, she's able to make a bus ride down Oxford Street sound like an adventure. Over cheese scones, tomatoes from Neil's latest crop, and dainty cakes from Harrods, she regaled us with tales of her recent activities and encounters. She had to get a new vacuum cleaner because her household help broke her old one: "Twenty-five years I've had it, and it would have lasted me, too, and Lily said, 'Oh Maud it's a pity it broke when I was using it.' and I was thinking, Lily, it wouldn't have broken if you hadn't been using it!"

Then she described how she went to get a new one with some of the money she has sewn in her curtains—for her funeral expenses—and how she saved ten pounds on it, but that the notes had been in the curtain so long they were no longer legal tender and she had to exchange them at the bank. Then she decided to assemble it herself: "You only had to put the handle in the thing, you know, with a screw, and I said to myself, 'Maud, you're not stupid, you can do it yourself.'" Well, she couldn't quite manage it, so at ten at night she went down and collared the building's plumber to come up and do it for her. Just so nobody would think anything was amiss, she's put an I.O.U. in the curtains for the money she used to buy the vacuum.

I finally got the opportunity to ask Maud how she met her husband, Bert. An excellent story—he was a friend of her boyfriend, and was intended for her best friend, Margaret. However, when Maud met him she fell in love because "he wore kid gloves and a watch and had his shoes all shined up, you know." A quick word with her best friend, and the two girls swapped beaux. Maud married Bert three years later, at nineteen, and her best friend married the ex-boyfriend one year later. They are still friends, and apparently when Bert died, Margaret and her husband were very good to Maud.

She told me she had received my card for her birthday, and was very pleased with it. With amused disdain, she mentioned that the birthday card from her own daughter had been a week late, sent by second class post, and didn't even say "From," never mind "Love," on it. Though such filial coldness, often typical of England, appalls me, she merely chuckles and accepts the situation, knowing with the wisdom of age that there is nothing to be done about such rudeness. "I never see my daughter," she commented once. "I don't mind; don't miss her, really." Her unexpected frankness is one of the qualities I am learning to adore about her, though it takes even me by surprise sometimes.

Gran also told us about her early life when she first came to London. At fourteen years old, she came down to London from her home in the north to "go into service." In other words, to work as a maid in one of the wealthy mansions of the between war period. I find it hard to reconcile the image of wit and strength she presents with her past as a meek and frightened servant; part of the below stairs set, not meant to mingle with the upper classes. The only time I've ever seen a shade of that past life was when she called to thank me for her birthday books. I know she is passionate about history, so I got her a book about being a parent during the Blitz in England, which I thought she would identify with. In thanking me for the volume, however, Gran said it was really meant for someone better than she—by which she meant better educated, of a higher class. It took me aback. She is so clever and capable—reading everything she can get her hands on, making beautiful crocheted works of art, sewing her own dresses—it just never occurred to me that she still had a sense of being below stairs as they call it here. After seventy years as an autodidact, in which she has gained more knowledge than some Ph.Ds, she still feels ashamed of not finishing her formal schooling. It makes me wonder what valuable gifts have been lost to the world in these past generations, women with the minds of engineers and architects and captains of industry, reduced to constructing woollen mittens and making the Sunday roast stretch to two meals.

We spent the afternoon at the Lanesborough Hotel, an early celebration of Maud's eighty-third birthday. It's becoming a tradition for the three of us to have a private party before Neil and I leave on vacation, since Gran's birthday is at the end of August when we are usually away. I don't know who enjoys it more, us or she. A proper English afternoon tea is now purely the reserve of the tourist industry, but still has echoes of an earlier time for someone of Maud's generation—though in her case, she was probably serving it up instead of enjoying it herself. In any case, it's a delight to be with someone who can appreciate a well made scone with clotted cream and lemon curd. The opulent Saudis swathed in robes and the birdlike Japanese tourists who occupied the other tables didn't have half as much fun as we did at our heaped up table. Only the over enthusiastic pianist banging away at close range could dim our little party, as it further complicated Maud's challenged acoustics. At one point she sighed pointedly and commented that it would be nice if his batteries ran down; although when we told her he was playing Happy Birthday she perked up and beamed grandly at the room.

Afterwards, we ensconced ourselves in the nearby lounge to let our digestions settle and have Maud assist me with my crocheting. Impressed by the works of art she has created, I had begged for lessons, but they have turned into quiet rituals of humiliation. She's an excellent and patient teacher, but every now and then she chuckled in sheer amazement that someone with a university education could be so breathtakingly clumsy with a crochet hook. "It's easy!" she insisted, while I threw filthy looks at Neil who was snickering behind his newspaper. Like tennis, flower arranging, and well-cared-for clothing, needlework of any sort is clearly not in my gene pool. However, I'm determined to continue because I feel that Maud's skill deserves a new generation. Each new baby in her growing family tree has been showered with frothy delicacies of wool and ribbon, booties and mittens, caps, sweaters, and blankets, while the older ones receive wardrobes for their dolls. The handiwork is exquisite, and would command a fair price in any upmarket boutique. Her offspring seem indifferent to it, making me all the more determined to struggle on with my lessons.

This bond I have with Neil's grandmother may seem strange since we come from backgrounds that are worlds apart, our only common touchstone being Neil. I certainly have been unable to connect with the rest of his family in a similar way; I am just too different, and there is intolerance on both sides. So why is it that I feel such an admiration for Gran, delighting in her company and conversation, and blossoming under her affection? She is certainly unlike my real grandmother—cultured, witty Mom, who had the mind of an engineer and command of several languages—whom I ache for still and whose face I am growing into. It is strange, too, to think that Gran could easily have been one of my great-grandmother's maids, and that Nana would have taken one look at the tower block where Gran lives and delicately wrinkled her well-bred nose.

However, I believe there is a commonality there that crosses the boundaries of culture and class, and one that serves me as a role model. Despite her humble background, and her unspectacular lifestyle, Gran has imbued her life with an energy that comes out of being her own person. At eighty-three years old she is independent, clear about her beliefs and values, thorough in her pleasures, and equally thorough in her disapprovals. She has dealt with everything that life has thrown at her, and come out with her joy untarnished by daily trials. She is a harbinger of the best of old age, having achieved the peace of mind that should rightfully come after so many years' experience. Strangely, people don't expect this of the elderly, and I think that is why I admire her so. In her own way she has kicked over the traces of stereotype, refusing to be timid and vulnerable, and woe to those who think otherwise. In that we have something in common, both small (vertically at least— Maud is a bit more horizontally endowed than I) and seemingly innocuous—until we open our mouths and react.

Maud takes great pleasure in recounting tales in which she has defied assumptions. Once, a British Telecom engineer came over to help with an equipment problem she was having. Obviously bored and disinterested, he glanced at the gadget (a gift from Neil and me to display the phone numbers of incoming calls), said there was nothing he could do, and that he would have to charge her for the visit because the equipment had not been purchased directly from his company. Bad choice. Maud went into full gear then, saying how BT was supposed to have a special policy of helpfulness with its older customers. She had read their brochure, and personally she didn't think he was being anything but rude. She said she had a heart condition and the stress of it all could well give her a heart attack (never mind that she is in bursting good health). She commanded him to take his coat and leave, and said she would be on to his superiors straight away. By the time she finished with the hapless chap, he was well on his way to having a cardiac arrest himself. In the end, it turned out that all she needed were some fresh batteries, which she went out and purchased herself; donning her close work glasses and installing them with great satisfaction. I suppose the other aspect of Gran that I admire is her forthrightness, unusual in a country that so values polite circumspection. If she doesn't like something, she just says so. Doesn't yell, just calmly states her opinion and that's it. You may not agree with her, but at least you know where she stands and can respect her honesty and integrity. People around her may shudder with horror when she shatters the inbred code of politeness, but she doesn't leave you doubting her genuine feelings. When she says she enjoyed a letter or a gift, you know she means it—it's terribly refreshing.

I reached a milestone today. For the very first time, I visited Gran on my own. We had a smashing afternoon together, but I realize something more extraordinary has occurred—at a time when most of my peers are losing or are distanced from their grandparents, I have gained a brand-new grandmother. My solo visit was like the last step in an adoption process, and her delighted cry of "Here's my girl" and enveloping hug were the official stamp. She will never replace my natural grandmother, of course, but in her own way she is a guide and a paradigm for me, unravelling the mysteries of adult life in general and of this confusing country in particular. In all the time I've lived as a foreigner in England, unhappily trying to grasp the slippery handle to this impenetrable culture, she is the one person who has taken me by the hand and, with a cheery calmness, drawn me into her world. I may not get the sense of cultural continuity from her that a blood relative imparts, but in return I'm receiving the warmth and wisdom that only an older woman can pass on—and getting it at an age when I am beginning to appreciate its importance. Never mind that the language is of gardens and tea cosys, holidays in Cornwall and wartime rationing cards. The lessons of independence, mingled with delight in the smallest details of life, are the same, showing me that a woman's older years can be just as precious as those that come before.

So maybe, just maybe, I have put down a few roots here after all, grafted onto the British culture by the diligent welcoming hands of Neil's—our—incredible Gran.

◗

Not Just a Bubbe-Mayse

TILLIE'S STORY

Beryl Minkle

A CARD FELL OUT of the old, worn cookbook, landing on my kitchen floor. Curious, I picked it up. It was a Hallmark-style Valentine's Day card from Grandma Tillie wishing me "Love Across the Miles," and encouraging me to "buy some art subblies." I chuckled over her characteristic spelling error. She knew what I loved most, and while the ten dollars had not quite covered the cost of one good sable brush, her small contribution meant much more than that to me. My working-class parents had discouraged my artistic aspirations, hoping to convince me to become a secretary, a hairdresser, or a teacher. Maybe, my mother always added (because I argued with them so much), I might even become a successful lawyer.

I leaned over my kitchen table, contemplating my grandmother's blintz recipe in the faded red hardback, its binding torn and ragged from constant use. Cooking was my grandma's ticket out of destitute poverty as a child. Later, during the Depression, when she had her husband and young son, my father, to feed, she plucked chickens and sold homemade cookies door-to-door. Cooking became her lifeline to me, and her folk wisdom, derided by my father as superstitions or *bubbe mayses*, fed my imagination. Although she died nearly thirteen years ago, I am still learning from Grandma Tillie, my best and most wise teacher.

She told me she was born in a town somewhere on the Russian-Polish border. The town's name kept changing, as did the border. Her village was probably somewhere outside of a city, since laws and custom prohibited Jews from actually residing within. Grandma's birthday was also indefinite. There were no official records, so her family decided to celebrate her birth on Memorial Day once they got to America. Her mother Leah's family had been dairy farmers, but as Jews, they were subject to constant attacks by Cossacks. Around 1910, the pogroms drove Leah, her husband Samuel, their young family, and some cousins across the Atlantic to New York, and then to St. Louis, Missouri. The immigrants regularly sent money, clothing, and supplies to the family left behind. Eventually, the letters from home ceased and a friend said they should stop sending gifts because officials were stealing the contents of the packages and harassing the recipients. Leah and Samuel made frantic efforts to contact the family, until their worst fears were confirmed by a *landesman* who told them that the family had been killed and the farm and their home confiscated by the government. They never heard from another family member in Europe again.

My grandmother displayed her only photograph of her parents in full view as you entered the front door. They were a handsome young couple, standing against a studio backdrop in Russia. As I grew older I was struck by the injustice of how Leah and Samuel had married for love, yet her father later matched his own daughter in an unwanted marriage. I never forgave him for that.

I loved their photographic image. Leah slender, small, and intent, with long fair hair pulled up in a bun, and wearing a dark brocade dress. She appears to be in her early twenties and looks about five months pregnant. This might have been her second child, my Grandma. Samuel is six feet tall, fair, and serious, his bright eyes staring straight into the camera. Someone in my family told me her parents might have posed for this photograph soon before leaving for the United States. It was one of my grandmother's treasures. While remembering actual dates was never my grandmother's specialty, she could recall a lifetime of her many different apartment addresses and her dress sizes, typically linking up the two in her mind, saying, "When we lived at the beach, at 50 Paloma Court, I was a size twelve, and on Venice Boulevard in the duplex I was still a twelve, until we moved to the fourplex on Venice Boulevard and I wore a fourteen." Almost five feet short, heavy, and very large bosomed, Grandma Tillie radiated a contagious warmth. She told us she kept her gold hidden in the pouches of skin which hung under her ample, strong arms. Her clear, brown eyes shone for children, whom she always favored with a ready smile. She cooked and served food to three generations of children.

Neither of my grandparents wanted to talk about their family's lives in "the old country," and I remember Grandma saying, with unusual abruptness, that she didn't speak any Russian or Polish. When the names of dead relations were mentioned, Grandma would glance downward, and in a soft voice intone: "May she (or he) rest in peace— Amen." Although we always called our grandpa, *Zayde* (Yiddish for grandfather), and they conversed with family and friends in Yiddish, my grandparents were determined that the grandchildren should speak only English. When we tried to decode the secret language, Grandma only waved us away with her hand, protectively patting us on the head, muttering something like "my beautiful girls, *shayna maidels*, . . . it's so as not to be Greenhorns like us."

Despite this, my sister and I managed to acquire a semi-functional Yiddish vocabulary of hilariously imaginative curse words with which we amused our non-Jewish friends. A very mild curse was: May onions grow in your navel. Our unprintable favorites were suggestively earthy and specific. Somewhat linguistically confused, my sister was convinced that the English word "spatula" was really Yiddish because it sounded so much like Yiddish words we knew, such as *tsatskeleh* (always said by an adult friend or relative while lovingly pinching a child's cheeks), and the endearing *bubeleh* (little grandma).

Grandma Tillie was about ten years old when her mother died, a victim of the postwar influenza epidemic. The oldest daughter, she had to quit school and stayed home taking care of her four younger siblings while her older brother Abe went to work in the family store. Their mother died just two weeks before Abe's Bar Mitzvah. Tillie became the surrogate mother and housekeeper; as she said, "working like a horse" until she got so sick she was hospitalized and a doctor told her father "a young child shouldn't be tied up like this, with all these kids; you've got to find a different way." Determined not to break up the family by farming the children out to relatives, her father placed them in the orphanage, which Grandma always called "the home." It was a large building housing many children, where Grandma was just one of many older children who were put to work cooking, washing, ironing, and taking care of the babies and little children. Grandma was the first adult I knew who talked openly about hating another person. She hated Mrs. Martin, a matron she called "a snake," who had terrorized the younger children, beating them when they wet their beds at night. Grandma tried to protect the little ones by secretly changing their sheets, but Mrs. Martin never let Tillie forget that she held the power over their young lives.

Grandma and her siblings stayed in the orphanage while their father, who had sold the family store, worked as a horse-and-cart junk man. Keeping the *Shabbos* on Saturday, he visited them on Sunday, in-between his other odd jobs. It was a life I could only imagine through Grandma's stories, told over and over, until they also became my stories, and we shared them together.

Through her, I knew and loved all her siblings, and especially loved hearing stories about her baby sister *Faygele* (Aunt Faye), the sixth and youngest. Faygele's birth was shadowed only six months later by the death of their mother, and Grandma became her fiercely protective caregiver. Aunt Faye's winning personality, good looks, and musical talents made her a favorite at the orphanage and a number of families wanted to adopt her. Tillie, her father, and the other siblings objected to an adoption, and Faye became a foster child, living at the home while receiving special privileges from these families. Resentful of her deprivation and furious at being denied a life of material pleasures with one of these families, the very young Aunt Faye wished for an adoption into the good life.

Even though only about two years separated each of her six siblings from the next, it was as if there were at least two different generations of children within her family, with Grandma Tillie and her older brother Abe functioning as breadwinners, and the four younger ones as the little kids. In keeping with tradition, both Abe and Tillie's marriages were arranged, while the younger ones fought to lead more modern, American lives and ultimately chose their own spouses. The younger ones smoked, dated, and snuck out of shul to see their friends during the Jewish holidays.

As a young woman Tillie loved, obeyed, and then resented her father, who decided that Jack, her first and only boyfriend, was unacceptable. She thought Jack was smart, handsome, and funny. Her father, an Orthodox Jew, considered anyone less observant, not Jewish. He called Jack a Jewish *Goy*, coming as he did from a conservative Jewish family, and once dumped a bucket of cold water on Jack's head when he visited.

Her father was more impressed with Ben, a devout *davener*, a gifted prayer singer, who sat next to him in shul. Ben loved Tillie, but she said "it had to be two ways." For the first time, Tillie challenged her father, and said she did "all kinds of crazy things" to try to convince Ben not to marry her. Ben was a shy man, at the time a respected worker in the garment district, and she would taunt him, asking "Is this what you want? Do you know what you're getting into? Right now you're a big cutter, making $75 to $80 dollars a week. That money will have to support all the rest of the children because they're not working yet." Although she grew to respect and care for her husband, she never really understood or felt romantic love for him.

Grandma Tillie's resolve to stay with him was tested early. A few years after my father's birth, Zayde insisted they leave St. Louis and move to Los Angeles, settling in low-rent Venice Beach. In the '30s, Venice was an ethnic enclave shared by Jews, Italians, Chinese, Chicanos, winos, artists, and those who would later be termed Beatniks. For Tillie, the separation from her St. Louis family was wrenching, and she returned to them many times, taking my father when he was young. Each time, resisting her family's entreaties to stay, she returned to her husband, bound by honor and convention.

Over the years my grandparents held various jobs, and eventually leased a corner at 5th and Spring in Los Angeles, working long and hard hours selling newspapers in the heart of the old downtown financial district. Grandma Tillie would often join Zayde in the chilly predawn hours, dressed in layers of skirts and old sweaters, a scarf on her head, hauling bundles of newspapers and magazines to the corner where they were bought by judges, attorneys, and stockbrokers.

Zayde was also a bookie, friendly with the downtown professionals, a wizard at predicting horse races, and no stranger to midnight raids and lock-ups. His buddies, the "boys" in the newspaper sellers' union, usually sprang for him and got him home the next day. This involved expensive pay-offs to "fixers," lawyers who worked both sides of the law. Grandma Tillie was terrified that she and Zayde would be deported. When she finally went to court to obtain her citizenship, she easily answered the questions, but after she got her papers she panicked when the judge asked to speak to her privately. He said, "By any chance, do you know of a good horse?" She was terrified and answered that she didn't know race horses. He asked her if she was Ben Minkle's wife. She trembled, and as she looked around the courthouse with all the policemen, she thought this was some sort of test. But she felt bound to tell the truth. When she answered in the affirmative, he told her to tell her husband to place a bet for him on a winning horse. He said Ben would know the one.

For several decades their newspaper corner had been a place of social interaction and pride for my grandfather, but in the 1960s downtown Los Angeles dramatically changed. The loss of the streetcars and the movement of government offices to the suburbs cut into his business, and he was devastated by the changes in his familiar way of life. His depressions became more severe, and psychosis sometimes stole his mind. He embarked on what was to become a decade and a half of suicide attempts, mostly on Jewish holidays. When he finally lost the corner, he believed sinister forces were at work to destroy him.

For the duration of their marriage, Grandma Tillie was torn between staying with him and leaving him. Her devotion and loyalty guided her through bleak years of sometimes daily visits when he finally required the care of mental hospitals and nursing homes. She rode in the car with my parents for their week-end visits with him, and during the week she traveled alone, using several buses. Zayde became an undesirable patient, paranoid and unpredictably violent. He was shuttled from place to place because it was difficult persuading the staff at the better hospitals to keep him. He often wouldn't recognize Grandma after shock treatments. I wondered how she dealt with it, year after year. Grandma always told us to "talk to the walls—they listen and they don't talk back." She said that one of Zayde's doctors had given her that advice and she followed it to keep herself from being *meshugganeh,* crazy. She also believed that laughter was great medicine. Grandma and I had a standard joke at that time. She would ask me, "So, are you going out with some nice boys?" and I would respond, "So, have you met any nice men?" She would laugh and say, "What do I need with another *alter kaker* (old man)?" Then she would tell me about her conversation with some gentleman she had met in the lobby of the neighborhood bank where they served coffee and cookies.

Grandma adored children, and it puzzled me that she'd had only one child. Her small apartment burst with photographs of cousins, nephews, and nieces, and of course my parents and my sister and me. She made scrapbooks of pictures cut out from magazines with the neighborhood children for whom she baby-sat, and her conversation was primarily focused on the details of new babies, how the children were growing, and whether the grown-ups were happy with their marriages, jobs, and children. Whenever I asked her why she didn't have more children, she would only say how blessed she was to have my father and her grandchildren. Somehow my mother knew about Grandma's back-alley abortions that had caused infections severe enough to prevent further successful pregnancies. Grandma never spoke to me about this.

But Grandma Tillie was full of *bubbe-mayses*, which would unfold as we settled into her couch, or would appear spontaneously, as the situation required. As children, we had to be careful getting across the room. If my sister or I had stepped over the other's legs, we dutifully retraced our steps, undoing a curse which would inevitably result in the one with the crossed legs becoming crippled. We were watchful of the "evil eye," and looked away from nuns, who might put a spell on us. The superstitious *kenahoreh* complex still compels me to knock wood, look cautiously around, lower my voice and take back a piece of good news or a boast, for fear some evil might occur.

Cooking and serving traditional Jewish foods for family and friends was Grandma Tillie's delight, and we would beg her to join us at the table, to which she would typically respond that she was full. Towards the end of the meal she would pull up a chair and sit alongside one of us for dessert. I wondered if she surreptitiously snacked on food while she cooked, or if she mostly just ate desserts. Years later, I found other Jewish friends who were just as perplexed as I by grandmas who had hovered around the table, and then disappeared while the rest of the family ate. Were these grandmas, who refused all offers of help, so busy warming and serving food that they never got to sit down, or were there other cultural traditions which silently guided their behavior?

Grandma's spiritual tracts were her many cookbooks, which she pored over with a studious passion, not unlike the reverence shown by those pale, young cheder-scholars squinting endlessly over the Torah. These cookbooks were her guides to Jewish tradition. With her fourth-grade education and a lifetime of learning on the fly, a book was for facts, those she had found helpful, and therefore important. Her annotations and additions are like Talmudic commentary and interpretations offered by Rabbis and sages throughout the ages, her handwritten notes vying for the savory truth. When I was a child, Grandma's recipes seemed boring. Now, as an avid cook, I understand her passion and find stories in these cookbooks myself.

I've inherited her cookbooks, and as I look at them I see, in her un-schooled handwriting, her own and her friends' special recipes, scrawling across the pages, competing with the printed words for space. "Nettie's Noodle Kugel" appears in tight script over the title page of *The Molly Goldberg Cookbook*. On opposing pages in Manishevitz's *Tempting Kosher Dishes*, "Edith's Rice Pudding" and "Ruth's Noodle Pudding" spar across the copyright page and the foreword. Grandma's editorial comments: "No good," "Fluffy Knoedel," and "O.K. for dumplings (with the addition of an extra egg and 1/2 c more water)," carry authority. I treasure "Sweet and Sour Ribs"—less for its recipe value than for its delectably characteristic spelling errors, which list "three gloves" among the ingredients. (Did she mean cloves, or cloves of garlic?) There are many dessert recipes handwritten on scraps of paper and across printed pages, including personal favorites such as "Beverly Ap plesauce Cake," "Tillie's Honey Cake," "Bella and Brody Coffee Cake," "Sour Cream Cake, Apt. #4, Flo," and "Edith Goldstein's Matzo Meal Doughnuts (No.2)." Perhaps this may be construed as Grandma's sense of mystical delight in the multi-dimensional workings of the Creator through pastry. Mysteriously, "Sylvia Banana Cake" has a large X through it.

Flipping through the pages of *Tempting Kosher Dishes* I find Grandma's cookbook entries for a sweet toast cake, known as *mandel* bread, including "Mandle Bread Brody," "Libby's Mandel Bread," and "Pecan Mandel Brot, apt. #5, Goldstein." I wish Grandma could tell me how each cook created her particular mandel bread with such singular density and texture. These women, who were so important to my grandmother, emerge from their recipes, each one a distinct personality.

In my kitchen I now read these notes eagerly, recalling briskets and fragrant potato kugelettes, crunchy in their glass custard cups. When my parents visit they always insist I use mixes, because they are quicker and I have so little time in my life, with work and children to raise. What they don't understand is that the artist in me comes alive when I cook. I adore the sensuous preparation of food.

I follow Grandma's potato latke recipe, improvising as she did. Despite my more unconventional approach, the taste and smells are deliciously like her own. Unlike Grandma, who wore her knuckles raw on a grater, I enlist a Cuisinart, and have discovered a way to protect my stinging eyes from the onions (I wear my swimming goggles while I chop, grate, and mix). Grandma never offered formal cooking lessons, and her measurements were always imprecise. If I happened to be at her side she would demonstrate with "a handful of this" and "a pinch of that." As her self-appointed apprentice I was watchful, smelling and tasting. Later, on my own, I would experiment, knowing it was right when my cooking matched her flavors and brought vivid recollections of specific places, people, and events.

I wish I could talk with her, cook to cook. We would have to discuss the use of that staple of Jewish cooking, *schmaltz* (rendered chicken fat), in an age of vegetarian and cholesterol-conscious diners. I have revised a number of her recipes, but always with nagging doubts. Would she think we lose the taste and the essence if we substitute with Canola? What are the implications if we microwave, instead of cooking the *Shabbos* chicken in the rotisserie for twenty-four hours, her ritual marking the end of the old week and the start of the new? Grandma honored the religious laws prohibiting work on the *Shabbos*. There is something special about this particular and exaggerated emphasis on time and space dimensions in cooking, as well as on the absence of human involvement for this sacred time. The very length of cooking time enhanced our senses, living as we did for one full day and night with the mouthwatering aromas of roasting chicken, heavy with garlic, onions, thyme, and rosemary. The potato and lima bean *cholent*, a richly flavored stew, was probably invented as a poor-person's *Shabbos* meal, perfectly suited for long, slow simmering, enveloping us in its familiar savory embrace. I mourn how ethnic distinctions melt away in the pot of Americanized cookery, and yet I am also willing to embrace the culinary possibilities of new and substitute ingredients, so that a *tsimmes* is still a *tsimmes* is still a *tsimmes*.

A recipe written on Union Pacific Railroad stationery, evokes joyful memories of when I was five years old and Grandma Tillie and I traveled on the Union Pacific and Santa Fe Railroads to St. Louis; the trip she had taken so many times when my father was young. This time it was just the two of us, a grandma eager to show off her grandchild to adoring relatives, and me, excited about the upcoming wedding where I was to be a flower girl. Together we crossed the states by day and changed trains in steamy, smoky, crowded stations at night. A highlight of the voyage was riding in the Domeliner Car, eating her endless supply of roasted chicken, packed as pieces and also cut up in sandwiches on thick rye bread with caraway seeds and cornmeal crusts.

I search in vain for the sausage recipe that is linked in my memory with my family's eventful trip to Sequoia National Park, our only foray as a family into nature, other than picnics on the sand at Venice Beach. My parents, grandparents, sister, and I swerved in our station wagon up one-lane winding mountain roads to stay in adjacent log cabins. My parents stayed in one, while my sister and I migrated between theirs and Grandma and Zayde's. Grandma had brought along homemade sausage which she hung from the cabin's rafters. While we were in her cabin, we noticed that a large group of bears had gathered outside our window. We looked out at the bears, wondering why they were there, until it occurred to us with frightening clarity, that they craved our sausages. One bear tried to put its paws through our window screen. In a split second, Grandma yanked down the meat and started throwing it out the window. Outraged, the rangers shouted at us, "Don't feed the bears!" Of course, we weren't; as we saw it, we were saving our lives. That night around the public campfire, the rangers made us the center-piece of a morality tale whose message was "Never, ever, feed the bears, no matter what."

Torn from the pages of the *Jewish Free Press*, (July 19, 1968, p.18), is a "Sweet and Sour Stuffed Cabbage" recipe submitted by Phil Gluck-stern, owner of the famous New York deli of the same name. On the other side, however, is a column, "The Rebbetzin's Viewpoint," by Reb-betzin Esther Jungreis, a sort of Jewish Ann Landers who answered poignant letters from troubled readers. In this installment entitled "Hypocrisy," the writer's problem has something to do with a domes-tic conflict. Unfortunately, the compelling part of her letter is missing and the Rebbetzin's response is unavailable. But, the fragmented letter pulls me in, "I was raised in an Orthodox home . . . I am ashamed . . . our marriage . . . children . . . sorrow."

Like biblical apocrypha, the meaning is obscured, yet the woman's humanity and yearning engage my concern and make me think about my own Grandma, her hard life, and the lessons she taught me about hope and coping with life's disappointments and bitterness. Like this letter, I realize the impossibility of filling in the gaps of what I want to know about her.

My move away from home to college was difficult for Grandma Tillie. She asked if I liked college and my work, but the details of what I learned and did were less important. "Move back home, where you be-long," she ordered me on the telephone, adding, "or move in with me.

You can sleep in the sofa bed, or I'll sleep in it and you can have my bed." My long, thick hair, which she wished I would pull out of my face, worried her. It stood for all the ways our society and I had seemed to change. "Are you eating enough? You're too thin. Move your hair out of your face," she intoned. "Those poor children, the hippies, if they would only get that hair out of their beautiful faces." Looking at me slyly, winking, she said with finality, "You're a hippie, aren't you? Why don't you trim your hair?" She still laughed at the absurd, the foolish, but became serious when warning me to be careful about my politics, my boyfriends, and nearly everything else. Grandma carried with her from childhood a keen sense for ferreting out any bad news which might affect young people, and she was prescient in recognizing emerging medical and social crises, like drug abuse and sexually transmitted diseases. Later, in the early 80s, she worried about the "Herbies" (herpes) and before its etiology or mode of transmission was identified, the "Abes" (AIDS).

When I stayed with her, Grandma and I shared the same bed (other visitors occupied the sofa bed) and during one of my visits I stayed awake, silently terrified that if I had caught AIDS,I might unwittingly pass it on to her by kissing her goodnight or breathing near her face. One of my roommates with whom I had routinely shared food turned out to have a lover with AIDS. Endlessly, Grandma lectured me to settle down, get married and have children "already!" She was impatient for *everyone* to produce grandchildren. Years later I made the mistake of telling her that my husband and I were taking our time, working on our careers, and researching the issues about having children. "Research!" she wailed to my sister. "What are they researching? You mean they don't know how to do it?"

The last time I saw Grandma standing was at my wedding. There is a picture of her leaning against an apple tree. Now I see that she was actually propping herself up, holding onto the branch above her head. The crippling pain was due to more than her old nemesis, "arthuritis." The following week she was diagnosed with bone cancer.

Tillie's remarkable cooking stopped, and the family took care of her. As we spoon-fed broth into her reluctant lips, she slid on a trajectory from home-care, to living with my parents, to a nursing home and then hospice. She fought cancer to get back onto buses, out on the street, out on her own. She was terrified and enraged. The disease ravaged her body and the dislocation from home disoriented her. Grandma, who rarely asked anything for herself, begged us to bring her home. When she could no longer even get up to go to the bathroom, she would ask me to get her walking shoes and put them on her feet. One time, I was able to get her up, with the help of her cane, and into the hallway. "Take me to that wall," she ordered, as I carefully supported her dwindling body with my strong arms. Heaving with the exertion, she breathed softly, "Go get my coat and my purse." She inched her way slowly down the hall, leaning heavily on her cane and the wall railing.

Shocked by the contrast between her physical frailty and her determination, I said urgently, "Grandma, what are you doing?"

She answered matter-of-factly, with a defiant, though fading voice, "I'm going home!" A passing orderly rushed to her aid and chastised me for getting her out of bed. It was the first time I really faced what was happening to her.

I flew across the country to be with her at every opportunity. The telephone connected us, my strong, hearty voice reassuring her faint, distant one. The calls late at night came more frequently, until the one that brought me speeding to the airport and the hospital. Within several hours I was donning a greenish gown, stepping into the Intensive Care Unit in Kaiser-Permanente Hospital. I felt dizzy standing there, as if engulfed in some invisible, thick padding that kept me removed from the sterility of the place. I felt miserable, small and hopeless.

In the ICU Dad and I were pretenders to the institutional regime, shuffling softly in hospital issue booties and over-laundered green gowns. I wanted to lightly massage her legs as I had done before. She used to say that it helped the pain. The staff told me not to touch her legs. My fervent desire to help her mingled with my forlorn wish that she could reassure me. Suddenly, from a dull distance, she squeezed my hand, harder and harder. She regained color and strength. Jolted, I returned to myself. She mouthed dry sounds, familiar, but nonsensical. The gibberish continued, her voice rising with urgent emphasis, her white-knuckled hand was more like a claw, clamped tightly around mine.

Someone official garbed in green said, "She's getting agitated . . . tranquilize." It all happened very quickly.

This was my beloved Grandma, possibly on her deathbed. Did she really need sedating? Was she delusional? Was this how people died? Was she losing her always agile mind? Finally, one question rose above the others: I asked Dad if he knew what she was mumbling. With a wry smile, he said that she was talking in Yiddish. He explained that some Orthodox Jews believe you can trick the Angel of Death into believing it has come for the wrong person by changing your name. How could I have questioned her mental health? I had nearly betrayed her through my ignorance. I was stunned, and then eager to participate in this fragment of our people's ritual for death and dying. According to Jewish law, such things as a name change require the presence of at least ten observant Jews. This group, or minyan, was unavailable to us in the ICU. What a struggle we had! Grandma insisted upon a rabbi, insisted that the minyan should be male, and made clear her intention to get out of bed and into shul. It was all we could do to keep her from pulling out her tubes as she tried to escape. Dad and I protected her, holding back the green-gowns and their drugs a while longer.

"She's not crazy," we carefully explained, hoping to convince them, our own credulity teetering precariously on the slim chance that her thoughts were sound. Against all regulations, they agreed to give it a try, allowing themselves to be hastily organized into an ad hoc minyan of less than ten uncomprehending, male and female, non-Jewish staff people. We all assisted her in her ancient and clever plan.

She became calm. She schemed for life. She bargained, returned to her old Jewish name of *Toba* (Hebrew for "good") and added *Chai* (Hebrew for "life"). Not knowing what else to do, we said a Shema. It seemed, finally, she had fooled the Angel and surprised us all. Exhausted, but lucid, she rallied the strength to leave the ICU and survive another series of battles with cancer.

It has been nearly thirteen years since her death, and yet sometimes I feel as if I am with Grandma, half-expecting to see her lying in her hospice bed. I remember her piercing awareness during our last visit together, when she said, "I won't ever get to see you again."

After she died, I kept wanting to call her up on the phone. "Hi Grandma" I'd say into a dial tone. I even dialed once to hear the message, "This number is no longer in service."

She was still present in my dreams. I dared to believe they were her dreams too, and we were together just like old times. They continued even after I had Noah, the long-awaited first grandchild who was conceived within hours of her death. But something was unsettling. She and I would be together and then I'd want her to meet Noah. In the dream I would go get him and when I came back, she wasn't there. Or she was in the other room and I could never get the two of them in the same room together. Introducing the two of them was the greatest goal of my dream-life. Yet it was slowly occurring to me that death was irrevocable, and the new people in my life could never really know Grandma's love firsthand. My next pregnancy was difficult and my baby and I nearly died during labor. With Aaron's birth, the dream changed. A small part of me wonders if our close brush with death shifted some time/space barrier that allowed us contact with Grandma. It makes as much sense as her tricking the *Malach Ha'Mavess* (Angel of Death). At last, I dreamt that I introduced my two children to her. She held them. I sat next to her and finally felt contented.

She, who never before spoke of angels, had held death at bay, grasping at a shred of mystical Jewish faith. Despite my American mind, I too have a *bubbe-mayse* (one that I made up) that I have passed on to my children. I tell them that we are always connected by a strong, infinitely elastic golden thread, which holds us together during hard or scary times, when we might miss each other because we are apart. Before going into the hospital to have Aaron, I told Noah about this strong golden thread connecting us, going from my heart to his heart. "This thread is so strong and elastic, it can stretch anywhere and not break. It always stays connected, no matter where we go and how long we are ever apart." I wanted to prepare him for my time away giving birth. It was also a way of preparing myself to leave the little boy whom I had never left before. When I nearly died in childbirth, the golden cord became an important symbol of our connection to each other. Frightened by how I looked when he visited me in the hospital, Noah refused to talk with me and told a friend that the cord was nearly broken. Two days later, his visit with me in the hospital went better, I was more like my usual self. He said that the cord was starting to mend.

The image of the cord has eased many transitions over the years. Aaron wonders now about the golden cord, asking, "How do we know it's there if it's invisible?"

I tell him, "We know it's there when we feel ourselves thinking about someone we love so much and missing them."

Nora Dunne ("Gran"), County Cork, Ireland
Courtesy of Patricia Traxler

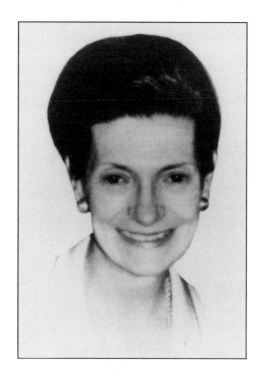

Valerie Galembert
Courtesy of Michele Cloonan

Maud Harvey ("Gran") and Laurence B. Calver
Courtesy of Laurence B. Calver

Tillie Minkle ("Grandma Tillie") and Deryl Minkle
Courtesy of Tillie Minkle

Laura Weiner
Photo by Robin Becker

Mary Kao
Courtesy of Christina Chiu

Grandma Luis with her husband, Liu Ch'eng-yü
Courtesy of Aimee Liu

The Rub of Love

Bread Pudding

Jean Gould

I WAS EIGHT YEARS OLD the time I thought my grandmother's bread pudding might poison me. She could not have been much older then than I am now, but in that time just after the Allies had won the war, the lines between young and old were more distinct than they are today. Of course, with her certainties about the value of hair nets in the kitchen and good manners everywhere, she seemed very old to me. And the ability to make sauce from apples and something she called "cobbler" from peaches rendered her magical as well. The sounds and meanings of words had already impressed me by that time with their power to add dimension to ordinary life. I had known only the cobbler who fixed shoes.

You didn't mess with Gramma. If for example, you forgot to put your dessert spoon on your saucer and left it in your dish by mistake, you were in for it big time. Character (carrotter was how I first heard it and colored it orange) was one of her important words. And that went hand in hand with the rules and the principles (the prince of pulls) of society (so sigh a tea).

Minnie Guntheroth Peters's world was one of ironed sheets, cro-cheted handkerchiefs, and proper enunciation. Don't get the wrong idea here. My grandmother was Minnie as in Wilhelmina, regal and dignified, never as in Minnie Mouse (who at that time was only a few years old and the only other Minnie I knew). Gramma was extra tall for a woman of her generation. Everyone said so. The oldest of six children and the mother of four daughters, she was the family problem-solver. Even neighbors came to her for advice and listened carefully when she told them what they ought to do. She had divorced my grandfather before the First World War and with only a sixth-grade education, managed to support herself and her children by selling curtains at Marshall Fields Department Store. Maybe because of having immigrant parents, she fell in love with language. That's what she told us anyway. She rose from sales clerk to buyer because she was so well-spoken and direct with words. It was all part of her story.

Whenever she played "hangman" with me, she usually won. Later, after I finished college, she would beat me soundly at Scrabble. I wish I had known the word "matriarch" when I was eight. May tree ark. Gramma generally pronounced me foolish when I had fun like that with words, telling me I would never get ahead in the world unless I were more sensible.

The most important thing in my life that year was winning at jacks, and while Gramma baked in her antiseptic Chicago kitchen, I practiced "peaches in the basket" over and over and over again under her black tie shoes on the linoleum floor. With both the war and sugar rationing now finished, she was back to making thin-layered pastry, although my favorite was her chocolate mahogany cake with white butter frosting. I would be nearly twenty by the time I discovered mahogany was a kind of tree and even then I imagined its texture dark and rich and delectable, so great was the impact of that cake on my psyche.

We were visiting from Philadelphia, my parents, teenage sister, and I. And having just come "down from the farm," as they spoke of my father's birthplace somewhere north of Peoria, the second half of the trip was to my mother's "people." That's how they talked about relatives in the Midwest in those days. The end of the war allowed us to buy a new Packard, and we'd driven "back home to the farm" this time. Except for gathering eggs from the henhouse, I'd had a fine time on the farm, milking cows and pumping water in the courtyard outside the house, but Mother and sister Pat were less enthusiastic. There ought to have been screens on the windows, said Mother. And Pat refused to drink the milk unless it was homogenized. Having had several heart attacks and at least one major stroke by that time, Daddy was probably already brain damaged. But for a few weeks every summer, we made the trip nonetheless. Maybe he was happy to be back where he grew up, although his mother, my other grandmother, apparently never forgave him for becoming a capitalist instead of a priest.

To my eye, the farmland was so flat as to be two-dimensional. All you could see were corn, soybeans, and alfalfa. And while Mother and Pat generally stayed indoors, I walked along the edges of the fields with Daddy, hand in hand, sometimes picking up the dark soil and letting it run through my fingers the way he did, and later, listening carefully when he spoke to the tenant farmer about the crops. It was true that the milk we drank was thick and sometimes buttery with cream and that it was never quite cold enough, but words like "alfalfa" and "manure" held me in the music of their attenuated syllables. And if the farmer's ten kids looked at my city clothes with wide eyes, I envied them the feral fragrances of their lives. After a time, I learned to gather eggs so that the chickens stopped pecking at me.

On that visit, my mother and sister spent hours, it seemed to me, pouring over photo albums with covers of thick velvet they retrieved from heavy wooden trunks in the farmhouse attic. Like many others from Ireland, the Colgans had come to America during the potato famine, through Canada, and homesteaded the land in the Middle West. Tanners and cabinetmakers, Mother's people, the Guntheroths, came from Germany, from Berlin, and went directly to the city of Chicago. The farm photographs showed page after page of large family picnics in the fields or class pictures of barefoot boys and girls at the local one-room schoolhouse. The Colgans wore overalls and carried hoes. Even Fulton Sheen, a distinguished bishop with a cape on television, an old classmate of Daddy's, wore overalls. Although my Irish grandmother lived in Peoria by that time, she took her shoes off when she had company and sometimes burped out loud. After dinner, we all had to kneel in what she called her "parlor" and say the rosary together. After the farm part of our trip, Mother was probably relieved to recover in Chicago. My father's mother was as rigorous and unbending about Catholicism as Gramma was about her own code of behavior, which, by the way, had no room for organized religion.

Gramma lived with and kept house for my Aunt Trudie, Mother's older sister, and her husband Bert on the north side of the city. Although Trudie had no children, she knew exactly what I liked and saved all her old sequined dresses and high heels for me to play dress up. She made jewelry from seashells and wore eye makeup. Bert taught me to play poker, always letting me win, and when I sat on the floor with my legs splayed like vees, he made a bet with me that when I was fifteen I wouldn't be able to do it anymore. As the bells of the two churches in the neighborhood pealed each morning and evening, I sometimes missed the convent school I was attending then, before I remembered it was summer vacation and heard Gramma singing, "Bring the nickels, bring the dimes." The Papists—she actually made the word hiss—would take whatever money they could get from you, she said. I don't suppose I had any notion then that she was referring to the Catholic Church, because I remember agreeing with her that the Papists, whom I assumed lived only in Chicago, must be very bad indeed to take money from people who needed it. And it also never occurred to me that Gramma was one of "those heathens" the Sisters of the Sacred Heart were always talking about, a pagan recruited by Satan himself to do evil in the world.

During the last year, I'd become a picky eater, a fairly glaring phenomenon given the fact that my sister ate everything in sight. As I lost her to her friends after she got her driver's license, she turned into a different person from the one I'd known. And she ate, if you can believe it, onion sandwiches, sometimes with liverwurst. She was starving, she said. Daddy, on the other hand, who had more and more trouble swallowing, occasionally lost his meal over the freshly ironed damask cloth. And my mother, striving for peace, or at least for neutrality, said nothing about our eating habits.

The night of the bread pudding incident, we had roast beef for dinner. At the head of the table as usual, my grandmother did the carving. Bert had given his place to Daddy who sat at the other end, and Trudie wore a new green dirndl skirt which matched the walls in the dining room. I loved the way she said "hunter green," as if she were a movie star. Pat complained that the roast beef was over-cooked, and we all laughed when I called her a cannibal. Uncle Bert ate the cauliflower off my plate before anyone noticed. Gramma had made mashed potatoes for Daddy—it was the only kind he could eat—and he complimented her on her tasty gravy. Mother said nothing when Gramma put string beans on my plate or when she later saw me drop them into the pocket of my shorts. And while I wouldn't have used the word "undercurrent" then, I knew I could get away with my string bean maneuver because Mother's attention was on other matters.

I don't know what happened that night to cause such a ruckus at the dinner table. It had been one of those overheated days in Chicago, and Daddy had taken me to Lake Michigan to swim while Pat and Mother went downtown shopping. I had prickly heat on my neck, I remember, and Gramma gave me a bath with baking soda after we got home, while I sang "Down by the Old Mill Stream." It was a song she also knew, but when I tried to harmonize with her, she told me I was singing off-key. The lake water had been too cold for me to get into beyond my knees. I loved it when she sprinkled me with dusting powder after toweling me off.

Although there was tacit agreement that Gramma would call the evening meal "dinner," while Daddy called it "supper," the two of them still had two major agenda items every night. He insisted on water at the table; she insisted on milk. Worse, he made us all say grace, and she would have none of it, either leaving the table or talking about the weather as soon as he crossed himself. So that could have started it off. Or maybe the summer heat had gotten to Gramma in her kitchen. Baking bread every day, as well as pastry, she rarely had her oven turned off. But even the usually oblivious Pat stopped eating when Daddy asked for water and Gramma told him to get it himself.

One of the wonderful things about my grandmother was that her jaw was as certain and square as Dick Tracy's. She used to let me tease her about that, and even though she said I was wasting my time reading such trash, she knew who he was and even sent me a Sparkle Plenty doll that year they were popular. When Daddy suggested that Mother get him a glass of water, Gramma's jaw got tight just the way Gary Cooper's would a few years later, right before the gunfight in *High Noon*.

"I'll get it," I said.

"Don't you move," said Gramma. "Stay where you are."

I remember the string beans moist and hot in my pocket. If I went to the kitchen for the water, I could throw them away. But I sat there, half in and half out of my seat. There was a shiny brass chandelier hanging from the ceiling that cast a textured shadow over our meal. "Ruckus" was an unrefined word, one my Irish grandmother might have used.

"That's it," my father said. "I've had enough. Pack the bags."

"If you leave my house, don't expect to come back," said Gramma. The story was that she had quite literally swept her husband out of their house with a broom shortly after my mother was born.

We were not a family of everyday volatility. As the insults darted back and forth across and around and back over the table, I thought about grabbing the gravy boat and drinking its entire contents. I thought about that first day in the chicken coop on the farm when the hens came pecking at my arms and face, and how their flying feathers obscured my passage to the door. Under the table now, Pat kicked me, and I kicked her back.

Just because Daddy had a big Packard car, Gramma said, didn't mean he was such a fancy pants. I remember that phrase, "fancy pants."

And that was when Daddy started coughing. We all held our breath when that happened, because you never knew if he'd get over it, lose his food, or simply pass out. With all eyes on him, I ran to the kitchen for the water. I couldn't figure it out; what was so bad about a pitcher of water on the table? Or even one glass full of the stuff? In those days we didn't know as much about water as we do today; that you shouldn't drink it from the tap, not ever. In fact, we didn't even know that adults were supposed to limit their consumption of milk. But I had no clue about why two different liquids were unable to coexist on my grandmother's dining table.

"Oh Tom. Oh Tom." That's what everyone said when Daddy coughed. Usually they helped him loosen his tie, or sometimes they got up and patted him on the back, but mostly they just sat there and probably hoped he'd stop. At home recently, his face got purple in his coughing, but this time when I got back to the dining room with his water, the siege was over, and everyone was smiling with relief. Even Gramma. Pat ate the rest of the roast beef and potato from my plate, and I drank Daddy's water myself before realizing what I'd done and passed it to him, forgetting about Gramma's germ rule. With a barely audible "excuse me," Mother rose from her chair and fetched a clean glass from the kitchen.

Trudie cleared the table, chattering all the time in that way she had of making everyone around her feel special. Although she had already had three husbands by then, she would never really leave her mother. The most beautiful and the most sickly of Gramma's four daughters, she had only one kidney and that, we were told, was tied precariously to a rib. I tried to imagine the organ dangling inside her like an ornament from a Christmas tree, and when I made a joke about a kid's knee, for once no one laughed and I knew I'd said the wrong thing. Because she worked at Zenith Corporation, the family had one of the first televisions in their neighborhood. Gramma was the only one who watched its round screen now and again, hoping for old Charlie Chaplin films, but laughing loud enough to hear upstairs when Laurel and Hardy came on.

She brought in coffee and dessert on a silver tray. My heart sank. Pat and I had significant eye contact. Bread pudding. In my whole life, I had never been able to figure out the importance of pudding. Daddy's favorite was rice. Mother liked butterscotch. But not one kid I ever knew liked pudding, which to my mind and palate was generally lumpy and tasted, Pat and I decided, more like runny stuff from your nose—we would never have said "snot" aloud—than anything else. Jell-O was bad enough, wobbling as it did like blobs in the ocean that stung you. But for some reason, Gramma never served Jell-O. Sometimes she made Grapenut or tapioca pudding. But the absolute worst was the stuff with bread.

How is it possible all these years later for me to explain that I was convinced I would die if I ate Gramma's bread pudding that night? I would have no dessert, thank you, I said. I was full, I said. I just couldn't eat anything else. These are all things I said. And, of course, with the table empty of its supper/dinner dishes, it was impossible to give Bert my dessert or to spoon it into my pocket with the now cold string beans.

Gramma spent hours cooking for us, Daddy said, now actually taking her side. She baked bread every day, bread that was folded into this delicious pudding, along with fresh farm eggs and cream, and, he added, her love for us, for her family. Many children didn't get dessert, he said. I was one of the lucky ones.

We'd be happy, my sister and I said, to share our pudding, in fact even give it away to some other kids. We weren't selfish, we said. And Pat was not even a glutton, although that's what I called her when we were home, when I didn't call her "garbage pail." She did eat everything. But even she had to draw the line somewhere.

Gramma had won gold medals for waltzing at the turn of the century when she and her father led the grand march at clubs in Chicago. I had seen photographs of her from those days when she wore long ball gowns and held all the corners of her beautiful face in knowing smiles. I tried to think of that as I looked down at the glop in my dish and my stomach threatened to back up. My spoon held just the smallest bit of bread pudding, but I could not raise it to my lips. And even though the others, including my sister, now ate their own desserts without fatality, I knew there was poison in my dish and that I would not survive the end of this meal.

And somehow now, they were all gone. Gramma's daughters and their husbands often went walking together after dinner, and Pat was probably upstairs reading true love magazines in the bathroom. Night had fallen, and Gramma and I sat alone at the white linen tablecloth with its blue and white dish of bread pudding in front of me. Characteristically—she had not raised four girls on her own by being wasteful—my grandmother did not turn on the electric light in the brass chandelier which loomed ever larger in the darkness. I suppose I shed tears.

In the power that children assume over their worlds, I imagine now that I thought whatever rift existed between Gramma and Daddy was my fault, or that, in fact, his illness had something to do with me. As we know today about the dangers of water and milk, we have also learned that children absorb such tensions. I shouldn't have gotten Daddy the water. I shouldn't have drunk from his glass and then passed it to him. If only I had eaten the cauliflower and string beans, things might have been different. And maybe I had annoyed Gramma by playing jacks under her feet all the time. Why wasn't I one of those good children the nuns were always talking about? I had made my confirmation that year, but I still got C-minus in Obedience on my report card.

I was small for my age and too thin, I was often told. As my feet dangled from the chair, I thought again of Trudie's kidney hanging from her ribs. If you did what Gramma said, she could keep you alive. Wasn't that so? Even Daddy now agreed with her about the bread pudding.

The two of us did not sit there until midnight as I expected. We probably were not at the table for more than a few minutes after everyone left. I don't remember if Gramma spoke to me or just silently rose from her seat, took my dish, and made her way to the kitchen. But I followed her. After all, I was not frightened of her; it was the bread pudding that I thought would kill me.

My grandmother was not a demonstrative person. Some people might say that's a German thing, but I think that's just the way it is in some families. Even so, that night she sat by the porcelain-topped kitchen table, stood me in front of her, and removed the beans from my pocket as delicately as if they were pickup sticks in a world championship. Just as carefully, she gathered me onto her lap. Her apron hung from its hook in the corner beside the shelf where I was allowed to keep my jacks. Then as Gramma spooned the yellow custard toward us, she directed it into her own mouth instead of mine.

She always liked her own cooking best, she said. And we wouldn't need to tell anyone that it was she who had eaten my dessert, would we? The pile of limp beans also disappeared one by one. The taste of vegetables was too strong for most children, she said, but she knew that one day I would change my mind. I would acquire certain tastes as I grew up, she said. "Acquire" was a new word for me, sharp like a cough with its "ack" sound. I might even learn to like bread pudding, Gramma said. I remember her powerful arms around me, and I wanted to believe her. But I knew I would never, ever eat bread or any other kind of pudding, even if it were made with the love that Daddy said Gramma put into it.

The following winter, when Daddy was really sick, Gramma came to stay with us in Philadelphia and continued her fight with the Catholics, although she no longer spoke openly of the Papists. Daddy could have his pitcher of water on the table, and she was even pleasant to Father Gafney when he came calling, pouring him a few fingers of the awful smelling whiskey he liked. Mother was out raising money for the church. Perhaps she had made her own covenant with God for Daddy's recovery. And while Gramma had made her "bring-the-nickels bring the-dimes" sing-song comments about the collection baskets at Mass on other visits—just as she did in Chicago when the church bells chimed, this time she was quiet when Mother told us at supper that she had made more money for the church with her weekly card parties than anyone in the history of the parish.

On Fridays, however, Gramma always packed a chicken sandwich in my lunch box and instructed me to inform the nuns it was tuna; although to tell you the truth, I'd have preferred simple grape jelly on white bread. Either way I suppose I was sinning, wasn't I? But it was a tough choice; that between God and my grandmother. No matter what they said at school about hell and purgatory, she told me, as she heard my catechism lessons, there was no such thing as a place where flames burned you up. And while some of the commandments were acceptable, why didn't they include something about cleanliness? What good were novenas if you were unaware of basic hygiene? Even Daddy agreed with her about cleanliness; checking our hands and fingernails before meals preceded grace in the family ritual.

When Gramma was in Philadelphia, I stopped boarding weekdays at school, and each afternoon promptly at three, there she was at the convent gate in her long sealskin coat. She never let go of my hand on the long walk home, instructing me at every intersection to look three times each way before stepping into the street. In our galoshes on the often slushy sidewalks we reviewed my day's performance, and she grilled me on the multiplication table until we finally turned into our driveway.

She had clearly taken charge of our household that winter, and in the kitchen that was now hers, I learned to soak bread or rice or tapioca in milk for exactly five minutes. No more. No less. After adding sugar, butter, and salt, we poured the whole concoction over eggs. The most important job, she said, was to add just a bit more vanilla than the recipe called for. After doing that, I got to lick the measuring spoon, and she placed the pudding in the oven to bake. At the table, I could just pretend to eat, Gramma told me, but I was not to make a fuss. And in case I was still hungry after meals, I could come to the kitchen for plain bread and milk.

Nobody ever mentioned the night I was so terrorized by Gramma's bread pudding, and eventually she returned to Chicago. Mother went out and got a job, and my sister went off to college. I was glad to be returned to the convent where the Sisters of the Sacred Heart were more like my grandmother than she would have wanted to know.

Even if I preferred to climb trees, I could still wear white gloves or curtsy when I had to do so. And in the 1940s you still had to do both. When the nuns told me that any organization with the name of a historical figure was communist or that if I went into a protestant church my soul would be blackened by mortal sin, I nodded in agreement. But in the long afternoons my mother had arranged for me to be away from the convent for music and dance lessons, I did my own research. Of course, eventually I was found out when the piano teacher reported my absences, but I had had ample time to explore the world forbidden to me by then and discovered nothing too dreadful would befall me in uncharted territory. Gramma and I had made a sort of pact that night in her Chicago kitchen which somehow accommodated the hazards of my childhood. I had learned about the important art of subterfuge, a lesson that was to serve me well in the years ahead as my wild nature tangled with the limitations of the conventional world.

The Geraldine Easton Story

Monty S. Leitch

AFTER LOLLIE AND I had celebrated our fifteenth birthdays, I was constantly on guard. I figured there wasn't much time left before Grandmother truly got her hooks in. Then she'd turn Lollie into another Geraldine Easton. From little shepherd, to Big Angel, to legend-in-her-own-time. Geraldine Easton. The youngest Big Angel ever to sing in Grandmother's Christmas pageant. Just sixteen years old the first time, and then the Big Angel three years in a row. But finally, a disappointment. Such a disappointment. Every Christmas Eve I squirmed through the story. "An audition with the Metropolitan Opera," Grandmother hissed, clutching her once-a-year Scotch. "The Metropolitan Opera! That girl could have had everything." But Geraldine hadn't shown up for the audition. She'd chosen, instead, to run off with Billy Ray Janney and debut three little towheaded children, one, two, three, in a row. Grandmother never forgave her. And every Christmas Eve she tortured me again with the story instead of letting me open my present. I tortured her back by gleefully imagining her, red-faced and pacing, alone in front of a panel of big-bosomed women and portly men who kept checking their watches. Grandmother's heels clicked like castanets when she was single minded and impatient, which was most of the time, and finally, in my Christmas Eve daydream, the big-bosomed women and portly men snapped, "Mrs. Covington, will you please stop!" And I snickered.

"I don't know what you find so amusing," Grandmother spat. "To have talent, real talent, and fail to use it." An angry slug of her Scotch. "Go get your present, Pudge." Christmas Eve was always a big letdown for my grandmother. The pageant was over. The Big Angel had sung "O, Holy Night" from the balcony a capella, and everyone had filed reverently into the night, reeling once again with emotions provoked by Grandmother's masterful staging. Grandmother was reeling, too. "The Metropolitan Opera," she repeated, over and over. In a little town like ours, even adequate voices were appreciated, otherwise I'd never have been allowed to sing. But lovely voices were few and far between, and genuine talent so rare that legends sprang up. Like Geraldine Easton. Like, I was convinced, my best friend, Lollie.

I'm talking now about those years between 1963 and 1968. And I'm talking about a small town in Virginia, a town in which *Jim Crow* was so accepted, so ingrained, that schoolchildren were flabbergasted to learn that laws had been required. Like all her friends, my grandmother had had *colored help* for most of her married life; but by the time I was ten or so, which was 1960, Hilda Johnson was coming only on Christmas Eve and other special occasions. Grandmother told her just how everything was to be done, and Hilda did it that way: salad forks, stemware, crème de menthe over the ice cream. My parents and I ate our formal Christmas Eve dinner in the dining room with Grandmother, each of us careful not to drip gravy on our clothes, while Hilda sat with a cup of coffee at Grandmother's kitchen table. Then we dashed off to the pageant, where jobs awaited each of us, while Hilda washed up the dinner dishes, put them away, and set out the fruitcake and Scotch for our later revelries under the tree. One Christmas Eve I asked Hilda while she was mashing potatoes, "Who's fixing supper for your kids while you're at our house?" The potato masher banged against the pan. Thunk, thunk, thunk.

"Get on outta here, Pudge," Hilda finally said. "You got me nervous as a cat in a room full of rocking chairs." Hilda Johnson was my grandmother's age and her children's names were Van Johnson, Shirley Temple Johnson, Princess Margaret Johnson, and Mickey Rooney Johnson.

In 1963, when the first black students integrated our school, Mama told me, "Try to make them feel welcome." A suggestion that baffled me, since they so clearly weren't. But in homeroom I sidled up to Anna Johnson anyway and said, "Hi." I already knew her, of course; she was Mickey Rooney's daughter, Hilda's granddaughter, and she'd come once or twice to help with Grandmother's Christmas Eve dinner.

"Hi yourself," Anna said back. But those were nearly the last words we spoke. For suddenly I saw the gulf that had lain between us for years, the gulf that Anna must have understood nearly from birth, and it yawned endlessly. I lacked all courage. More than that, I lacked all motivation. So I just went on, as much as possible, with life as I'd known it; sitting next to Lollie in class, calling her every night on the telephone, trying to figure out how to keep Grandmother off her back when the time came.

For, you see, I knew what was going to happen. It happened to everyone who got anywhere close to Grandmother: you'd be tripping along happily in your life when Grandmother would swoop through, intent on something that had to be accomplished, usually "for your own good," and then she'd see to it that it was done. Mama and Daddy and most of the people in town were frenzied wrecks every year for weeks because Grandmother's pageant plans got bigger and bigger. "I want the Kings in real velvet this year," she'd say, and someone would dash off to the fabric store. "Spotlights," she'd tell Mack Austin, "there, there, and there." Did she care that her "theater" was on the Virginia Register of Historic Landmarks?

"Miz Covington, we can't do that," Mack tried saying.

She answered, "Work something out. Put one there, too, while you're at it." She never seemed to notice, or to care, how many people lived their lives at her beck and call. But I noticed. Nobody stood a chance against my grandmother. You could run, but you couldn't hide. And Lollie would be next.

In fact, it had already started. We were in two choirs: Grandmother's at the church, and Miss Sullivan's at school. "Gloria in eggshell-cis deo," my grandmother directed. "Eggshell-cis." That, she told us, was the proper Italian pronunciation. She'd spent three days in Venice on her European tour; she should know.

In chorus at school, though, crisp Miss Sullivan insisted, "None of these eggshells. The word is ex-sell-cease. Gloria in ex-sell-cease deo." She directed by moving the tip of a short, cork-handled baton in tight, little arcs.

"Who do you think is right?" Lollie asked me one time.

"Miss Sullivan, of course," I said. Back then, I thought I knew everything. I was expert at remembering when to sing eggshell-cis, and when ex-sell-cease was right.

Lollie had real talent: a clear, high soprano that never wavered. Naturally, as soon as she got old enough, Grandmother had her singing solos in every pageant. Even the first was spectacular. Just the kind of stunt Grandmother loved. Lollie hid behind the pulpit and sang the first verse of "There's a Song in the Air" a capella in that hush just after the shepherds have come with haste and found Mary, Joseph, and the Babe lying in a manger. You could see the thrill pass through the congregation. They didn't know Lollie's voice yet and they couldn't tell where it was coming from. They thought they'd heard a real angel, singing from beyond.

Then Lollie rose up slowly (with Dan Caldwell hiding behind the pulput, too, to help her), easing herself up a stepladder and singing about the tumult of joy occasioned by the wonderful birth. To the congregation, it looked as if her tinsel-tipped wings would lift her straight up to the Star of Bethlehem, as if the very light of heaven was streaming over her face. When all the Heavenly Hosts, among whom I was a minor voice, burst forth on the chorus, an audible gasp passed through the congregation. It was a showstopper, just like Grandmother knew it would be. Every year after that, people started asking Lollie on Halloween, "What'll you be singing for the Christmas pageant this year?" I knew she'd have to be the Big Angel when the time came. Only my grandmother knew The Geraldine Easton Story better than I.

It was at chorus tryouts at school that I discovered Anna Johnson could sing, too. That's when we all discovered Anna could sing. We were sitting in the auditorium, trying not to giggle as one measly adolescent voice after another struggled through "If I Had a Hammer" or "Climb Every Mountain," when Anna stepped up to the piano, the last tryout. "You don't have to play the music," Anna said, when she handed Miss Sullivan her tattered song book. Snicker, snicker, snicker, throughout the auditorium. Anna's was the only black face in the room. I heard someone in back say "jungle bunny." Snicker, snicker, snicker.

"Do you want your pitch?" Miss Sullivan asked, and Anna shook her head. Then she turned to face us all, with her hands folded at her waist. Snicker, snicker, snicker.

"Were you there when they crucified my Lord?" Anna seemed to whisper. I squirmed. "Were you there when they crucified my Lord?" Her voice rose and the auditorium quieted. "Oh-oh!" Anna wailed, and I felt the tears welling up in my eyes. "Sometimes it causes me to tremble. Tremble," she breathed. "Were you there when they crucified my Lord?"

Never in my life had I heard such a voice. It wasn't just that the notes were true. Anna was living the crucifixion all over again while she sang, and she was making us live it, too. When she finished, you could have heard a pin drop. Then there was shuffling and snuffling and rumbling around the auditorium. Books hitting the floor, kids punching each other and saying, "Ow!" Miss Sullivan finally said "Thank you" and handed Anna her book. We couldn't get out of there fast enough. I would have rushed by Anna in the hall, too, if Lollie hadn't stopped.

"Boy," she said. "That was really good." Anna murmured thanks. "I didn't know you could sing like that!" Lollie said. Anna just looked at her. Then she looked at me.

"Yeah, it was good," I said. "Come on, Lollie, we'll be late."

"That was great," Lollie kept saying all the way down the hall. "Just great!" Until I told her to shut up, it wasn't as good as her. And she said, "Pudge, you're so ignorant."

After the school's fall recital, the cat was really out of the bag. Even Grandmother must have heard about Anna's performance, although, of course, she wasn't there. Hilda Johnson and Mickey Rooney's wife Arcelia were the only women in the auditorium wearing hats. Miss Sullivan didn't care much for popular music, so she'd had Anna sing "Sheep May Safely Graze." Lollie had only a couple of little solo parts in other songs. But life went on. Lollie and I had our fifteenth birthdays. Carolyn Williamson struggled through the Big Angel's part in Grandmother's Christmas pageant, rehearsing secretly, as tradition demanded, and then squeaking forth on Christmas Eve, not quite the miraculous voice from heaven she was supposed to be. Although Carolyn did the best she could, it was clear she was one Big Angel who'd never suffer the full force of Grandmother's attention. And so once again Lollie stole the show, this time with "I Wonder As I Wander." Grandmother had her dress up like a bare-footed shepherd boy and wander around the sanctuary while Mack Austin projected "stars" on the darkened ceiling.

At Christmas Eve dinner beforehand, I'd heard Grandmother ask Hilda about her granddaughter, "the one who sings."

"She sings right well," Hilda said.

"Is she getting any training?" Grandmother had asked.

Hilda had answered, "Miss Cherry Sullivan's taking her."

After the pageant, Grandmother started The Geraldine Easton Story by saying, "Cherry Sullivan couldn't find her way out of a paper bag. You know, she and Geraldine Easton were thick as thieves."

Remember, now, that Geraldine Easton, at sixteen, had been the youngest Big Angel Grandmother had ever had. So the year after "I Wonder As I Wander," I was particularly mindful of any advances Grandmother made against Lollie. At a summer picnic, when Grandmother asked Lollie if she'd thought about college yet, I grabbed Lollie's elbow and said "Let's go swimming!" as fast as I could. Grandmother narrowed her eyes at me through her cigarette smoke. But she was always doing that. "Pudge," she'd say, with her narrow eyes, "when are you going to do something with yourself?"

For Miss Sullivan's fall recital, Anna and Lollie sang a duet which nobody, including Anna and Lollie, liked. And they looked so odd standing there together. It was a showstopper of a different sort, but Cherry Sullivan didn't notice. While the audience clapped politely, Miss Sullivan positively beamed.

Then it was time for Christmas pageant rehearsals to begin. "You don't have to be the Big Angel if you don't want to," I told Lollie on our way to the church. "Just remember that."

"You don't even know if she's gonna ask me," Lollie said. "Besides, there's plenty of better voices around."

"Ha!" I shouted. "Ha! You just watch. I know my grandmother!" We sauntered into the sanctuary, red-cheeked, breathless, smug. At least, I was. Ready to face Grandmother and the world. And there sat Anna Johnson, cool as a cucumber, leafing through a hymnal. Well, of course you know why. Anna was there to be the Big Angel. Lollie would be the Virgin Mary and sing "The Coventry Carol." But "O, Holy Night," the pivotal moment, the culmination of all the emotion gathering through the show, that would belong to Anna Johnson. She of the sooty cheeks and fat lips, she of the yellow-backed eyes. Grandmother pretended like nothing was wrong. She barreled ahead, just like always, single-minded and impatient. Mack Austin walked in with his tool belt jangling, took one look at Anna, and walked right back out again. Two altos and three tenors—less straightforward—came less and less to rehearsals and then stopped coming at all. Joseph had to be recast three times until finally the preacher, who couldn't sing a lick, took the role, even though that meant we'd have to find new readers for the scriptures. And all the while there was Grandmother, tossing her head, waving her arms, adjusting the program over and over, all business, and business as usual.

On the days when she was rehearsing Anna alone in the balcony, I lay on our living-room floor and wailed at Lollie, "She's ruining the pageant!"

"Pudge," Lollie said, "Anna will be wonderful."

I said, "What difference does that make? You know nobody will come."

Lollie just sighed and told me, "They'll be missing one heck of a show."

"I don't know how you can just sit there and let that Anna Johnson steal this away from you," I said.

"You've been telling me for months," Lollie started.

To which I shouted, "Don't try to make sense of this! My grandmother's just a selfish old witch who only thinks about herself and her stupid pageant, and that's all there is to it!"

I sulked. I pouted. At rehearsals I deliberately sang "Gloria in exsell-cease deo," until Grandmother, exasperated, exhausted, clapped her hands and shouted, "Someone's still doing it wrong!" She looked right at me, and I glared back, grinding her romantic eggshells in my fist. Maybe you don't know this, but balconies in Southern churches were put there for the slaves. That was my one consolation: that Big Angel Anna Johnson would still be stuck in the balcony.

About a week before Christmas, Mama sent me over to Grandmother's house to get more yellow thread. She was sewing some extra project for the pageant that she couldn't tell me about; which wasn't unusual. I banged on Grandmother's back door, thinking no one was home, and almost ran into my grandmother and Hilda Johnson, embracing in the middle of the kitchen. They broke as soon as I walked in, even more flustered than I, and Grandmother snapped, "Were you raised in a barn?"

I turned around to close the door and heard Hilda say to my grandmother, "Cecelia, I can't tell you how much. . . ." More stunning than the fact that Hilda Johnson had been hugging my grandmother was the fact that she'd used her first name.

"I couldn't have done it without you," Grandmother said to Hilda. Then, to me, "Pudge, show Mrs. Johnson out."

When I got back to the kitchen, Grandmother asked me what I wanted before I could even begin. So I got the yellow thread and went on home, where I told Mama what had happened.

"I guess Hilda Johnson is your grandmother's best friend," Mama said. Then she went back to her sewing.

Now, doesn't this seem just the place for me to say, "I kept all these things and pondered them in my heart?" Except that that's not what I did. I poured what I'd seen like gasoline onto the fire in my heart, over which I continued to twist my grandmother's writhing form. She'd known about Anna for years! She'd been stringing Lollie along!

The last couple of rehearsals before the pageant were miserable. We were used to rehearsing without all the scenes in place; Grandmother liked surprising the choir as much as she liked stunning the audience, so at least one scene was rehearsed in secret every year: in addition to the Big Angel, of course. But that year, the very first scene was a secret. All through rehearsals, we'd be going along just fine and then Grandmother would say, "There'll be a scene here. Just watch me for your cues." Also, two of our readers couldn't attend the final rehearsals. So Grandmother would say, "Read, read, read, read, read. Just imagine it for now. Then we go on with the next song. Keep alert. Follow my lead." Adding to the confusion was Grandmother's sudden revelation that we wouldn't be closing with "Silent Night."

Somehow she'd cajoled Mack Austin back to the show, and the two of them kept growling at each other over in the corner. "It won't work, Miz Covington. Dagnabbit, I tell you, it just won't work," Mack kept saying. Which was the only clue, as far as I could see, that anything would work at all. Everyone was jittery at Christmas Eve dinner. Hilda was dressed to the nines and she kept crying out in the kitchen, "Oh, Lord have mercy!" We ate quickly, and almost in silence, then all of us, even Hilda, dashed over to the church.

I was wrong to think that nobody would come. The place was packed. But there were as many women wearing hats as not. Even Lollie was jumpy, fidgeting with her blue Virgin Mary costume. She and Joseph would have to walk in barefooted from the back of the church with only the 40-watt light from the Star of Bethlehem to guide them.

"At least Reverend Dickerson knows the way," I tried to joke.

Lollie said, "This thing around my face is so tight I don't think I can sing." She'd been rehearsing in secret, too, and wouldn't tell me a thing.

At last it was time. The choir filed in and Grandmother took her place. Then the whole sanctuary went dark. Just when it seemed like the crowd would start mumbling, Anna's voice floated out of the balcony. "Let all mortal flesh keep silence," she instructed. And it did. "Ponder nothing earthly-minded," Anna sang. "Christ our God to earth descendeth, our full homage to demand." We knew what she meant when she said it, too. As Anna sang, Mack was opening up a spotlight on her. Little by little she was revealed in the balcony: the biggest, most magnificent Big Angel ever to stand there. The golden costume Mama had made her floated as if in a wind. And Anna must have been standing on a chair, because she seemed ten feet tall. "Rank on rank, the host of heaven spreads its vanguard," Anna sang. "That the power of hell may vanish—as the darkness clears away!" Just as she said those words, the whole balcony lit up with lights like stars and planets. And we saw that it was filled with angels the likes of which we'd never seen in our pageant. Black-faced, brown-faced, yellow-faced angels with enormous glittering wings, and they were letting forth with "Joy to the World!" before we could even catch our breaths.

When Grandmother finally caught our eyes, back down in the choir, it was to cue us for an intricate twisting in of "heaven and nature sings" from up above that nobody had expected. But it worked. Then we sat, the stars in the heavens dimmed, all but the Star of Bethlehem, and a man stood up in the pulpit and began reading, "And it came to pass in those days . . . " It was Mickey Rooney Johnson. While he read, Lollie and Reverend Dickerson started in from the back of the church with the Baby Jesus; they got themselves settled in the stable just as Mickey Rooney said, "She brought forth her firstborn son, and wrapped him in swaddling clothes, and laid him in a manger, because there was no room for them in the inn." Then Mickey Rooney lay aside his Bible and began singing a song I'd never heard. "Mary, Mary had a little baby. Um, um, pretty little baby. Oh, oh, pretty little baby. Glory be to the newborn king!"

While he was singing, the heavenly hosts from the balcony were filing up the side aisles and taking their places all around the stable and pulpit, adding their voices as they came. "Star is shining, shining on the manger. Oh, oh, welcoming a stranger. Glory be to the newborn King!" Then one voice separated out of the heavenly hosts, a thready but true voice, and I realized it was Hilda Johnson. "Mary, Mary what you gonna call your baby?" she asked. And Lollie answered, "Some call him 'Mannuel, think I'll call him Jesus," and all the heavenly hosts rejoiced, "Glory be to the newborn king!"

My grandmother was a genius. There wasn't a dry eye in the house.

Not a single one of the shepherds that year was more than ten years old. They straggled in from all over the place, too, coming out from behind the pulpit, out from behind the heavy curtains in the windows, out from the back of the church. God only knows what Grandmother threatened them with to keep them quiet until it was their turn to appear.

As they came, we sang "While Shepherds Watched Their Flocks By Night," then "Angels We Have Heard on High." We all sang "Gloria in eggshell-cis deo," too. Even me. Then the little boy and girl shepherds sang "Away in a Manger" and Lollie sang "Infant Holy, Infant Lowly." You wouldn't think it could get better. But it did. Because after Lollie sang, Reverend Dickerson stepped from his place as Joseph and said from memory, "The people that walked in darkness have seen a great light; they that dwell in the land of the shadow of death, upon them has the light shined. For unto us a child is born, unto us a son is given."

You didn't even realize that Mack Austin was lowering the lights until Reverend Dickerson finished with, "The Everlasting Father, the Prince of Peace." Then you saw that the only light in the sanctuary was once again the Star of Bethlehem, and Anna was singing "Lo, How a Rose E're Blooming" while Joseph returned to his place. When the Kings processed in slowly from the back, we all saw that our school janitor Mel Wilson was among them.

"Myrrh is mine," he sang, "its bitter perfume breathes a life of gathering gloom."

Then Judge Marshall stood from his place in the congregation and boomed out, "Arise, and take the young child and his mother, and go into the land of Israel!"

To which Anna answered from the balcony, like a trumpet, "Children, go where I send thee!"

"How shall you send me?" Mickey Rooney asked her from the pulpit.

"I'm gonna send you one by one," Anna sang, and Lollie stood up with her baby doll Jesus and started down the aisle. "One for the little-bitty baby," Anna commanded. Then all the heavenly hosts started clapping and answering, "Born! Born! Born in Bethlehem," while Mary and Baby Jesus disappeared into the night. "Children, go where I send thee!" Anna's clarion voice commanded over and over again, with Mickey Rooney answering each time, "How shall you send me?" Next out were Joseph and the oldest shepherd, then the three Kings, then four, five and six little shepherds. Then seven, eight and nine of the heavenly hosts walked out, until all the aisles of the church were filled with angels, clapping and shouting and singing.

Suddenly they fell silent again. "Children! Go where I send thee!" Anna commanded, and Grandmother turned to the choir and directed us to stand. "How shall you send me?" we asked Anna, knowing without being told that that's what we were supposed to do. "I'm gonna send thee ten by ten!" Anna sang, slow as a bell. "Ten for the Ten Commandments!" Grandmother turned to the congregation and motioned them to their feet, too. As everyone stood, the heavenly hosts started the litany again. "One for the little-bitty baby, two for Paul and Silas," getting louder and louder all the time. "Eight for the eight that stood at the gate! Nine for the nine that dressed so fine!" Until everyone in the church shouted out "Ten for the Ten Commandments! Born! Born! Born in Bethlehem!"

At that very moment, the lights went out. All but the Star of Bethlehem. And there stood Lollie, right under it again, alone with the Baby Jesus in her arms. The church was absolutely quiet. "Oh, holy night," Lollie sang, in her clear, sweet voice. "Fall on your knees," everyone answered when the time came, just as we had at every Christmas pageant we'd ever been in. "Long lay the world in sin and error, pining," Lollie told us. And we answered, "Oh, night divine."

Of course, Grandmother's house was a mess when we got home. No fruitcake set out, no Scotch. Dirty dishes all over the table. "What a show," Daddy said. "The best ever, Mother." He still had smudges on his face from where he'd blackened it so he could slip around setting up lights without being seen.

Grandmother kicked off her shoes and sank into a chair. "Remember this night," she said, looking straight at me. "Because some day you'll be able to say you heard Anna Johnson sing before she was famous."

Daddy handed Grandmother her Scotch and said, "You bet."

"Geraldine Easton had talent," Grandmother said, "but she lacked ambition. I have ambition without any talent. But Anna's got both. And now she's got opportunity, too. That's what it takes, Pudge. That's what it takes."

Nothing was ever the same again after that night. Except my grandmother, of course, who remained Byzantine, rococo, selfish, brilliant, and courageous to the end. I don't know why she thought she lacked talent. I suppose because she lacked the talent she most desired. Dreams are such fragile things, aren't they? As delicate as eggshells.

The New Deal

Robin Becker

SHE WAS STANDING in the doorway of her studio apartment when I got off the elevator on the ninth floor.

"Hello, *shanah punum*, my sweet one," she said pressing her palm to my cheek. She pushed me ahead of her. "So let me look at you. Are you taking care? Do you need a coat?"

Her shove still carried conviction—a good sign. Like a camel's, her back rose and fell with its hump, and her hair stood upright, supported by a lacquered spray. She wore a long-sleeved navy wool dress and matching heels. On her collar was a Star of David with the words "Jewish Home for the Aged" embossed in gold.

"No, Bubbie, thanks. I've got a coat."

"Then why," she queried pulling on the sleeve of my parka, "do you wear this orange *shmatta*, rag, like you're going on a hike?" She draped my coat on the back of a chair. "What are you, a boy scout?"

She settled in a straight-backed chair, straining to sit erect, and clasped her hands in her lap.

"What's new by you, Jesse?" she asked.

"Do you remember Lindsay?" I attempted.

"It's a terrible thing trying to get work nowadays," she commented, ignoring me. She rose and walked to the sink carrying my jacket, preparing to attack a stain. She wasn't ready. I'd have to wait.

"In Roosevelt's time," Roosevelt was very popular with her, "he would find jobs or he would make them. He was the only president

who ever cared about the Jews. He went to all the big world confer-
ences, but no one wanted to talk. They got rid of all the big topics before he got there. Like Roosevelt," she concluded, "I've always been for
the underdog." She was about to sit down, knees bent, arms gripping
the sofa when she changed her mind and walked to the bed to smooth
the spread.

"Bub?"

"What, child?" Her hands were busy tucking and pulling.

"You know my housemates, the people you always talk to when you
call?"

"What about them?"

"I think we're splitting up, the whole group. Everyone wants to go
her own way. It makes me sad to see the house break up."

"Only because you want to live in a commune like a hippie. What
kind of crazy, half-baked idea is that?" Her face reddened. "All those
people sharing one kitchen and two bathrooms! It's not nice!"

She lunged for me: I snapped back, but she caught my forearm and
twisted it like a wet sweater. Then she dug her nails into my arm and
glared at me.

"I lived," she pressed, "in a tiny Russian village with my mother and
my grandmother. All I ever wanted was to live in a city with a man."
Blue veins appeared in her neck. "I know what you want—to live with
that woman, and I'm telling you, go find a man and be his wife!"

"What's right for you isn't necessarily what's right for me," I replied.

"What's right for you is right for the devil." She dropped my arm.
The visit had begun.

"Lindsay and I broke up," I said. She jerked towards me. "Lindsay's
going to try to be with a man."

She pointed a gnarled finger at me. "Your friend Lindsay is no fool.
She knows she has to eat meat and potatoes. That's why she's going
with a man where she belongs. You think you can live a whole life on
desserts, with women, but a person has to eat a balanced meal, Jesse."
she shook her head. "Take a lesson, *farcockta kind*, crazy child."

Now it was my turn to point the finger. "I'll talk to you," I retorted,
"when you're ready to listen."

She got up and walked to the closet. In a moment, she was by my
side carrying a heavy black coat with a fur collar.

"Let's go for a walk before it gets too cold," she said. "Your Bubbie's
old. She can't take much air."

We wound our way towards the double glass doors. For almost thirty years she'd lived on Locust Street. Every Sunday I'd go with my mother in the Chevy to pick her up. She'd come walking down the stairs and my mother would comment, "she's walking well" or "she looks tired."

Outside, we trudged along the flagstone footpath lined with benches. The November air was warm; I sweated in my thin parka. Seated, propped up with canes and metal walkers, the old ones were packed four to a bench like kids in their mufflers and hats. I remembered how my grandmother used to give us a sign when we'd drop her off, her hand, and then her face, and the her whole head and upper body, leaning from the third floor window, calling in her heavy accent, "Thank you, drive carefully *kinder*." She had seemed vigorous, agile, light.

In the distance I could hear the traffic, the shouts of the city transportation workers at the car barn a few blocks away. But here, strolling along the paths surrounding the Home, there were no children, no teenagers, no sign of the comfortable middle-aged these women had spawned. Old people. Everywhere. Walking in pairs, standing to catch a breath, sitting on wooden benches.

The Jewish Home for the Aged rose twenty stories; a driveway swirling right up to the double glass doors. Like the big hotels in Miami, the facade promised a jazzy interior with its tile mural and pink stucco. Every few feet, my grandmother stopped to introduce me to an elderly person buried deep behind collars and scarves. It was as if she could pull them back from the distant world towards which they drifted.

"I'd like you to meet Mrs. Cohen, a dear friend of mine. Ruby?" she asked bringing her face close to Ruby's. "This is my granddaughter Jesse from Boston."

I shook Mrs. Cohen's hand; my grandmother frowned. "Like a man," she hissed. "Act like a lady!"

"Mrs. Schwartz," she whispered as we promenaded, "is a real brain. To listen to her talk is the greatest pleasure. Such a learned person you could sit at her feet."

I hugged her shoulder.

"You know *mein kind*, she looked at me and winked, "I never got no education. Russia was a *farcockta* place, and only the boys went to school, but I learned all the things a girl needed to know: cooking, sewing. You kids," she sneered, "you kids don't know nothing."

We walked in silence; this was our way. When she was ready, she would give me a sign, a gesture, and we would resume talking. She scowled, made a clucking sound with her tongue, and gripped my elbow. Maybe she was thinking of Russia. Did she see herself, I wondered, an illiterate peasant girl making do, waiting for marriage? Was this woman the child who ran to the rabbi? "My mother," she used to tell us, "opened a chicken once and found a nail in its intestine. I was only five years old, but my brothers were away at heder, religious school, so I had to ask the rabbi if we could eat it, if it was kosher. 'Go ahead, child,' my mother said, and I rushed into the tiny village. I knocked on the rabbi's door once, twice; but no one answered. I saw a face peering down at me, the face of the rabbi's servant. He cracked the door. 'What do you want?' he snarled. 'I have to ask the rabbi if the chicken is kosher! We found a nail!'

" 'Wait here,' he spat. It was bitter cold. I waited and waited. Finally a woman came and let me in. She took me to the fire where I stood to get warm. After a while, the rabbi's man appeared. 'The rabbi will not see you because you are unclean.' He left, muttering something to the woman. She put the chicken in my arms and led me to the door. '*Es ist Kosher mein kind*,' she said.

"And I've never forgotten that story to this day, Jesse," she would say. "That same rabbi went around in the town with eggs in his beard so everyone knew what he ate for breakfast. And he called me unclean! Pale, weak men! Study, study, study, that's all they could do." She would knit her eyebrows and make a face. "Phooey! Who needs them! That's what I'm asking."

On Castor Avenue, black girls played jump rope on the pavement and cars whipped by, reeling on slick trolley tracks. We walked in a pumping motion like two old adversaries flung together.

"Am I walking too slow? Tell me," my grandmother said suddenly.

"No, Bub. You're walking fine."

"It's these shoes, they're too tight."

The shoes. The false teeth. The glasses. The way the tailor altered the suit. All the little things she never could get just right. I watched the mound of her shoulders rise and fall; she was terribly hunched over. But every summer when I was small, she stood tall, gripping my hand on the beach in Atlantic City. In that memory, I'm weary before her tirelessness, shy in the face of her self-confidence. She was on intimate terms with the bandleader at the Breakers Hotel. She whispered her requests into his ear: "I'll Be Loving You Always," "Love is a Many

Splendored Thing," "Three Coins in a Fountain." She danced. I sat at a little table with my sister sipping a Shirley Temple. We yawned, bit into chewy macaroons. Bubbie reached for two women and they did the *troika* across the floor. The crowd clapped. She spun in a tight circle with an elderly man. He hardly moved, but her eyes glowed. "You are one of my favorite partners, Mr. Goldman," she said. He kissed her cheek. "Laura, Laura," called the men and women who loved her dancing, her attention, her grace. "Sing for us, Laura," they shouted.

She stood very straight. The hall was silent. She breathed. "A-loo-loo-loo, hush a bye; a-loo-loo-loo, don't you cry; a-loo-loo-loo-loo, hush-a-bye." She made the room whirl with color and music. Later, out on the Boardwalk, past Planters Peanuts and the Diving Horse, she marched us proudly, introducing us to her friends.

Dry leaves blew against our coats. She tightened her hold on my arm.

"Do you know where we are, *kind?*" I nodded. "This is the Weiss Building. I want to see if Mrs. Meyer is here. Do you want to come in?"

"Who's Mrs. Meyer?"

"The woman whose room I got. You know there's a long list of people waiting to get in. When someone is moved to the Weiss, it means they can't take care of themselves. Her mind is okay, but her body doesn't work."

I tried to imagine my grandmother transferred to this wing, being dressed and fed by attendants. Instead, I kept envisioning my own mother, lifting her mother in and out of the bathtub, bringing her meals.

We entered a glass hallway and walked through a turnstile into a room the size of a gymnasium, filled with old people strapped into wheelchairs. I felt her hand on my arm like ice. At first I thought the old ones were playing some sort of game. Why else would fifty people be scattered across the room, strapped into straitjackets? My grandmother steered me across the floor. A steady buzz broke into monologues as we passed each person. One whined, "I will not come; you can't make me." Another whimpered like a baby. One woman repeatedly banged her head against a plastic guard, yelling, "This is no place for me, I tell you, Irene. Who do you think you are? I tell you, Irene." Each one of them created a little play, dramatizing their particular grief. Their sounds were hardly human—howls, whines, yelps—and I wanted to stroke each one, caress arms, massage feet, smooth matted hair.

Women stared at us with blank faces. In a small section cordoned off by rope, a group huddled in a circle watching a portable television. Ignoring the ones strapped into chairs, my grandmother walked directly into the circle.

"Where's Evelyn?" she asked.

"We don't know," a woman cried. "We haven't seen her all day."

Starved for company, they threatened to swallow her whole, to keep her there with them. She kissed the top of the white head closest to her.

"Laura, come visit us soon," they called. "Be sure to come soon!"

They were like the dead calling to Eurydice as she made her way back to earth. They were the ghosts of the hunted animals come back for revenge.

She was old, weak, her resistance was low, but I remembered how she used to catch our rubber balls rebounding off the garage door; how she used to try to teach us the letters of the Hebrew alphabet. She was resilient then, she could take a joke; we teased her and she teased us back. "*Alef, Bet, Gimel, Dalet, Hey, Vav, Zayin, Het, Tet, Lamed.*"

"No! No!" we screamed. "You forgot one," we laughed. "You skipped one, start over."

She turned from the group and shoved me ahead of her. This was her prerogative: to bully, to belittle, and then to turn a dignified face on that which pleased her. For a moment I saw the woman who sat year after year at the head of the Passover table, calling for everyone's attention; "*Me-mitz-ray-im, mots-ei-an-nu. Day-day-ei-nu, day-day-ei-nu.*" She led them and they followed. Old shaman-woman. Released from her body, she would send her soul to haunt me.

Late afternoon. Up in her apartment we sat on the upholstered sofa. I imagined the place swept clean, stripped bare, ready for the next resident, a housemaid humming in the hall with brooms and dustpan, daughters arriving to pack up the paraphernalia of a life.

"Bubbie, Bubbie," we used to say, "tell us the story of how your father died and how your mother took the horse and wagon. Tell us what the holy one said and how beggars came asking for onions and potatoes. And tell us the names of the towns in White Russia where you handed the thread, the scarves, and the cloth to the servants who ran to the marketplace. And tell us how you lied to your mother and carried your basket of berries deep into Gypsy camps after you promised never to take your shoes off or dance with the boys in their bright

shirts. And tell us how you called to the workers on the hot summer afternoons, singing Gypsy songs, the sweat staining your face like juice."

Our visits always took a political turn mid-afternoon. From politics
she leapt to the Old Testament, proving one point or another.

"And it came to pass," she began, "when men began to multiply on
the face of the earth and daughters were born to them, that the sons of
God saw the daughters of men—that they were fair; and they took
wives, all of which they chose. Do you know what that's from, Jesse?"

"Genesis," I answered mildly.

She offered me the red and black lacquered candy container on the
coffee table. The three dividers held Kraft caramels, Hopjes, and lemon
sour balls.

"Ever since you were little, you loved the candy."

She squinted. She was flirting, looking away, glancing back, and
then a smile breaking and a high wheeze escaping. She was laughing,
teasing, listing.

"Carmel popcorn, you were a great one for it in paper horns on the
Boardwalk. How about that sticky cotton candy, eh, that stuff always
ended up in your hair. Fancy mint logs, you ate all of it, nothing was
left. Black licorice, oh *gutteneau,* and toffee bricks."

Suddenly she was quiet. I waited. More religion? Back to politics? I
stood to look out of the window. It had started to snow. I thought of the
ballrooms in Atlantic City that I entered on my grandmother's arm.
This was our paradox: the past bound us together—helpless before our
memories—but forbade us our dissensions. I carried her judgments of
me like amulets around my neck.

"How's the writing going? Still with the poems?"

"It's slow you know, but I'm still working on my manuscript."

"Listen! If I told you once, I've told you a thousand times! People
like a good story. If you have to be a writer, you may as well try for Tolstoy. Now there was a writer, *mein kind.*"

"Bubbie, not everyone can be a Tolstoy!" I laughed.

"They could try! You have to aim high. Now there was a man who
understood life. He knew about many things, self-control for example,
and the love of man and wife. If I could read English, I'd study *Anna
Karenina.*"

"What's this," I asked, holding up a cannister of Lemon Pledge.

"What do you think it is?" she snarled. "I came to your place in
Boston, and I think you could clean it better."

"We have Lemon Pledge in Boston," I replied sourly.

"Use it then!" she commanded. "And read some Tolstoy so you know good from bad."

Good and Bad. Russia and America. Oh, Bubbie, tell us how you hid your brother when the Czar's bad men came with rifles and they flung your mother and grandmother across the room; how you told them he had gone to Kiev with the other boys to study. And tell me how you waited for days with your mother for the man with the papers to send your brother to New York, the person who made arrangements for you to travel to Bremen where you watched the others leave the line. How you ate candy in Germany, lying about your age, your home, your family, your religion, and how you finally collapsed in steerage where a blond man held your head and you vomited for days, seasick, with the smell and squalor churning in your stomach.

"Christ, Bubbie," I said getting up. "Even the scholars argued with God. Who's to say what's good or bad? The Talmud is filled with contradictions."

"But they're learned contradictions!" She stood tall and raised one arm in a toast. "Great is the Lord, and greatly to be praised." Her arm dropped. "Who do you think you are?" she questioned. "I've been around a lot longer than you. And don't act so smart."

We sat in silence, each waiting for the other to risk a topic.

"Your mother told me," she began, "you ran a race last weekend. What kind of a race?"

"Six miles," I replied. "It was Lindsay's idea."

"Did you win?"

"Bubbie, there were three thousand people in the race."

"Did you fall?"

"I finished."

"The same day?"

"It took about an hour."

"Where there any other girls?"

"It was all girls."

"That's just what I mean, *mein kind!*" She slammed her fist on the arm of her chair. "You would pick a race that was all girls. How do you expect to meet any boys if you run in a race that's all girls?"

"Bubbie, it was a race!"

"I don't care what it was. If you run with girls, you run with girls. Don't give me no backtalk!"

We were losing ground. But the burden was on me. I had to work to get along with her.

"Don't you think," she continued, her voice modulated, "that I'd like a little *nachas* like the other grandmoms? A wedding? Maybe a great grandchild?"

She was beginning her pitch, as familiar to me as the shape of Lindsay's body curled in sleep against my back.

"*Kind*," she said, "in *Anna Karenina,* one of the greatest books aside from the Talmud, Levin learns to love his brother's dying body. Now his brother is very sick, child, and smells terrible, and he's got no control over his bladder. Still, Levin loves him at the end. Don't you think you could learn to love a man, especially a healthy and handsome one?"

I leaned over and took her hands. "Listen to me."

"I'm listening."

"I like women. I like their companionship."

"Companionship I understand. Making a life is something else. You think Lindy's going to take care of you when you're old like me? You think Lindy can be your family?"

"Lindsay and I aren't together any more, Bub. You know that."

"See? What did I tell you? She gets a new idea in her head and she forgets your name. A man! What are you doing? Looking for another woman? I never heard of anything like this in my life, *kind*."

"Let's look at the cousins. Is Julie happily married? Karen? Elsie? Peter?"

"They're divorced, " she roared. "At least they had their accomplishments. At least they tried. Elsie had two accomplishments."

"Bubbie," I yelled, "Elsie was divorced twice! You think it's easy for her raising David and Rachel alone, with no help from Dan?"

"Every life has sadness, Jesse. Peter and Julie and Karen and Elsie all gave marriage a chance." She shrugged. "It's the times. I've told you before. It's bad times for marriage."

"Look at it this way then. My life with Lindsay was like a marriage. Can you see it? And now we're divorced."

She sat very still. "Sometimes," she mused in her professorial tone, "does a woman run off with another woman?"

"Sometimes," I answered.

"What kind of a world is this?" she cried, beseeching the sky. " I see those queer boys on television, those *fagallahs*. Some of them are so handsome you could die."

I shook my head. "Can you say something new?"

"Does the Torah say something new each time another person picks it up?" She raised her head. "The economy is in a terrible way. A girl needs to start looking for a husband a lot earlier."

I raised my eyebrows.

"You know," she said sadly, "if I had anything to give you, you would have it."

"I know that, Bub, and I appreciate it."

"All I can give you is a piece of my mind, *kind*, because your father took all of my money for a bad investment."

"I remember when that happened, Bub, and I'm sorry."

"Just remember your father is a good man at heart, even if he has mean ways. But he's a lousy businessman. Men! Who needs them? But your Pop-pop!" She leaned back in her chair. "Now there was a man, my child. A real gentleman. Thirty years since your Pop-pop passed away."

For thirty years, we used to visit the cemetery during the High Holy Days. Was she thinking about that too? She closed her eyes. I pictured my Aunt Sarah, my mother, myself. That was childhood: going with the women to the fish store or the cemetery. At the cemetery they drove round and round, getting lost on lanes called Rosewood and Evergreen.

"I think it's over there, *mein kind*," Bubbie would say, pointing her finger.

"All right Mrs. Know-it-all, stop pointing." my aunt snapped.

"Talk to you and talk to the wall." my grandmother sighed.

My mother drove, her face a rigid web of lines.

When we finally parked, my grandmother limped towards the graves mumbling in Yiddish. I walked beside her.

"Sweetheart," she said, shoving me forward, "say hello to your grandpop."

"Hurry up, Mom!" my mother called. She was sitting on a low gravestone smoking a cigarette. Behind her, my aunt picked flowers.

My grandmother steadied herself, held the stone out in front of her and wept. "Oh, my Julius, I miss you so."

"Hi, Pop-pop," I said somberly. I thought of the picture of the dapper Russian man that had sat on my grandmother's dresser for as long as I could remember.

She sniffed.

"If I knew how to get here by public transportation, I'd come more often." She took out a Kleenex and blew.

"Throw a little grass on your grandfather," she said handing me a clump. I heaved it towards the stone. She took out a black lace veil and placed it on her head. It fell softly on her face. Eyes closed, holding the stone with both hands, she murmured the Yiddish prayer for the dead.

It was dark outside when I rose to turn on a lamp. Six o'clock. I thought she was dozing, but as I reached for a quilt to throw on her legs, she called to me.

"*Kind?*"

"What?"

"I'll never in a million years accept your kind of a life. I love you and you'll always be my granddaughter no matter what, of course, but I find the whole thing disgusting."

"I hear you, Bub," I smiled, thinking of how we'd start again in a few months.

"It's no life, I'm telling you," she concluded. She sighed and stood blinking at the darkness outside.

I went to the closet to get my coat.

"I'm telling it as I see it, *mein kind,* and I just can't see it."

"See what, Bub?"

"What you do with women."

"What are you talking about now?"

"I'm talking about sex. You say you don't want a fellah, and I can understand that, but how can you be satisfied? Sexually, I mean?" She looked sincere, curious.

"Well, I am," I said defensively.

I'm sorry, *mein kind,*" she said, "but I just can't get it. I try and I try. All day sitting here with you, I've been trying to visualize what two women can do with each other and I just can't imagine it."

"Maybe you'll get it by Passover," I said.

"*Kind?*"

"What, Bub?"

"Will you see her?"

"Who? Lindsay?"

She drew her hand across her forehead and sighed. "Her parents must be fancy people to give her a name only a professor can say."

I knelt beside my grandmother. She turned her face away from me.

"Bubbie," I said gently, "I probably won't see her for a while. And after some time has passed, I think we'll be friends."

She put her hand on my head, conferring her particular blessing. "I only hope she doesn't turn against you. Now that she wants a man, maybe she'll be ashamed for what she was."

"Maybe she will," I answered.

"Love is love," she said pressing on my crown. "You cared for her very much, *kind?*" she said releasing me.

"Yes," I said standing.

She blinked at me. "She won't forget you so fast."

I pushed "L" and waited for the elevator doors to close. I'd promised to call when I got back to Boston; to alleviate her anxiety about other drivers, people drinking, and other people taking their eyes from the road to scream at their kids.

She stood in the doorway and yelled out, "I'm praying for you day and night, and if the good Lord spares me and listens to the words of an old woman, you'll be married or engaged by *Shevouos.*"

Every visit ended the same way; her wish for my expedient engagement by the next Jewish holiday. It was part of our routine. I had lost Lindsay to a dream she had of another life; but I had not yet lost my grandmother. We gave what we could and let the rest stand.

The Peak

Christina Chiu

THE SKY IS LIKE a brightly lit screen. From Grandmother's room on The Peak of Hong Kong, I watch a black hawk dive feet first into the jungle trees. A vine reaches around the trunk of a papaya tree, twisting like a parasitic vein. Out of its reach, a greenish-orange fruit dangles heavily from a branch. When I was five—after my grandfather died from bone cancer and Grandma moved here to live with my aunt— Grandma and I took after-dinner walks to the overlook. A fragrant papaya in hand, we sang Chinese songs, counted the lights in Central or the ships blinking in the harbor.

Inhaling the familiar scents of Joy perfume and stale cigarettes, I try to recall Grandma's favorite song about the moon. *Yueh liang zai na li? Where is the moon?*

The rest of the lyrics escape me now. On the altar by her bedside is a black-and-white photo of Grandfather, a slender, balding man dressed in a western-style, pin-striped suit. A candle sits in front of the picture. I notice that I have the same pudgy nose.

"You have to be careful," Grandma whispers conspiratorially. Without dentures, her cheeks and lips cave inward. Against the severe, tattooed eyeliner and eyebrows, her face seems ghoulish. The Grandma I remember would never have allowed anyone to see her in such a state. As if suddenly aware of my thoughts, she reaches into a glass, withdrawing two rows of teeth and slipping them into her mouth. Her painted lips have thinned, but still reveal her trademark pout.

"Yes, careful," I mumble, laying my aching body in the reclining chair next to hers. What drama is she going to invent this time? During my last visit, Grandma was convinced that her mother had been smothered to death by her father's second wife. When I told my father how distraught she was, he informed me that her mother died of TB. "She loves making up stories," he said. "She's alone all day. It gives her something to do."

The aircraft's odor lingers in my hair and clothes. With the layover, the flight from New York took close to twenty-four hours. I couldn't sleep. Each time I closed my eyes, I thought about my fiancé, weighed the positive against the negative of marriage, and then dwelled too long on the word "forever." Is he the one I want to share the rest of my life with? Will I get like Mom—bored but dependent—resigned to sharing the rest of my life with someone I no longer love? Will he? I fidget with the ring. I haven't told him how I feel. Fatigue weighs heavily on my lower vertebrae.

"Are you listening?" she asks, impatiently, her large, blind eyes on me. I yawn. My aunt and uncle should be home any minute now. I'll say my hellos and then retire to bed.

"Yes, Tai," I say, respectfully.

"Do you know what people are saying?" she snaps.

I pat her soft hand and let my sore eyes draw shut. "What are they saying?"

"They're saying that you've been with many men," she says coldly.

Heat flushes my face. My mind darts into the past, overwhelming me with the taste of alcohol and the faces of the college boys I slept with. "Excuse me?" I ask, straining to keep my voice steady.

Outside, the hawk reappears from out of the lush purple and olive leaves, a limp rodent clutched in its claws. Grandma stares as if through me. Just how miserable I was during my last visit eight years ago rushes back to me. The general consensus, she had said, was that I was too fat, I dressed like one of those hippies, and since I had just graduated from college, I needed finishing school.

I start to wheeze. Upholstered wall cabinets stuffed with tailored and designer clothes surround us on three sides, reminding me of a cushioned silk casket.

"It's terrible," she says. "After all, you are a *chi jing xia jia*."

I twist the ring around my finger. Why did I bother to come here? Why did I think things would be any different this time? How am I going to survive an entire week of this?

"I'm engaged," I say, my voice rising.

"Do you know what it means to be a *chi jing xia jia?* It means you are lady." Didn't she hear me? Doesn't my engagement count for anything? I should have expected this. He's not Chinese after all.

"Tai," I shake her hand roughly. "I'm engaged."

She quiets, pulling free. A glutinous film textures the surface of her eyes. They wander in the direction of the cabinets facing us. "Take a look through my clothes," she says. "If there is anything you want."

"Thanks, Grandma," I say, straining my voice, "but I have too many clothes already."

"When I was little, the fortune-teller told my father that I would die young. My father spoiled me. I had a new dress to wear every day."

"Yes," I say, finishing the story for her. "Two tailors lived in the house solely to make your outfits."

She clasps her hands over her lap. "That's right," she says, proudly. For a moment, I think she's going to break into a reverie about her father's pet lions or the expanse of her dowry, which included trunks of silk and pearls, gold ingots and precious pieces of jade. There's the chance she might dwell on her mother's fictitious death or make up a new calamity from out of the past.

"Oh, I have a beautiful jacket that I bought yesterday," Grandma says, about to get up. "It would look pretty on you."

"No, thanks," I say, catching her by the arm. My feet wiggle into my slippers.

"You must be hungry," she says, sensing that I'm about to leave and pushing a tin between us, prying it open with her long, manicured nails. "Have a cookie."

They are my favorites, but I tell her, "No." If only I could shake her.

"They're very good," she says. "You like them."

"I'm not hungry," I say, jumping to my feet. "I'm going upstairs to get some rest."

Trying to replace the lid, the tin slips from her fingers to the floor. Cookies spill on the carpet. I toss them into the garbage.

"My favorite cookies, too," she says, her voice cracking. Her hands are shaking. I regret being so harsh. She's an old lady, I tell myself. Be patient. Who knows how much longer she's going to be around? This could be your last visit.

"I'll get another box for you tomorrow," I say, stroking her arm.

She nods. "The kind with the jam in the middle."

It occurs to me that I'd made the same request when I was little. "Strawberry jam, right?"

Her eyes light up. She takes my hand, exploring the small diamond between thumb and forefinger. It's less than a carat, but she doesn't say a word.

Drifting into sleep, I feel my body relax as if my bones were melting into the mattress. A sound jerks me upright. The room is dark, foreign. The hair on my arms stands on end. I fumble out of bed and race out the door.

"Eh!" Grandma screams. "Eh!"

I race down two flights. In the hallway outside her room, she stands a step up from the landing.

"What's wrong?" I say, taking her by the arms. "Are you hurt?"

"I was calling and calling," she says in a hoarse voice. "Where were you?"

Checking my watch, I realize it's been two hours since I left her. "Upstairs."

"What were you doing?" she accuses.

I blink, trying to focus. The backs of my eyes feel like dry sand. Her teeth are out again. "Sleeping," I say.

"You've had enough sleep," she tells me. "Why don't you keep me company for a while and then go back to bed?"

"Where's Aunty?"

"They went to a dinner party."

"When will they be back?"

"Soon. Now, try this jacket," she says, pushing a red Chinese style *si mi* at me. It is patterned with tacky, gold leaves.

"No, thank you," I say. "You keep it."

"Try it," she says. "It's beautiful."

"I have one already," I say, lying.

"You must try it," she says, picking at my clothes with her red nails. "You need to dress better."

"I don't like it," I blurt.

She pauses. "You understand what I was saying earlier? You come from a very good family. You wouldn't want anyone to think you were anything less than a lady, would you? You know how people like to gossip."

"Why do you listen to them?" I scream, banging my fist against the banister. "You're my grandmother. If you don't like what your hear, then don't listen! It's that simple."

She slips down a step onto the landing. I catch her by the forearm.

"Oi, I fell!" she mutters, clutching her chest. "My heart. See what you've done? See what you made me do?"

Air clumps in my throat. I recall that she did this the last time I was here. I was so frightened, it triggered a three-day asthma attack.

"That scared me nearly to death," she says, breathing heavily.

"You need rest, then," I say, leading her back to her room and depositing her firmly in her chair. "I do, too, okay?" I march out of the room. On the stairs I catch a glimpse of her. In the large reclining chair her figure seems fragile, even childlike. The dark eyeliner makes her seem owlish; perpetually stunned. She shuffles to the altar by her bedside. Quietly, I duck behind the banister. Kneeling in front of an icon of the Virgin Mary and Grandfather's photo, she mumbles something I can't hear, taking the matches into her hand. She strikes one, then, with a steady grip on the candle, lights it on the first try. So she can see, I think. She can see light. Why hasn't she told anyone? She whispers her prayers, the flame flickering with her breath.

When I think of Grandfather, I recall the wailing sound of the *erhu*, a Chinese violin with a long, thin neck, which he practiced every morning, and the ostrich marionette he gave me the summer he fell sick. Grandma told me then that he had a bad case of the flu. "He'll be all better tomorrow," she said.

But when I marched Oscar the Ostrich into Grandfather's room to wake him the next day, Mom shushed me, dragging me into the kitchen for a scolding. "Grandma says Grandpa needs to get back on schedule or he'll never get over the flu," I said.

Stunned, Mom answered, "Grandpa's very, very tired. You tell that to Grandma."

Years later, at his grave site, Grandma told me: "He was so good to me. I didn't even get to say good-bye." She polished the headstone using saliva and a full purse-pack of tissues.

Grandma crosses herself. The flame dances. I climb to the guest room and shut the door.

Grandfather comes to me in a dream. Propped on his knee is the *erhu*, its neck like a crane's. The strings shimmer like gold. His fingers move over them. With his right hand, he slides the bow horizontally over the strings, producing the low sound of sadness. He looks at me. The *erhu* sings, "Take care of Grandma."

I wake. There is the sound of the *erhu* outside. Peeking out at the overlook, I try to locate where the sound is coming from, but the jungle trees hide this secret. For a moment, I wonder if Grandma is listening. Changing my clothes, I circle down the stairwell to Grandma's room. The air conditioner rumbles loudly.

"Who is it? " she asks. I notice her makeup has been removed and her teeth are once again soaking in the glass.

"*Xiao Mao,*" Little Cat, I say, using my nickname.

"*Bau, bau,* my sweetheart." She smiles. "It's almost dinner time."

"Let's go for a walk," I say.

"Oh, no," she says. "We couldn't do that."

"Why not?" I say, gently brushing a strand of hair from her cheek.

"Well, just look at me," she says.

"You look fine, Grandma, you really do."

She shakes her head. "Oh, no, I couldn't. It's too late. Besides, I couldn't walk that far."

"It's just outside."

"Too far. It's not safe."

"Well, okay, but there's a papaya just across the street waiting to be picked," I say, in a sing-song voice.

"Oh, really?"

"Wouldn't it be nice to share a big, juicy papaya in the morning?"

She licks her puckered lips. "It's just across the street?"

"I can see it from here," I say.

She slips on her slippers. The dentures re-enter her puckered mouth. Grabbing her cane and changing into shoes at the front door, she slips into the damp night.

The papaya plucks off into my hands, dew from the tree's leaves showering me with raindrops. The fruit's sweet aroma fills me with hunger. We are standing in a mist, enveloped by the lingering dampness of monsoon season.

"Smell that," I say, offering the papaya to Grandma. She has her back to me, listening to the *erhu.*

My chest lightens. It's one of Grandfather's favorite tunes "You hear it?" I say.

She walks toward it, as if in a trance. When we get to the overlook, Grandma becomes silent. Sweat dots her nose and brow. She gulps, searching with blind, desperate eyes. Directly below us, I spot a silver-haired man dressed in Chinese pajamas. I swallow my disappointment.

"Wang Goong Goong," Uncle Wang, I say, respectfully, waving at my aunt's neighbor.

He nods, continuing the song. The voice trills. A lover beckons. In the valley, a million starry lights illuminate Central. Ships flicker in the harbor.

Grandma takes my hand. There are tears at the rims of her eyes. She must be thinking about her duets with Grandfather. Withdrawing a tissue from my pocket, I dab at the corners of her eyes.

"Don't cry," I say.

"Is he good to you?" she asks.

It takes a moment for me to realize she is referring to my fiancé. I can picture his tender blue eyes watching me; his soft kiss on my lips before he leaves for work each morning.

"Yes," I answer. The papaya's fragrance fills my nostrils. "Very."

She looks up at the full moon. "I'm scared," I want to say. But she's from a different world, one that chose a love for her, and then expected that they grow toward one another.

She touches my cheek, wiping the tears from my face. "Do you see the lights?" she asks, pointing her cane toward Central.

"Can you?" I ask.

She smiles, a smirk curled at the corner of her mouth. I hug her tight and cry. The *erhu* lulls me. I close my eyes. In a moment, I feel our bodies swaying slightly. A thick mist moves in over The Peak and into the valley. Small droplets settle on our skin.

Yueh liang zai na li? Grandma starts to sing. Where is the moon? *Yueh liang zai na shang?* From where does it rise?

Wang Goong Goong switches tunes to accompany Grandma. The two sounds merge. Wind sweeps through her hair, tickling her shirt. She is the grandma I remember from when I was five. Beautiful. Alive. Suddenly, I realize it's more than just a song about the moon. It's about "home," China, where, after all these years, she still yearns to return. Only now, if she were to go, she would have to do it alone, without the man her heart still belonged to. I fault her for constantly dwelling in the past, yet I'm paralyzed because I can't stop fretting over the future.

Grandma sings: *Zao zai wo di fang,* earlier it was shining in on my room. *Zao zai wo di chuang,* earlier it was shining on my bed. The papaya feels soft within my grasp, its fragrance sweet and forgiving. I think of my fiancé curled on the futon next to his cat. If only I could kiss him the moment just before he wakes. I rub the papaya with my thumb.

Its skin is smooth. I love him, now, I think. Now is what matters. Our love, like my grandparents', might grow.

I open my mouth. A voice, both woman and five year old melded into one, emerges from my lips. Hugging Grandma, I sing, *Yueh liang zai na li . . . Yueh liang zai na shang . . . Zao zai wo di fang . . . Zao zai wo di chuang.*

Searching for a Grandmother

What I Know About You

Aimee Liu

NOTHING FITS. I've spent thirty years collecting stories about you, Grandmother, trying to understand. But each piece seems to belong to a different puzzle. You destroyed too much evidence, took too much with you when you died, and left behind a collection of images—each filtered through the eyes of a son or daughter, daughter-in-law or grandchild—that refuse to jibe with the facts.

Starting with my own memory . . .

I am nine years old. We have just arrived at my aunt Loti's villa in the Hollywood Hills after a two-week drive from Connecticut. It is the first time I've met my California relatives, my father's side of the family, and I am frankly overwhelmed by aunt Loti's insistence on addressing us as "Dahling!" and by her ruddy blond husband's equal insistence on plying my parents with highballs. I'm trying to find an inconspicuous corner to hide in when suddenly my father's voice rises above the rest. Grammy Luis is coming.

Grammy Luis, who spent more than twenty years in China married to my Chinese grandfather, then left him there, never to see him again when you returned with your children to America. If not the whole truth, this is the gist of my parents' preparatory briefings. At the time of our visit you are an invalid and live in the guest house across Loti's patio. You rarely venture out, but, in honor of our visit, you've agreed to join us for dinner in the main house.

The grown-ups surround and painstakingly seat you. I am summoned.

Nine years to eighty-four, we face each other. Your very age terrifies me. Your once blue eyes are clouded with cataracts. Your gnarled fingers grip your seat. The rose-colored bedjacket that my mother sent last Christmas is tied at your throat by a velvet ribbon, and a pair of cloisonné combs sweep back your soft white hair, but this disguise does not reassure me. Should I curtsy and kiss my grandmother's hand? Should I hug her, pretending love?

I stand before you and mumble hello. Your breath sounds like sandpaper. Your rouged lips pucker, stretching crepe paper cheeks, and you squint to see me through those veiled retinas. At last you deliver your verdict.

"My, you're a chubby girl, aren't you?"

This to a child on the verge of adolescence, smack in the era of Twiggy.

You were absolutely right. I was a chubby little girl, but the fact that your strongest impression of me happened at the time to be my greatest weakness, deafened me to any further exchange. I backed away, never saw you again. It would be years before I considered that maybe you never meant to insult me at all.

Yet I was hardly alone in misreading you, Grandmother. To this day, every member of the family seems to view you through a different lens. My mother recalls you officiously telling her how to peel carrots and wash diapers during the three months in the forties when you crowded into her one-bedroom Greenwich Village apartment. At the time, Mom was juggling a job, her first baby, and a journalist husband preoccupied by the global politics of the "New Post-War Era." She barely had the patience to look at you, let alone tease out your life story.

My two aunts remember your uneven handling, overprotecting the eldest, Blossom, while taking an almost prurient interest in the younger and more beautiful Loti's willful escapades. Do *you* remember the night in L.A. when Loti, then an "exotic Eurasian starlet," was being wooed by a Hollywood producer, and you, in the next room, put a glass to the wall, the better to hear the moaning? Blossom remembered, still resentful in her seventies, even passed the story down to her own daughter. "My mother the busybody, I'll never be like that."

Of course, the more egregious offense was lying to Blossom's fiancé. "No," you told him, "She doesn't want to see or marry you. Never come here again." And you slammed the gate and let Blossom think that he'd abandoned her. Were you really so cruel, Grandmother? Blossom claimed that she and her beau each married on the rebound people who reminded them of each other. Both marriages died painful, lingering deaths, and it was all your fault. That's what I heard, and I wonder . . .

My father, your eldest son, remembers you in a starkly different light. He says you were shy, sickly, a virtual shut-in. Once, in China, another American married to a Chinese man came to call, doubtless hoping to find a kindred spirit. This stranger stood at the door and knocked, rang the bell. You watched from the upstairs window and ordered the servants not to answer. Finally the woman left a chit and slowly walked away. You read the chit, a suggestion that you meet the other woman for tea, but you never replied.

There were occasions, too, when the family was stranded, amid the perennial political unrest of Shanghai or Peking in the 1910s and 20s, or in the remote mountains of central China, without a father or money. Once, Dad remembers, in the mountain village of Kuling, you told him to go to the Chinese police chief and plead, as eldest son, for the chief to extend you credit. More than once you sent Blossom and Loti to beg money from the white neighbors in Shanghai's foreign settlements. The girls were children and half-Chinese. By implication, you, a white woman, could never stoop so low.

Yet they all loved you, Grandmother, forgave you, cared for you, in their ways. Even though she blamed you for ruining her life, Blossom considered you her best friend. Loti, by marrying well (husband number one had a family fortune, number two connections in Hollywood, number three—the highball enthusiast—a senior position with a major airline) was able to shelter you through your old age. Your baby, Herb, came back from World War II duty in France to raise his family near you. He saw you through life-saving surgery in your seventies. And Dad annually flew across country just to take you shopping for pretty new clothes in your waning years. In spite of everything, you were the mother who gave them life, who kept them well through twenty years in China, who survived another forty to give advice and criticize and pronounce that "East is East and West is West and never the twain shall meet," ignoring the blatant evidence of your own dutiful half-Chinese children. As I say, the pieces don't fit.

But if we could push ourselves out of the way and let the facts of your life speak for you, an entirely different woman would emerge; has emerged since I took the bait and began to research these facts.

This other you was fair and smooth-skinned, barely five feet tall and slender with translucent blue eyes, long dark hair that was once, in childhood, strawberry blond. A beauty by some lights, by others you were handsome, even hard; but the hardness came of caution. Your mother died young. You were raised in Kansas by a fellow pioneer family while your own father was off selling snake oil, running cattle, or grubbing out worthless gold mines. You grew up wary of men and, more, of the realities of marriage. When you arrived, solo and well into your twenties, in turn-of-the-century Frisco, the city's sailors and swindlers and fat, mutton-chopped politicians hardly reassured you. You supported yourself by tutoring new immigrants in English, and, over time, concluded that your Chinese students were the truest gentlemen the Bay Area offered. For all the bad that was said about Chinamen—specifically, that they were lazy, shiftless, dishonest, unclean, promiscuous, rat-eating coolie gamblers—your educated scholars proved themselves right honorable. One, in particular, intrigued you more than any white man you'd ever known.

Liu Ch'eng-yü (you chose Don as his American name) was a bona fide revolutionary, even had a price on his head back in China for trying to overthrow the Imperial government. All your other Chinese students wore queues—pigtails—as required proof of their subservience to their Manchu rulers. Don cut off his queue while studying in Japan, and now he could be beheaded in China for this offense alone, though it was hardly his sole violation. When he wasn't attending classes at the University of California (or tutorials with you) he was editor of a revolutionary newspaper in Chinatown, and he actively solicited money from merchants and laundrymen to fund rebellions back home. His hero was Dr. Sun Yat-sen, who believed that China was ripe to become a modern democratic republic; and if Don was any indication, you thought, maybe Dr. Sun was right. Tall and broad-shouldered, his lank black hair scissored close to the head, Don wore Western suits and pastel ties. His shirt collars lifted like wings. His ears were small and flat and precise, skin as smooth as amber, and his face, dominated by high, wide cheekbones, was a perfect oval. Amusement softened his lips and eyes. His mind seemed always engaged.

But here the few surviving photographs and recorded dates become ambiguous. Were you already in love with "Don" Liu Ch'eng-yü when he rescued you after the Great San Francisco Earthquake? Did you know he was widowed from his first (arranged) marriage, had two children living with his mother back in China? Did that bother you,

Grandmother? Surely Grandfather had feelings for *you*, or he wouldn't have put his life on the line, a Chinaman giving aid and protection to an unmarried white woman. Conflicting stories of this episode have been passed down, but whether his heroism consisted of rescuing you from a burning boardinghouse, or carrying your belongings to one of the refugee tent cities erected following the Quake, or guarding your tent against ruffians hardly matters. The fact is—and here the evidence starts to shimmer again in the form of a hand-scripted marriage certificate—you and Grandfather were wed just six weeks after the Quake and in direct contravention of California law. Wyoming was the nearest state that would allow a Chinaman to marry a white American. It took you three days to get there by train, riding in segregated cars. As if this weren't discouragement enough, Grandfather's mother in China was cabling threats to disown him if he married you. I cannot believe this was a sudden or shallow romance.

However daring you may have been in marrying the Chinese Liu Ch'eng-yu, you entered his name on the certificate as Don Luis, a *Span ish* name. The Spaniards, you reasoned, had dark hair and tawny skin like your husband's, but they were also California's original European landowners. With this name, at least on paper, you and Grandfather would appear respectable.

The pseudonym was clearly a concession on Grandfather's part. On returning to China following the long-awaited defeat of the Manchus in 1911, he reverted at once to Liu Ch'eng-yü. But you would remain Mrs. Don Luis for the rest of your life.

Nearly thirty years you and Grandfather spent, six in America and the rest in China, producing four children, losing two more to stillbirth and infant death, moving from one temporary home to another, finally building a house of your own in the Kiangsi mountains just in time to be driven out of it by occupying armies. You suffered war, loss, disease, poverty, countless separations. One hour Grandfather was the consummate western-style senator in suit and tie, debating taxation and land reform on the floor of China's Parliament. The next, he resumed the role of scholar, donning long silk robes and hosting banquets and mah-jongg parties, drinking ficry *pai kan chiu* and sing-songing verses with fellow poets late into the night. Meanwhile you struggled to keep your children clothed, fed, and alive through the regular periods when Grandfather's government salary went unpaid (when a little chubbiness in a child can be a saving grace, I hear you chiding, Grandmother).

And you maintained your own pride and decorum, in spite of the fact that your mother-in-law was a true Dragon Lady, with bound feet and an ebony throne, who instructed Don's two Chinese children never to speak to their "white devil" stepmother. In spite of the fact that there was no one more reviled in Shanghai's foreign settlements than a white woman who would lower herself to bed a Chinaman, let alone marry him and bear his half-breed babies.

The annual family photographs show immaculate white clothes edged in ruffles and lace, healthy children—wide-eyed, dark-haired, gorgeous children—and you looking afraid to breathe. After the first few pictures taken in Frisco, in which he holds baby Blossom on his lap while you lean against his shoulder, Grandfather does not appear in these family poses, but the babies are unmistakably his, and they do keep coming, right up through the year you turn forty-six.

Grandfather was there and not there, in other words. There to make babies, to rescue you and his children periodically from the brink of poverty, to borrow, rent, or build a house where you could stay while he went off, ever plotting and campaigning for a free, democratic China. But he was not there in 1917 the night a hostile warlord invaded Peking, forcing you and the children to flee by donkey cart into the countryside with only a manservant for protection. Nor was he there later that night, when you became delirious with fever. He was not at the Chinese inn where you were forced to stop, where you commanded your children—the youngest barely one year old—to sit on the table away from the rats whisking across the floor. Where the Chinese doctor refused to treat your diphtheria for fear of being blamed for a white woman's death. Fortunately, your manservant, Yen Ching-san, was devoted to you. One day he would hang your portrait at the entrance of an inn bought with his accumulated tips from serving drinks and barbecued pork at Grandfather's mah-jongg parties. But that night, Yen ran ten miles to fetch the English doctor who saved your life.

Ten years later, Grandfather was again absent when twenty-year-old Blossom staggered home after being escorted to "tea" by one of Shanghai's missionary priests. She was disheveled, disoriented, remembered nothing beyond arriving at the party and sipping a little punch. Only when it became clear that she was pregnant did Grandfather reappear. His solution: he would arrange a marriage. No one, he said, would believe the word of a Eurasian girl against a European priest, and, regardless, no honorable man would marry her any other way now. If not for the fact that Blossom, alone of your children, was born in America, his argument might have held sway. You, however, were adamant. Blossom was a U.S. citizen, not some concubine for one of Don's cronies. Instead of marriage, you arranged Blossom's abortion. But from now on, you would insist on screening the girl's callers, and refused virtually all of them. Your old mistrust of men was revived. You took personal possession of Blossom's ill fate, for better and for worse.

"What we went through," my father, now in his eighties, murmurs when I ask about his childhood. This is just some of what his family went through in the China. He claims he barely remembers, the squalid, ruthless China that you, Grandmother, so longed to escape. Some came to China and were enchanted; you always said you loathed the place. You'd seen human heads dangling, caged like birds. You'd stumbled over the blue corpses of infants abandoned in Confucian temples. You were assaulted each day by countless beggars with their dripping sores and stumps and blindness. You'd watched your own children suffer and die, felt the slow torture of abandonment yourself as Grandfather slipped further and further away, back into the clothing and habits and language of his native home. China was never your home.

For twenty years you argued with Grandfather, begged him to let you return to the States. But he reminded you that your father had died in the time you'd been away, the friends of your youth had all scattered, you had no one left in America. I think Grandfather was afraid he'd lose you, so he told you there was no money, no way to get a visa. By marriage, you were not American. You were a citizen of China. International limbo.

Finally the time came for your eldest son, my father, to go to college. Grandfather used his government connections to get Dad admitted to the University of Southern California. He even rounded up the money-bags in his home province, Hupei, to sponsor the tuition—Chinese money sending a Chinese-American to an American school. But the irony of this was lost on you, so busy were you cajoling Grandfather into letting you escort Dad to the States. By the time he relented, the only berths left were in cabin class, so while Dad sailed in luxury at Hupei gentry expense, you and Blossom and Loti and Herb jammed into a single cubicle next to the ship's boiler room. On that blustery New Year's day in 1932 when you stepped off the boat in San Pedro, you could hardly wait to find a lawyer.

I have your petition for citizenship, stamped and certified. It says you were reinstated on grounds that you had "not acquired any other nationality by affirmative act." As if you had married against your will. You named your residence as Los Angeles, your husband's as Shanghai, and just for good measure, you changed your name, from Jennie Ella to Dorothy, though keeping that pliably respectable Spanish-American Luis for your surname.

So you had your U.S. passport again and your feet on American soil. Why, then, before the year was out, were you back on the boat to China? If the pictures taken that gray day are any indication, there was nothing you wanted less. Your face is pinched, your mouth set as if you're in physical pain. Was it lack of money that drove you back? Fear that you couldn't support the children in the middle of the Depression? Or were you forced to leave? Though you had your citizenship back, Herb and Loti were China-born and subject to American exclusion laws.

I think all of these were factors, but I also think you'd made a deal with Grandfather. If he let you go, you would return. "Papa always wanted to keep the family together," Dad still maintains. At the time, your youngest was only nine and Grandfather's favorite, by all accounts. Loti was sixteen and a handful, Blossom twenty-four but still under your guard. And you, at fifty-five, remained Mrs. Don Luis.

You returned to a rented apartment in Shanghai. Grandfather, now in the Executive branch of the Nationalist government, begged you to bring the children and live with him in the capital, Nanking. You reminded him there was no foreign concession in Nanking, no international protection, as there was in Shanghai, against China's next (inevitable) political upheaval. And you refused to change the children's schools. So for two years he commuted, making the day's journey back and forth every couple of weeks. But even as he appealed for family unity, Grandfather was preoccupied with the Nationalists' dual campaigns against the Communists in the west and the Japanese in the north. In 1934 his inside information told him the country was headed for war. Not the standard patchwork of skirmishes and sabotage between warlords that had been China's norm for as long as you'd lived there, but a full-scale invasion by Japan. As the family tells it, Grandfather decided you and the children must return to the States for safety. As you later told it, you agreed to separate because your marriage was finished.

Whatever the truth, Grandfather didn't see you off. You said your goodbyes a day or two early. He had to get back to Nanking. So he left you to finish packing up the apartment, dismiss the remaining amah, bid a final farewell to Yen Ching-san at his inn with your portrait over the desk. Grandfather left you to hire your own cab to the wharf, guide the children up the thronged gangplank. He was two hundred miles away when you took your place at the steamship railing. The whistle screamed. The gulls circled. The Western spires and rotundas of Shanghai's skyline shrank away. That was all.

You arrived back in California for the second time after twenty-two years in China. You leased an apartment, enrolled Herb in school, and sent your daughters out to work. The anti-Chinese sentiment had ostensibly diminished over the decades, and for a time Hollywood, where you were now living, was gripped by *Good Earth* fever. The Pearl Buck classic was being made into a studio film, and casting calls were out for extras who could pass for Chinese. Your "Eurasian" children fit the bill, and Loti, as sing-song girl, succeeded in launching her brief career as a casting-couch starlet. But America's passion for China was no more genuine than the producers' ardor. It was the late thirties. World War II was heating up, and, while America was technically China's ally against the Japanese, most white Americans couldn't tell one Asian face from another. "Chink" and "Jap" were used interchangeably, and with equal contempt. Having suffered your fill of epithets without returning to America for more, you instructed your almond-eyed children not to mention their father, not to discuss their life in China. You suggested that, when anyone asked why they looked so "Eurasian," they should say they were American Indian.

Meanwhile Grandfather continued to send you letters, signing them, "Your husband." He used his official pull to get jobs for Dad in Washington after college. And he sent what money he could, though his salary was slashed as the war took its toll on the Nationalist coffers. Then, in 1937, he and the rest of his government fled Nanking, with the Japanese at their heels.

He spent two years making his way up the Yangtze River. His only belongings were some summer clothing and a blanket from Shanghai. In the winter of 1939, when he finally reached the new western capital, Chungking, his English was poorer than it had been when you tutored him in Berkeley. I have the letter he sent on arrival, brushed onto government issue paper, mostly in pidgin.

Japanese air-plan have bombarded every day. Surround my home all de-

stroyed or burned. . . . I received a letter from Hankow, said that my house in Hankow was burned by government order before they leaved there. My property will be lost all. . . . Tho condition in here will be passed quickly, I do not know how to do in future.

You and children well,

Your husband, Don Luis

The plea, not stated, seems clear enough to me; though perhaps this is just hindsight. "My property will be lost all. . . . I do not know how to do in future." Please help me.

At the time, Dad was working as a journalist. Your eldest daughter, Blossom, had taken her rebound husband and was living in Arizona. You and young Herbert, then fifteen, were living with Loti on her first husband's Hollywood estate. It was within your means to help Grandfather, and indeed, you did send a few dollars, some penicillin when he was stricken with pneumonia. But no more.

Grandfather stayed on in Chungking through the war years, taking shelter in mountain caves when the Japanese bombed the city, and later, after the annihilation of Japan's own Hiroshima and Nagasaki forced the end of World War II, he remained in China, retired. While his family cultivated amnesia about their Chinese past, he visited with old friends and wrote his memoirs and poetry. He reverted so completely that even his letters to you were now written in Chinese.

But the peace was illusory. The ongoing civil war between the Chinese Nationalists and Communists only escalated with the surrender of the Japanese, and by 1949 the Communists were making their final victory sweep across China. Too old, ill, and low down the Nationalist chain of command to flee with the wealthy to Taiwan, Grandfather had only one hope for getting out of China.

You, Grandmother. You were his only hope.

He sent his final plea through the son of a friend, a diplomat who met Dad at a conference in Canada and passed the letter hand to hand, as Dad then passed it to you. Hand to hand. If you petitioned the American government, if you promised that your husband would have a home and a means of support with you, a U.S. citizen, then he might be granted an entrance visa. He might be allowed to leave China.

You never answered that letter. It's finished, you said. We're old. It's too late to start over. . . . No.

"We didn't know," my father protests when I grill him on this point. "No one knew how bad the situation was over there. So much time had passed. Fifteen years. Papa was in his seventies. He had never suggested leaving China before."

But I hold the earlier, 1939 letter in my hands, and I am not so sure. "I do not know how to do in future."

In 1957 Dad learned, during a meeting in Hong Kong with his father's former secretary, that Liu Ch'eng-yü had died sometime after the Communist takeover. Thirty-eight years later, in Taiwan, I requested information from the Kuomintang archives, learned that my grandfather had, in fact, died in his hometown, Wuchang, in 1951, at the age of seventy-six. Whether of natural causes or political retribution we will never know, any more than we know whether he would have survived an attempted escape to America, but none of this alters the larger fact.

You did not want your husband, Grandmother. You felt that he'd betrayed your trust in a hundred different ways, and you were too embittered to forgive. "East is East and West is West, and never the twain shall meet."

Why, for all the times you quoted this line of Kipling's, did you never teach your children its ending? I suspect, because it undermined the pretense you were living. "For there is neither East nor West, Border, nor Breed, nor Birth, when two strong men stand face to face, though they come from the ends of the earth!" Once you, too, were strong enough to believe in this happy ending. You could not have chosen Grandfather for your husband otherwise. But the ordeal of your life and love wore you down, made you brittle and pitiless, and turned you against your own history. That's why you destroyed your old letters, birth announcements, newspaper clippings. Why you trained your children to forget, and clung to this invented name that no one would know was twisted Chinese. Why you buried the father of your children in the rampage of history you pretended not to notice.

You'd given up hope that the pieces could fit. You didn't think we could understand.

My father alone of your four children reclaimed the family name Liu. My Luis cousins grew up never knowing they were part Chinese. It's a typically American pattern, I realize, this submission to the melting pot; a tactical evasion of prejudice and sorrow and disappointment. The name—the association—you left behind might have been Jewish, African, Armenian, or Slavic. I understand this, Grandmother, just as I understand your refusal to give Grandfather asylum. Still these decisions sadden me. For Grandfather's sake and the family's, but most of all for you.

You were an extraordinary woman. You lived a fascinating life. And you loved a remarkable man, however distant, however frustrating. I wish you'd been able to take pride in this love instead of trying to hide it. For your story is a cautionary tale, but, more, it is a tale of courage. East may be East, and West may be West, but once upon a time you and Grandfather dared to stand face-to-face and defy the ends of the earth. I admire you both for that, Grandmother. I admire you.

My Lebanon

Paula Gunn Allen

I AM PAULA, daughter of Lee, son of Narcisco, son of Elias. I am an American of Lebanese descent, cut adrift from Lebanon by the meanders of time, history, place, and the private decisions of my family and myself. Because the course of my family river has been diverse, I have no central myth or legend, no single point of view, to enclose me. I have death, grief, snatches of history, and memory of song. I have tolerance, passion, an oddly persistent memory that can't be mine of a spring graced by the healing power of a female god, a sprite, an ancient water being. I know the sound of finger cymbals. But I don't know how to do the dances, was made foolish at my *lileeah*, my engagement party, by that lack so many many years ago, when I married a *Hanosh*, my great-grandmother's great-nephew. As her name was Haula (Paula in English), her family in Lebanon was particularly excited by the match. "Haula is coming home," they rejoiced. I am told that my picture occupies a place of honor in their home, or did a a few years ago, even though I divorced my Hanosh cousin twenty-five years ago. Or maybe the house and the picture have been bombed. Maybe all her relatives are dispersed or dead.

In my mouth sometimes I carry the taste of food, on a tongue that stumbles in saying the names: *kibbe, leben (or Laban), hemos, duele, mamoul, mehle, butujin, risbe habeeb, hibs, cusa mitwe, babaganoush, eftire, kibbe sinea, kibbe erst, yubra, yuhne, halewe.* Some of them everyone knows: Halvah, for instance, my father calls *halewe. Mehle*, that in Amer-

131

ica is called baklava. *Duele,* dolma, grape leaves. *Risbe habeeb,* rice pudding, rich and sweet, studded with fat raisins, rich with cream. Others are too strange in America, and that's too bad. I can't spell them because they don't spell in English. Not the way I hear them in my ear. I carry a little of my Lebanese people's language in my ear, a few of their stories, their ways, their history both here and in the old country; only a little, but no more. ("*Poco, poquito, pero no más,*" Jido is saying in my memory, in my ear. "*Pero no más.*").

Lebneni (*lubnaani*); Syrian; Arab. When I was young, I was told that in the east, in New York and New Jersey, they had signed up in certain places, hotels, restaurants, "No Syrians or Jews Allowed." I was told that meant us, too, because they called all of us "Syrians." I guess there were no Lebanese in the minds of the anti-semitic sign makers, just as there was no Lebanon for so long that it is still difficult, almost impossible, to find mention of it anywhere except on the news on TV. Does that mean that there is no Lebanon, really?

My Native American grandmother, Agnes Gunn, remembers being excluded from the group at Indian School in Albuquerque, from the group at home in New Laguna: "They used to tell me to go away. They wouldn't have anything to do with me. So, I did."

She went away to Cubero in geographic location. She went away to the home of the German-Jewish immigrant she married. She went away to whatever version of America she could manage in that tiny Spanish-speaking village, my grandmother Gottlieb who never learned to speak Spanish and forgot as much Indian as she could, who internalized the scorn and loathing directed against her and against her full-blood mother by their Laguna community, who turned as racist against Indians as she could, for as long as she could. Not because the whites rejected her. But because the Indians did.

And my mother, her daughter, who was not the biological daughter of the Jewish immigrant, but who was his stepdaughter, was stoned by the Cubereño children, her peers, after school. "They used to chase me down the hill," she remembers, "throwing rocks at me, shouting 'Judea! India!' as they chased me." Those children were Mexican American, Spanish, as they said of themselves in those days, before the new age of militancy and radicalism came into vogue. La gente. La Raza. "Viva la Raza! Venceremos!" They have every reason to hate the child they stone. Is she not the enemy? The despised Jew? The loathed Indian?

And me. La India. La Arabe.

Like my Lebanese relatives I love the mountains and the sea; like them I am drawn to the Madonna, the Mother; like them I feel safest when there is a spring nearby, as there was in my childhood Cubero, a spring I can speak with and know that the sacred sprite who lives within replies. And like them I know that the tradition may change in time and place, but that in essence it remains the same, and that it is in the stories that the sacred essence survives. Perhaps, more than anything in my life, I take that love from them.

So I have much from them. Even my body, which at barely over five feet is not much taller than my grandmother's. My father says, talking about her, "She was broad," he gestures with his hands, "hefty. Like you, and Kathy." Kathy my sister, is five feet tall and weighs over 150. I am about five foot one and weigh around 190. When he says that, I am proud but a little dubious. Not about matching Mama Mine in size, but in face. He says, "You look like my mother." I think, "No, Kathy does, I don't." Because I have heard them saying that one of my aunts looks exactly like her mother, and I know that Kathy looks almost exactly like that aunt. I think my father says that I look like his mother because our dispositions are a lot alike.

My body. From my mother's family I inherit arthritis, sinus trouble, hay fever, and perhaps lupus. From my father's family I inherit size, low blood pressure, a tendency toward diabetes, and heart trouble. And thick, thick, curly, almost kinky hair. From them I inherit my skin, a pale olive that turns a lovely brown with the summer sun. I have one farsighted eye and my father is farsighted. I have one nearsighted eye and my mother is nearsighted. A little of this, a little of that: a person is made up of too many pieces, a patchwork quilt, a horse designed by a committee. The single most important part of me I inherit from Lebanon: my body. My very unfashionable, unthin, uncool, un-American as it can be; my round, big-breasted body. But even that is half-breed, for while its size is of my father's people, and though my hair is thick and tightly curly, almost kinky, I am otherwise quite hairless. Is that Indian? My mother has thin hair on her head, virtually no hair on her arms. She plucked her eyebrows thin when she was in high school in the early thirties and she says, they never grew back. They are thin. My eyebrows are thin too. I notice that my mother's grandmother has thin eyebrows, and I don't imagine she ever plucked them. So even my body is part-Lebanese. Though what it matters, I am not sure. I think it matters to me, to know about my own proclivities, inclinations, and dreams. To know whence they are, and in that way, perhaps, to know whence they will proceed. Or maybe it's just that I'd like to know which side I, American mongrel, am on, and whether that side is or isn't "right." To know how I can justify the thoughts and emotions I experience, sometimes overpowering in their intensity, when the subject of Zionism, fascism, genocide, good guys and bad guys in the Middle East comes up in conversation or on television.

I also have a Lebanese ability to talk, wildly gesticulating. I have a love of loud parties, dancing, drinking, hollering and bonding, and eatingeatingeating. I have a love of full cupboards, laden tables, plenty for all the guests, and lots left over. I have an expansiveness, a sense of cunning, a love of storytelling, a love of place, a sense of history, a personal sense, a delight in mystery, a delight in ritual of the Christian kind, a weakness for children, a tendency to humor them, to indulge them, a respect for nuns and priests that comes close to patronizing them. I enjoy doing business, I love to try to get the best of someone in a business deal. I have a pride of heritage and a quick anger, a quick biting irritability. I have a strong sense of family, of propriety, of place. I have a sense of martyrdom, of melancholia, of great age. I have a liking for difference, a love of complication, a joy in intra-familial conflict, a sense of daring, of adventure, of the folly of humankind. I love to gamble, and I love to win. And I have a huge pile of memories to go along with the pile of memoirs I have also collected, and they include the best and the worst moments of my life.

My father has a piece of wood that he says is a piece of the cross that Jesus died on. He says Grandpa brought it from Lebanon. Grandpa used to peddle goods from Turkey to Jerusalem. My father says we are of the House of David, descendants of the same family that gave birth to Jesus. He says that Lebanon was the first nation to convert to Christianity. Long, long ago. Lebanon's patron saint is Mar Elias. According to the story, Elias and Moses joined Our Lord on the mountain peak. And the apostles, overcome with awe, offered to erect a tent to shelter the three, but Our Lord refused their offer, bidding them to simply watch and pray.

Elias, the assumed one, was so precious to the Father God that he did not die. They say he will return to earth in the last days, because like all men he must die. But not yet, they say, not yet. I wonder if somewhere Elias is being born, if somewhere some old patriarch named Elias is declaring himself present, present to preside over the final death of the Lebanese. Of us all.

In the church in Seboyeta, where my father was born and raised, Seboyeta that is nestled in the arms of the Cebolleta mountains on the eastern spur of Mount Taylor, Seboyeta that is one of the earliest settlements of the Spanish colonization of the northern territories of New Spain, now New Mexico, in that church, one that is very very old as things in America are dated, hangs a picture of Abraham preparing to sacrifice his son, Isaac. The picture is actually of Saint Elias. Or that's how the story goes, because my great-grandfather ordered a painting of Lebanon's patron saint to grace the church where he worshipped on Sundays and holy days.

I went back to the church because the new young priest sent word that he had some papers and other things that had been left at the old house in Seboyeta years before, the house that had been bought by the Gallup diocese and was now the priest's house. I wanted to walk around there, remembering. Go into the church and sit, and listen, and dream. Maybe talk to some ghosts.

It didn't quite work out that way, though I guess I did talk to ghosts as I listened to the young Anglo priest, bearded and "involved" in the dynamic way the new priesthood often exhibits. He then told me about the superstitious credulity of the local people, the Seboyetaños (descendants of Spanish colonial settlers of the region who were granted possession of the land by decrees of the Spanish crown a couple of centuries ago). His story concerned what he called a legend about the miraculous healing of an infant boy, sixty years before. The story, he said, was that some local child had had some mishap—something had happened that should have killed him. But the child's grandmother and his mother had taken the baby, wrapped him in a blanket, then crawled on their knees from the church to a shrine some several miles into the hills, praying the rosary all the while. They had begged the Virgin, whose shrine it is, to save the child, and had dedicated him to her for life if she would grant their petition. Well, the baby lived, or so the story goes. And saying that, the priest shook his head pityingly. He thought the story had probably been carried from Mexico, maybe from beyond Mexico, from Spain, a quaint example of old belief in the modern age. It was, he implied, yet another illustration of the magnitude of the difficulties he faced in this remote place.

I could see that he was university educated, and was quite taken with himself as a folklore specialist stationed in the wilds of New Mexico. He evidently didn't know that the story was quite true. That the infant in the story was my father. That the women—my grandmother and my great-grandmother—had indeed crawled all the way to Portales from Seboyeta, had dedicated the baby to Mary the Madonna, and that the baby had lived. The priest didn't know that after they did their religious best to save the child, they took him back to Seboyeta and then to the doctor in Albuquerque, who discovered that the immediate cause of his nearly lethal injury—a screw that his sister, then about three, had given him to hold and he, infant-curious, had put in his mouth and swallowed—had passed, like God in the night.

I do not know where, exactly, the village of my grandparents is. Or if it exists anymore, anywhere at all.

Déjà vu? I know how my elder half-breed Indian relatives felt. And why a full-blood uncle used to ride on the train, claiming to be Italian. I find myself obscurely humiliated, frightened, grieved, to be one who is identified as the enemy of righteousness and good. I think Uncle Charlie must have felt that way, as many Indians have testified to feeling; because Indians have been so long the enemy of the good as that good is defined by white eyes. And so I can only watch, horrified, as the mods, the shells, the bullets erupt. I can only listen, aghast, to my professional community as its many members denounce Lebanon and claim the right of the Arab to triumph, denying the right of the ancient-ancientancient Lebanese to live.

Walking to classes is painful. Today neon-orange stickers adorn the elevators, demanding that the imperialist Israel and the United States get out of Lebanon. The demand was made that all foreign powers get out; that Syria, the PLO, Palestine nationals, the Soviet Union, Iran, or whoever else is in Lebanon minding its business and murdering its citizens, at least as much as the so-called imperialists, cease their genocidal war on the people of Lebanon, the people of the mother's breasts, her milk-giving breasts. Lebanon is a cognate of laban, milk. Because the map of Lebanon is the map of two mountain ranges that are divided by a deep valley, the psychic-culture map shows a similar topography: the Lebanese display two towering ranges of knowledge and culture, divided by history, religion, diversity and oppression. Lebanon, recorded in the Book of Numbers as a land enslaved to Egypt, who quarried stone to send to the Egyptian rulers, carried it out of the quarries through the mountain ruggedness so Pharoah could have palaces fit for Egypt's might. Lebanon, conquered by the Aryan Turks, who split the children from the mother, who tore the son from the tree and ripped his body to pieces, and cast the pieces upon the sea; who cast the sacred dogs of the goddess into the sea where they waited long centuries to be restored by Nordic seamen during the Second World War, the war that finally resulted in the liberation of Lebanon, for however brief a time, the liberation of the mountain wild folk, the Lebanese.

I think about the ride up to Los Cerrillos Judy and I took a couple of summers ago. I wanted to find the house where my grandmother was raised. The store her father kept. Early that morning my father and I sat and talked over breakfast in my parents' apartment high above the plain. Mother was in her room, Judy asleep. We talked about how he felt, seventy years old. We talked about how he loses his memory, how it bothers him.

"Are you afraid of getting old?" I ask. Wanting to know something about him as he is to himself, in himself; wanting also to know for myself, later, so I will know where I am when I am where he is now. He doesn't answer, just looks at me quickly, in that way he has, eyes darting over to me, away. A bird, perching for a moment on the twig of a thought, then away.

"Your grandmother was raised in Cerrillos," he says.

"Where?" I say. "You mean Los Cerrillos, up in the Sandias?"

"Yes," he says. "Up There. Her father, your Jide Michael, had a store up there. That's where she was raised."

I think this came up because I asked him about his mother. Something I haven't done much because it makes him sad to talk about her. Or it always used to. But now, maybe because he's seventy, he talks about her, mostly without tears.

"How old was she when she got married, do you know?" I ask.

"Maybe fifteen or sixteen." He shakes his head, lightly. Not sure. Or sure about the age she was when she was married, but not sure how I'll take that. How it sounds.

"How old was she when she died?"

"Forty. She was forty."

"And how old were you?"

"Fifteen."

"She was young," I say. "She had so many kids in such a short time." I feel depressed, troubled. I try to calculate swiftly. Seven children that lived. Nine altogether. Fifteen from forty is . . . I give up the attempt.

"Is the house still there, in Los Cerrillos?" I ask. He doesn't know. It might be. "Wouldn't it be great to go up there?" I say. I tell my mother, "Daddy says Mama Mina was raised in Los Cerrillos. Isn't that amazing? I didn't know that! Maybe we could go up there, see if we could find the old house, the store."

"Well, why don't you go?" she asks.

"Maybe I will," I say. "Why not."

It is late August, and the mountain is a study in floral design we drive through: white and yellow, deep gold and dark green, fuchsia and orange. We drive east out of Albuquerque, through Tijeras Canyon, turn right onto Highway 10, past San Antonito. Turn to the right a few miles, later, swinging with the highway toward Santa Fe to the north. Past Golden, where the country-and-western twangs out on Sundays at the bar there, and the hip, the cool, and the alcoholics spend a long afternoon drinking and getting stoned in 2/4 time.

I take a lifetime of memories with me on the drive, twenty or more years of drives through this lovely countryside. I take curiosity, the unanswered questions of years with me. I take eyes that look and look at the passing land, trying to hold perfect every blade of grasss, every golden or purple blaze of color from the wildflowers, every stone juniper, every pine, trying to find what the land knows, what it remembers, what it means. Every period of my adult life is here with me as we drive, Judy and I, through the Sandias toward Santa Fe. My life rides in my eyes, investing everything I see with a memory, a meaning, a terror, a joy, a grief.

Somewhere is the road that goes among the tall pines where I went with some boy I was dating when I was sixteen. The road to the wilderness, the night, in the snow; where I was raped, though it took me over twenty years to acknowledge the event. Somewhere else is the road that goes up to the peak, that ends near a path I walked with a man to a round stone building that looks out over the 5,000–foot drop to the plain, the city below, that looks 50,000 feet up to the sky, 50 million miles to the stars through the openings in the stone. The round stone building where we made love and conceived twin boys. Conceived two, one of whom died.

And now, so long after, I drive that highway again, counting my life at various milestones, roads that run off here and there, at stops along the way. It's a habit I picked up from my father, and my Jido—this telling my life's stories in terms of the places we drive by. I wonder if I learned to experience my feelings the same way, from those same men. I feel filled with joy because the mountain is ever so beautiful: with melancholy because the thread that holds my life in place here or anywhere is so fragile, so tenuous. So many people I knew in terms of this mountain, these roads, that I have lost. Most of them I've never seen again.

Tristesse. I first heard that word over twenty years ago, when I went to Los Cerrillos for the first time. I was with the divorced man from Iowa, or Indiana or Illinois, the one who was an engineer, who ached for his children, his wife. "*Tristesse,*" he said. I forgot why he said it. "The sweet sadness." *Tristesse* is what rides with me, in my eyes, in my mind. *Tristesse* is what invests the wildflowered land, the beclouded sky that I look at for significance. I wonder as we go where they went, those Lebneni's who lived here once, who live here no more.

Finally we get there. It's farther from Albuquerque than I'd remembered. It's almost all the way to Santa Fe, through the mountains. We can't find it at first. We pass the turnoff a couple of times before we realize that the road that runs at an angle to the highway we're on leads to Los Cerrillos. I am filled with excitement. Sentiment, *Sentimiento. De me pensamientos.* My thoughts begin to move in awkward Spanish. Primitive Spanish, to be sure. But it is something that always happens when I go home, when I return in fact or memory to my father's house, to his land.

In the village we drive slowly up and down what we take to be the main drag, a wide gravel road. It hasn't been graveled in some time. Unlike many New Mexican villages, though, it has cross streets, stop signs, and even some sidewalks. Maybe because it's so close to Santa Fe. Or maybe because so many Anglo urbanites come up here to browse in the not-quite-quaint shops before they have dinner—if the fancy restaurant that was once here is still in operation. The oldest part of the village sports wooden sidewalks. Made of planks nailed together, raised a foot or so from the ground. Keeps the mud from covering it, makes it easy to dismount.

But we don't have a horse, and neither does anyone else. Or at least not for riding up to the cantina or *la tienda.* After a couple of slow passes, we park, catercorner from the wooden sidewalk, across from the few businesses that line the other side of the street. We get out, lock the car. I wonder why I'm locking it. This isn't the city. I don't have much to fear. But I lock it anyway, remembering my insurance man and feeling silly.

The questions haunt me. How long has it been since she lived here? I wonder. I try to spot a building that is old enough, built of adobe and roofed with galvanized steel. Red with age. But I know it's been too long for that to mean much. They'd have reroofed it long since. But I try. There's a building with a faded ancient sign; circa 1930, at least. There are several buildings that might be my Jido's store. Some that might be the old house. The house that in some sense I come from, but that I've never seen.

"I'll ask," I say. "I'll just go into some store here and see if anyone knows." I do. We do. We go into a secondhand store. It may be the same one I visited twenty-one years ago with the man from Indiana, but I can't be sure. There's a woman tending store, and I ask her if she knows the Michaels, or where they had their store. She's very pleasant, but of course she doesn't know. Maybe so-and-so up the block, or down; she forgets which might know. We leave and try the grocery store next door. They don't know either. Spanish American, Mexican American, Chicano. I imagine they've lived here for generations, but they don't know. It's been a long time since the Michaels lived and traded here, I think. It's not surprising that no one remembers them anymore. I can't even find the restaurant I ate in, so long ago.

How long has it been, anyway? Over seventy years? Over eighty? She must have been born in 1888, moved from here around 1903. Eighty years, then, since she lived somewhere called Los Cerrillos, though perhaps, probably, it was a different Los Cerrillos then. She was forty when alone and surely in despair, she died in a mental hospital in Pueblo, Colorado, in 1928, four years before my parents were married. Such a long time since she felt this wind.

We leave Los Cerrillos. Drive to Santa Fe for coffee. Or not (I get confused, trying to remember which trip is which, which journey takes me to what place). We drive back toward Albuquerque, the car behaving strangely. I discover it's because I've had the emergency brake on all the time. Days, probably. Maybe weeks. I release it, hoping I haven't done lasting damage, and we continue toward the city. Along the way we stop and walk around, tasting the mountain with our feet, our hands, our eyes. We take some chunks of a strange stone we find. One that's white and crumbles easily. Hard dirt, caliche, most likely. But it pulls me. I want it with me. We put it in the car to take to California with us, to the house we haven't found yet. We will have a piece of the mountain in our new life.

Back at my parents' apartment they ask about our trip. My father is in a jovial mood. He jokes around. He knows, far better than I, I suspect, how fragile is the past. How futile the attempt to recover anything from it. And how necessary. His mother lives in his memory, his feelings, his life. And in that way only does she live in mine.

"This is it," a friend said. "This is Rumie." I gaze at the tiny village, almost invisible in mountain mistiness, off to the side in the photograph. There was a picture of the ruin, high atop a hill just outside the village. "That's it!" I exclaim. "That's the place they showed on TV!" I hadn't seen much on the show, though, because the camera was focused mostly on the reporter. I remember his short-sleeved khaki outfit, my frustration at the cameraman. But the magazine spread includes a view of range after range of mountain juniper and other pine trees, sandy rocks, and a small paved road. "No wonder Jido said Lebanon was like New Mexico. No wonder they settled in Seboyeta," I said. "I always wondered how Grandpa found Albuquerque and Seboyeta, in all the world he had before him. Now I know. This looks just like home," I said. Not sure which home I was referring to in that statement. "It's very lovely. In fact, it looks just like I thought it would."

My grandmother, who we called Sitte—meaning grandmother in Lebanese—well, actually, my father's grandmother, worked in a silk factory when her husband—my grandpa Francis—came to the United States for the first time. He kept sending money home for her and their son, but his uncle wouldn't give it to her and so she was forced to go to work in a silk factory. (Grandpa Francis once had silk worms sent to Seboyeta from Lebanon so that his grandchildren could raise them and see where silk comes from.)

My friend Albert described the work of a silk factory to me: "They have huge vats of boiling water. The women drop the cocoons into it—you know, the worm spins a cocoon around itself and it's the thread of the cocoon that is used for making silk. The women put their hands into the water and take out the worms. They have to work very fast, because you can leave the cocoons in the boiling water only a short time, just until the worm is dead. So they would have to reach their hands into the boiling water, over and over, all day long." Albert thinks that the Arab word for bordello, *karkhana*, comes from *khafanu*, the silk factory—because the women worked nearly naked in the intense heat. "Wow," I think. "My Sitte worked in a bordello!" And this thought, obscurely, relieves me of some of that lifelong sense of shame.

I understood the anger in my father's voice every time he repeated the sorry tale of Sitte's humiliation at the hands of her husband's relatives. For no daughter of a landed family worked in a silk factory, like the poor were required to, yet she, his own beloved grandmother, had been forced to do so. I realized that this happened because Sitte, born Haula Hanosh, was from a poor family in the village. I knew it because my first husband's father, her nephew, had told me of his childhood and manhood, when they had suffered greatly at the hands of the Druse colonial armies of the Empire. "Five men work all day eb'ry day in stone quarries," he had said. "Five strong men. And for carrying rocks on our backs for twelve, sixteen hours," he said, emphasizing the point by counting the hours off one finger at a time, "one loaf of bread we take back to family, women, and all the little children. We died of the yellow fever, of diphtheria, of war. We were so glad when war over, and Lebanon made free of the Turks."

I realize that my Sitte, this man's aunt, had lived like that; so poor, so without food. She married into a family that would say, two generations later, "We never carried rocks on our backs. We were merchants, traders. We never carried rocks." Except for when we (she) worked naked in the bordello, *khafanu*. Her grandchildren would tell me about her suffering, but would display no understanding of what might have caused it: that because she came from a family that did carry rocks on their back, she was made to suffer physical and social torture at the hands of her husband's relatives when her husband was in America. Were her husband's relatives keeping her in her place? I imagine so, though I can only speculate. I know that later, after her husband returned, he found himself unable to live there amidst the multiple varieties of oppression, so he decided to emigrate permanently. That time he took her and their child with him. Over the years, he brought members of their respective families over, and for a long time he was the head of the circle of Lebanese Americans in New Mexico.

After his death, Sitte became the head. She lived to see her son a member of the New Mexico State Legislature; to see her nephews settled and prospering in various villages around the state. To see herself head of the sprawling clan of Lebneni from Rumie; and no one, man or woman, made personal, business, or political decisions without receiving her advice and concurrence. I bet it did her heart good, my Sitte.

Maybe she thought about the long road she had taken from desperate ignominy in *khafanu* to being the power center of a large clan of relatives in America, in those long nights while I pretended to sleep so I could watch her ready herself for bed, so I could watch her sleep.

My mother says that Sitte always greeted people by saying something that sounded like "S'lem or klem." It was probably *"Salaam o khalem,"* peace and greetings. *Salaam o khalem,* Sitte. *Salaam o khalem,* Lebanon.

In the Absence of My Grandmother

Martha Collins

WHEN I WAS GROWING UP, the only framed photograph in our house was of my mother's mother holding me. She was in her sixties; I was a few weeks old. She had taken the train from southern Illinois to Nebraska to care for my mother and me; my mother was the last of her three daughters to have a child, the last to benefit from the advice and care that were passed on in this manner by so many of that generation. In the picture, I'm told, she's showing my parents how to hold a baby so that the camera's focus is on the child, not the adult.

Three weeks later, she was dead. The diagnosis was meningitis, the first serious disease she had ever had: she had escaped her daughters' scarlet fever and whooping cough, as well as the usual childhood diseases, only to succumb to a malady that no one else in her small town seemed to have had. Where did she get it? On the train? If so, she would appear to have died because she came to take care of my mother and me.

I don't remember when I first put the facts together in quite that way, or how much my mother helped me do it; I do know that I grew up thinking that I had somehow both killed my grandmother and replaced her for my mother. It was much later that my mother herself made the latter connection explicit: *You took her place,* she told me; *that was how it had to be.* I know that, holding me, my mother mourned her own mother.

My grandfather's sorrow was, predictably, greater than my mother's;

that he never recovered from his wife's death was something else I grew up knowing. His own mother had died when he was ten; raised by an aunt and uncle, he had made his way in the small-town world of southern Illinois, finally landing in the town where my grandmother lived and worked. One of five graduates in her high school class of 1892, she had tried teaching but disliked it, and ended up working for the local bank until she was in her late twenties. She was a skilled and valued employee: when the adding machine salesman came to town, the bank owner said he didn't need one of those—he had my grandmother. He wanted to marry her, too, or so the family story goes. But then my grandfather came along. With only an eighth-grade education, he began by setting type for a Baptist publication, and gradually came to assume most of the major responsibilities for the town's daily newspaper. Drawn to him rather than the banker, my grandmother nonetheless kept her very practical head on her shoulders and insisted that he *buy* the newspaper before she married him. That was the last involvement she had with his business. Once, a few years before, the bank for which she had worked foreclosed a small mortgage and, in my mother's words, stole my grandfather's business; my grandmother went to the office to try to help with the books. But the disorder that disturbed her embarrassed him, and she never interfered again.

This was not the part of the story I focused on as I was growing up. What I remembered were my grandfather's achievements. And I remembered him. He mourned my grandmother for almost five years, and he was buried on my fifth birthday. But I remember the Christmas before, when he brought me blocks shaped like letters, and showed me not only how to make words, but also how, turning the letters over, to print them. Years later, I saw a home movie of that Christmas, in which I open a gift, a doll. Not knowing quite what to do with it, I turn it over, around, upside down. Then my grandfather enters the frame, holding out a book. I throw down the doll and turn to him, settling in by his side as he starts to read. That was my heritage, I thought for years. While my grandmother was still with us in Nebraska, he wrote me a letter on the Linotype machine that I didn't see until I was grown. *When you publish your first world-thrilling literary manuscript*, it says near the end, *be sure to send it to me for its first review.* That was some years before I published my first book of poems. And when I received my doctoral degree, my aunt sent me the Harvard Classics that had been, along with the Bible, most central to my grandfather's long process of self-education.

But I was not self-educated: like my grandmother, I had received the best schooling my culture had to offer. Or like my grandmothers, I should say. Remarkably, my father's mother was another of the five graduates in that high school class of '92. Unlike my mother's mother, she loved teaching children in the years before her marriage, and was still something of a legend among her former students when she died, during my second year of high school. I have her teaching copy of Longfellow's *Hiawatha,* and the colors of the rainbow are still in my mind where she put them long before I went to school. She wanted to teach me to read then, too, but my mother told her I was too young. I don't remember hearing that conversation, but I do remember that reading was somehow forbidden, a quality it retains for me even today.

Whether reading would have strengthened the bond between my paternal grandmother and me isn't clear. I remember a bathrobe she made for me, bright blue with lambs on the fabric, and the spice cakes she sent us on special occasions. I remember visiting her, though she never visited us; I remember how she urged us to eat, and I remember liking her chicken dumplings. But she didn't appear to take much pleasure or pride in the gifts she sent or the meals she made, and before I finished grade school she had begun to sink into the depression and illness that kept her in a nursing home for the final years of her life.

Nor were she and my mother close. Though marriage and motherhood had not particularly suited her, my father's mother was quite possessive of her son. And while I'm sure that my mother would similarly have benefitted from some kind of work outside the home, I don't think she ever quite forgave her mother-in-law for being the bitter woman she may herself have feared becoming. That neither of them was thoroughly content with her allotment of marriage and child was of course never voiced; but it was clear to me, even when I was young.

What, then, if my mother's mother had lived? Would my mother have been happier, able to maintain that first close tie? Would I have had a happier role model in that woman who traded in her bank job for marriage, but who apparently suffered no loss of self-esteem in the process? If she had been alive to give me a doll that Christmas, would I have valued it as much as the book? Would I have been able to balance those gifts? Would I have been able, earlier and more easily, to see my most capable self as female, or would my primary intellectual identification still have been with my grandfather?

It's impossible to answer these questions, of course; what's interesting is that it's only when I imagine my grandmother's life that I'm tempted to ask them. It's a life that has more appeal for me than I used to acknowledge. Coming out of the nineteenth century, when women were seen to have a special sphere of influence in the home, my grandmother took domestic management and community responsibility seriously. She was a founding member of the Domestic Science Club, whose members met once a month, in one another's homes; she was a pillar of the Baptist Church, where she played the piano and taught Sunday School, grateful for what she learned in the process as well as for what she could give. She quoted St. Paul, not the famous passage about obedient wives, but an obscure one I never heard in church, about the older women teaching the younger. She was much loved and appreciated throughout her town, a valued friend and acquaintance who enjoyed nothing more than a lively conversation.

Or so I imagine it. The more I try to say about my grandmother, the more I realize that my picture of her is shaped as much by my reading of nineteenth and early twentieth-century women's novels as it is by my mother's words. Which may explain why I began reading those novels even before feminist scholars began writing about them. What I found in the books certainly supported what I'd surmised about my grandmother's life: her position granted her a kind of respect that would be denied her today. It's true that contemporary women like me who have not experienced motherhood tend to undervalue women who devote a significant part of their lives to it. But even those who embrace what we now call family values do not grant wives and mothers the influential role accorded women in my grandmother's time: it's men who must assume leadership in the home, we're told by today's domestic neo-conservatives.

Even then, though, I don't think the life of husband and children and home would have suited me. I'm grateful for my grandfather's lesson in letters, for his words that blessed my literary career before I could even spell my name, and I'm probably grateful for the negative example of my father's mother as well: her unhappiness made it clear that marriage and children were not enough for every woman, even in a time and place when virtually everyone lived as if they were.

But like many women of my generation, I've paid a small price for my attachment to a male predecessor. In the early days of the current women's movement, some of us traced our heritage back through the constantly shifting names of our maternal lines: Collins from Essick from Harriss from. . . . Few of us could get much farther than that, but many could at least remember the woman attached to that third name. "I wish you'd known my mother," my mother used to say. I would like to have known her, that woman of intelligence and capability, of kindness to others and apparent contentment with her own life. What she would have thought of me, of the person I became, I of course don't know. But one thing I realize as I write this essay is that everyone in my immediate family would probably have been a little happier if she had lived a little longer. In the absence of my grandmother, I not only had to become her, for my mother; I've also had to invent her, for myself.

●◆

A Grandmother Twice Lost

Ann Kimmage

IN THE SUMMER OF 1950, *when anti-Communist sentiments and actions reached dangerous heights, I was eight years old. My parents, both active Communists, had to flee America illegally. Our escape to Czechoslovakia via Mexico, where we lived for the next thirteen years, changed irrevocably my country, my language, and my family connections. Ironically, the events of the McCarthy era steered me into the arms of the international communist family, taking me away from the Orthodox Jewish one I belonged to by birth. In my imposed exile I lived with memories of my grandmother that fueled my need for her exclusive love and made me long for the past to become, once again, the present.*

As soon as I got back to my room I called my mother, whom I always called Belle, a name she preferred to Isabelle given her at birth. My fingers were trembling and suppressed sobs filled me. I heard my mother's voice coming to me from their home in far-away Wisconsin. "Belle," I was sure I had shouted into the receiver, but my voice was thin and strained.

"Belle," I tried again, this time shaking with emotion. "How could you, how could you send me to visit her? After all these years and all we went through, didn't you know what would happen? Don't you know your own family?"

My voice picked up speed and the sobs raging within took flight, traveling through the telephone wires, from Spring Valley, New York,

149

to Stevens Point, Wisconsin. I repeated over and over, as if in a dream I could not manage to wake up from, "How could you, how could you do this to me?"

Finally I heard Belle's voice, "I thought it would be a good idea, I thought you would both make up for lost time, I thought . . . " I didn't let her finish. The intensity of my anger overwhelmed me. I was shocked to discover how fresh the buried hurts still were.

"She would not even acknowledge me as her granddaughter, can you imagine that?"

My reunion with my grandmother occurred after practically fourteen years, a visit my mother urged me to make. I was almost twenty-two years old and had only been back in the States for a few months. The world within and around me was filled with foggy recollections that failed to match up with the newly acquired impressions. Once again I was sitting in my grandmother's kitchen. But this time nothing looked or felt familiar in this house, except for the kitchen smells that reminded me of what I had known a long time ago and sorely missed. After a lunch of feather-light blintzes and my absolute favorite— crunchy *mandelbrot* that crumbled delicately in my mouth, she suggested we go for a walk. It was a warm, sunny day. We walked down the road. Relieved that we were beginning to feel somewhat comfortable with each other we started to converse as if the past had not happened, as if she might once again be the grandmother I had not had during my exile. And then it happened.

A middle-aged woman walked by us on the same side of the street. A broad smile appeared on her face when she recognized my grandmother. From the casual conversation in which they exchanged neighborhood information I deduced they had known each other for years. I stood there forgotten. I listened, too uncomfortable to speak.

This was my grandmother's world, one I knew nothing about and had not been a part of for many years. Their arrangements for the cake baking for the synagogue fund-raiser had nothing to do with me. I had never been in that synagogue, I did not even know where it was. Meanwhile I could sense the woman looking at me from the corner of her eye, no doubt wondering why this woman she had known for so many years would be taking an afternoon walk with a stranger "Oh," my grandmother said slowly. "This is Ann."

Suddenly she was in a rush to continue our walk. Now there was a heavy silence between us. A wall created by a family history distanced us. We did not resume our disrupted chatter. I could no longer contain the pressing question "How come you didn't introduce me as your granddaughter? Am I not your granddaughter?"

"Oh," she said awkwardly as her walk slowed down and the smile now completely vanished from her lovely, soft face. "Nobody in this community knows that I have a daughter."

I let those words sink in before I replied "So nobody knows you have two more granddaughters?"

"That's right, nobody knows. When the four of you disappeared, and the FBI pursued us for information about your whereabouts we were unable to provide, we moved from Spring Valley to Monsey. In Monsey we were known as Mr. and Mrs. Shulman and their son Avi. We had become a family of three; our daughter was lost to us."

I knew ahead of time it was pointless for me to ask "And you won't tell them I am your granddaughter?" By now we had reached the house we had left feeling comfortable with each other a short while ago. The past managed to stifle the delicate shoots of my attempted reconciliation, and I knew that my grandmother was lost to me for good. The permanence and inevitability of the rift between our two worlds, her Orthodox and my unorthodox one, horrified me.

Things had once been simpler. I thought of those days when my grandmother was indeed my grandmother, my country was America, my language was English, my family origins Jewish. But now? My thoughts were pulsing through my mind in Czech and my grandparents no longer claimed me as their own. I thought about those days when my childhood was still mine, before my parents' life commitments and political ideals for a communist future swept me into a whirlwind of events, depriving me of my right to be my grandmother's granddaughter.

I missed being in my grandmother's kitchen where I spent my days when I visited my grandparents in their Spring Valley home. For hours, I watched and imitated the particular motions of my grandmother's hands when she shaped matzo balls or cut the loaves of *mandelbrot* into thin strips. I licked the bowl with the cheese filling for the blintzes, and when I wrapped a perfect blintz that did not fall apart while she lifted it into the pan, I felt her approving smile. I was being initiated into the mysteries of flavors, smells, tastes, and traditions which my grandmother learned from her mother and grandmother.

I was becoming part of the history of my family when I repeated the stroking and shaping of the challah dough that we transformed into the golden loaf we put on the dinner table. Before we could eat, my grandfather recited long prayers during which I impatiently admired the braided challah I wanted to taste. My grandmother's connection to the family was in her kitchen, and the tasks she performed in her home and her community that lived by the same rhythms and priorities. Once my parents took me away from America, my family life became divided between the period before my exile and the years of my exile.

In Prague, I clung to the sensual thread that connected me to her, longing to retain the fading images. I remembered my grandmother telling me stories in her steady, soothing voice. I recalled the loving warmth of her voice instead of the content of those stories which vanished behind the darkness of my isolation. An unyielding desire to have what I had lost altered my childhood.

I imagined the love I had once felt in my grandmother's expressive eyes and soft hand and lap. Being in her kitchen, smelling and tasting her foods, and listening to her voice stayed with me. But what that kitchen looked like, what her voice told me, how and why she did things the way she did was beyond my reach. I realize now why I sought relationships with older ladies, forever seeking a replacement for what I had lost. I was looking for the grandmother I desperately wanted, and who had once been mine.

My grandmother Ethel was a short, delicate woman with a disarming smile that made me feel instantly at home. As an Orthodox woman she was not allowed in public with her hair uncovered. When I was a child, I never realized she wore a wig. While she did her chores she made me a part of her woman's world which was full of mystery and the importance of an efficiently run household. I followed her every move and obeyed her commands copying what she did. She had a ready laugh and while she worked in the kitchen she entertained me with her tales. I never noticed sorrow or sadness in her eyes. She did everything with natural ease. Though she had come from a wealthy family she ran her kitchen and home with the skill of a captain who had never done anything else in her life. My closeness to her was in strong contrast to my grandfather, who remained a distant shape. He was the one to observe the rituals and prayers before the meal or to read at the chair by the living room window far away from the kitchen. Unlike the lively textures of my grandmother's voice, his monotone uttered Hebrew, sounds I associated with a world that I knew nothing about and which I did not share with him. While my grandmother's voice made me smile and feel safe, my grandfather's voice accentuated my separation from him.

What I remember most from my early childhood was the contrast between the lively home of my parents with their friends and comrades who created their own rules, and the home of my grandparents and uncle, filled with commands and prayer that remained constant. My parents rarely, if ever, joined us at my grandparents' Sabbath table. Instinctively I switched back and forth from the subtle codes of one home to the expectations of the other, accepting that this is the way it should be. I also accepted that my kosher grandmother could not eat or drink in our New York home where my mother experimented with foods of all nationalities without abiding by kosher dietary restrictions.

Learning how to maneuver between the two alien worlds of my parents and grandparents was an unplanned preparation for the continued separation between my newly established Czech world that clashed with my parents' American one. When my parents, Abe and Belle, unhesitatingly fulfilled the party orders to keep our lives in Czechoslovakia a complete secret from all who remained in America, a choice had been made to place the needs of the party above those of family. None of my Czech friends lived the way we did, for their lives were rich with family reunions and grandmothers who cared, cooked, shopped, and played with them. Above all, the Czech families around me were part of each other's lives in good times and illness. Several of my friends came home from school to grandmothers who made them tea and snacks and listened to descriptions of their school day. Eva's grandmother sewed her clothes, Vlasta's grandmother crocheted dainty doilies for the living-room armchairs and dining-room table, and Karel's grandmother baked the most scrumptious cookies I had ever tasted. But my grandmother could not even send me letters or call me on the phone. Nobody in our Prague apartment lit the Sabbath candles as my grandmother had when I had visited in her home.

Though daily visits with my grandmother were torn from my life as a consequence of our exile, her absence continued to play a large role in my fantasies. Watching a child walk down the street holding hands with her grandmother would spark a flash of unexpected pain, reminding me of the unfulfilled need I had for her love. I would retreat into solitary skits in which I would imagine myself in my grandmother's kitchen following the motions of her hands with curiosity and answering her playful questions.

Then one day I noticed I was no longer conversing with my grandmother in English. My entire existence was immersed in Czech, and though I still had to speak English with my parents, the rest of the day I lived and felt in the Czech language.

When I was about twelve years old I discovered the beauty of one of the most important Czech literary classics, *Grandmother*. It is a story of Bozena Nemcova's own grandmother who lived in a little village in the nineteenth century and who shared her love and folk wisdom with members of the family and the village. She was the grandmother everybody held up as a model for generations of Czech readers, and she became my new companion. Every time I read the opening lines of that book I identified with Nemcova's memory of her dead grandmother and my unreachable one:

It has been a long, long time since I looked into that dear, gentle face, since I kissed those pale cheeks full of wrinkles and since I have gazed into those blue eyes in which there was so much goodness and love: it has been a long time since her old hands last blessed me.

I never saw my grandmother again after that disastrous reunion in Monsey, New York. I married a non-Jew, which made it impossible for me to re-establish a relationship either with my grandparents or my strictly Orthodox Uncle Avi, who lived with his wife and nine children a block away from my grandparents. I remained estranged from my uncle and his family as my own children grew into adults without knowledge of their cousins, uncle, and great-grandparents.

About three years ago I stumbled on a book called *Candlelight* written by my uncle Avi Shulman as a tribute to his parents, my grandparents. Here I learned about two loving people devoted to their grandchildren and shul. In my uncle's descriptions of my grandmother, I discovered the realities for which I had substituted the skits I replayed in my mind during my childhood.

Ethel Shulman's father, Mayer Kalmanowitz, was a highly respected and successful fabric merchant in the Lower East Side. My grandmother attended public school and had a private tutor who came to the house to teach her Yiddish. After graduating from high school she became a bookkeeper in her father's business. In 1913 Ethel married, and my grandfather Israel joined his father-in-law's business. For the next seventy years their home became a center of activity and inspiration for the learning of Torah and for support of students from the Talmudic

Academy. In 1927 when my mother was twelve, her parents took her on a journey to visit the capitals of the world and the land of Israel.

But far more interesting than the bare facts were the little stories about my grandmother's character. For forty years my grandmother was involved in yeshiva activities. On the opening day of school she welcomed the new parents and walked up and down the lines saying hello to each child. My grandmother was a renowned housekeeper and generous hostess. She set the table well in advance of each meal, and when she went to a meeting she left a set of written instructions as to where each course could be found in the refrigerator. On a hot day she would run after the mailman to give him a glass of soda. Every Thursday night she set the *Shabbos* table, a custom she learned in her mother's home and loyally followed throughout her life. During the last years in the nursing home she would ask a granddaughter to come on Thursday night to help her select and prepare clothing for *Shabbos*. I found it touching and gratifying that she had had such a large family around her in her old age, but sad I was not among them.

My uncle concludes his recollections of my grandmother's role in the community when he describes her annual appearance in the play the women of the yeshiva performed. Throughout my grandmother's seventies and eighties she was always given at least one line, just so that she could appear on stage. The last time she participated at eighty-eight years of age, the director graciously created a part so that she could walk onto the stage holding on to a carriage. Her tenacity and zest for life, my uncle says, commanded such respect that each time she appeared the audience responded with a standing ovation.

Perhaps there is no discrepancy between the woman whose lap, cooking, and warm voice I longed for, and the grandmother her other nine grandchildren and many great-grandchildren actually knew. She was like the grandmother in Bozena Nemcova's novel that everyone needs, but that I had lost my right to because of irreconcilable generational differences in religion and politics.

Today in my Plattsburgh home, when I prepare for the Christmas holiday and our grown sons return home from college, I spend long hours over the kitchen counter working with pounds of sweet butter, crushed nuts, powdered sugar, flour, and spices recreating the special cookies I had during my "Czech" childhood. When my sons were learning how to talk, I made them say the Czech words *medvedi tlapicky*, "bears paws," which is the name of my favorite Czech Christmas cookie. I made sure they felt the same regard for this pastry, representing everything that made that holiday unique.

Torn from the traditions of my grandparents, and uncertain about the lasting value of my parents' social and cultural experimentation, I have found a link to connect my uprooted childhood to my current family life. The subtle traditions that evolved in our family, and which only make sense for us, are a blending of my husband's Russian Orthodox background and the conflicts I have been left with. Evidently my grandmother's legacy has given me a foundation to build on. My desire to establish rituals of my own, rather than having a void, has provided a future to build on. My husband and sons have given me a reason to search for expression and self-definition. Most importantly, I managed to create something new from the fragmentation and discontinuity I inherited that has a vitality and significance of its own.

This annual ritual of baking several kinds of intricate Czech Christmas cookies has become an outgrowth of the intermingled strands of my identity. Ironically, my need not to deny the importance of my own past is in harmony with my grandmother's legacy. Perhaps I have come full circle in my search, continuing in spirit what had been lost in the act of living. My grandmother would marvel at the loaves of bread and challah that come out of my oven and which I share with my family and friends.

My parents' beliefs were as deep and intense as my grandparents', only my grandparents' Orthodox faith and my parents' communist faith excluded those who did not follow the commands from their circle. My parents turned away from their traditions during their youth and early years of their marriage when I was a child, concentrating instead on a radical future they believed they could create. Ultimately my grandparents lived out their lives with faith, while my parents' ideals led to a shattering disillusionment.

During the last days of my mother's life, when a spreading cancer made her approaching death inevitable, she asked me to bring her a birthday card she wanted to send to someone from the hospital.

At this point my mother and I were beyond conversations about our tangled past and family disconnections. We were consumed by the immediate concerns of managing the disease. I did not ask who the card was for. I handed my mother a pen and I watched her weak, shaking hand write the following words: "Dear mama, I am fine, Happy Birthday, your daughter Belle." I knew my mother's brother, who cared for his aging parents, requested she not upset them at this stage of their lives with the knowledge of her illness. But I did not know it was my grandmother's birthday and I did not know my mother had been corresponding with her. This was the last time my mother signed her name. Two weeks after I sent this card, filled with morphine, memories, and anxieties she could no longer articulate, she called out her last words "MAMA, MAMA" before she slipped into unconsciousness. I held her hand hoping she might think it was her mother sitting by her side whispering words of love and comfort.

I was the generation caught in the middle, left without a connection to the generations that preceded me, and left to my own resources to understand the childhood I had lived and the adulthood I entered. My memories of what I had and lost are part of who I am today.

Carrie Harris Essick with Martha Collins
Courtesy of Martha Collins

Malissa Dalton
Courtesy of Mary Helen Washington

Sitti Khadra Shihab
Photo by Michael Nye. Courtesy of Naomi Shihab Nye.

Emma Berg Mezger ("Oma Emma")
Courtesy of Anneliese Wagner

Berta Kahn Ottenheimer ("Oma Berta")
Courtesy of Anneliese Wagner

Anna Guzman ("Nana")
Courtesy of Marguerite Bouvard

Grandmother Histories

The Four Lives of Malissa Dalton

Mary Helen Washington

*Subscriber has for sale a negro woman, 32 years old, of fine
constitution and good character, and two children ages 6 and 11.
Sold for no fault but to raise money.
They will be sold altogether, or separately to suit purchaser.
1851*

BY THE TIME I WAS BORN in 1941 my maternal grandmother, Malissa
Dalton, was seventy-five years old. She had been married twice, widowed twice, and had borne nine children. Since my two older sisters
are from my father's first marriage, I am my mother's first child, my
grandmother's first grandchild. In the first seven years of marriage, my
mother, good Catholic woman that she was, produced five more children, making us, by 1948, a family of ten. My mother needed my
grandmother's help with this large family, and so she came every day
until I was about ten, when my father, in one of his bad moods, decided
to put her out. She moved around the corner into my aunt's house and
came when he was at work. My memories of my grandmother from the
1940s are fleeting, fragmented ones; she is always doing the work of
the house, mainly in the kitchen. I can see the long black pan on the
stove with the dough plumping up as she waits for it to rise high
enough to bake her rolls from her own recipe for the lightest, sweetest
rolls you can imagine. She sometimes sits on the white high-back kitchen
chair with a large brown mixing bowl on her lap and mixes the yellow

coloring packet into the white margarine to make it look like butter. At Bruder's Dairy, where there was sawdust on the floor, and where I seem to recall they sold live chickens, she selects one and waits for its head to be chopped off and its feathers plucked. She does the ironing for us. There is an old flat iron sitting in its brown tin holder on the ironing board next to the stove where she heats the iron and irons my father's crisp white Cleveland Trust Bank shirts to starched perfection. She keeps her money tied in a white handkerchief, money earned from her day-work job in Cleveland Heights, where she goes on the days she does not work at our house. In her nineties she was confined to a little second-story bedroom in my aunt's house which I passed every day coming home from St. Thomas Aquinas elementary school. Most of the time I went in to visit her, but even now the shame over the times I passed and waved and did not go in, fills me with tears.

Though most of the terrible sorrows of her life were behind her by the time she was forty, she was preoccupied for most of her life with raising children, taking care of the sick, burying the dead. But she had two good husbands, and the seven children who lived to be adults mostly prospered. She loved her youngest daughter and was loved by her in return. They never lived more than ten minutes away from each other. At age eighty-three, when my mother needed her most, she quit her job in the Heights and came to help take care of the eight of us. She lived to be ninety-three and was never once in a hospital. I never saw her cry. I never saw her afraid. For a black woman born in 1867, the daughter of an ex-slave, it doesn't seem like a bad life.

Growing up in the assimilationist 1950s, that decade of devotion to the melting pot, it never crossed my mind to ask my grandmother about her life in the nineteenth century or about her mother's life as a slave. I was in a predominantly white Catholic school in Cleveland, trying as hard as I could not to seem "different" from white immigrant children and not the least interested in being identified with a slave past. But I absorbed enough of Malissa's stories that when I went to Kentucky in 1990 to research family history, I had so many clues to follow that I was able to find the house my great-grandmother lived in as a slave, the same house where Malissa was born in 1867. What made genealogical research tricky is the resistance, especially among Catholics, to admitting their involvement in slavery. I was invited by Sister James Maria to stay at Nazareth Convent, about an hour's drive from St.

Mary, Kentucky, where my grandmother lived. St. Mary was part of the "Holy Land" of Kentucky, an area whose names indicate its deep roots in Catholicism: Nazareth, Gethsemane, Holy Cross, St. Rose, St. Stephens, St. Thomas, Loretto, St. Catherine, Calvary, St. Mary. Nothing in Catholic spirituality, however, seems to have prevented these Kentucky Catholics from participating in slavery. Priests and bishops owned slaves. Nuns brought slaves with them as part of their dowry so they could enter "religious" life. Catholics justified these practices by calling their slaves "servants" and by insisting that they never separated families; but the records show otherwise. Even in 1990 there was a reluctance to admit this past. To my persistent questions about religious orders trafficking in slaves, Sister said dismissively: "Oh, there was some of that."

Malissa's life divides somewhat neatly into thirds—one third of it lived in St. Mary, Kentucky, the middle third, in Indianapolis, the final third, in Cleveland, Ohio. Malissa Abell. Malissa Beaven. Malissa Dalton. Each surname representing a different epoch in her life, a different family, a man she outlived.

I found the first historical reference to Malissa in the Kentucky census of 1870 in the household of Peter and Elizabeth Abell. The first time my maternal family appears in history we are a family of three: Sarah, 30, Black, domestic servant; Tom, 7, and Malissa, 3, both designated M for mulatto. There is nothing here to indicate that until 1885 Sarah was "owned" by the Abells, that she was "sold" as a young girl on the auction block away from her mother and sister. There is nothing to document the relationship of Tom and Malissa, Sarah's children, to the Abells, but I know that the Abell's second son, George, was the father of Tom and Malissa. At some point in the 1870's, after Tom is killed in an accident, Sarah and Malissa Abell left the Abell household, where Sarah had been enslaved since childhood, and went to work for and live with a white woman named Miss Liza Beaven, a very devout Catholic, so devout, my mother said, that she left orders for the people who worked for her not to cry after she died. Instead, she instructed, they were to pray for one hour for her departed soul. At first Miss Liza took a great interest in Malissa, agreeing to let her be schooled along with her nephew and making sure that the men who worked in the stables (black) and in the fields (black) stayed away from her. But when she saw that Malissa was getting ahead of her nephew, she found more and more reasons for Malissa to miss school and gradually lost all interest in Malissa's education. She said there was just too much work to be done. That is all I know about Malissa's childhood, except one thing someone told my mother: Malissa worked so hard that she lost her beautiful looks.

The one man Miss Liza could not keep away from Malissa was Billy Beaven. My mother said Malissa considered Billy "wild" and for a while (years?) would not let him court her. He was persistent and apparently willing to give up whatever made him wild in order to win her hand. Unlike Malissa, Billy could trace his family back through three generations, through his father's grandmother (Charity) and his father's mother (Charlotte) because their names appear in the 1835 will of Edward Yates who bequeathed to his daughter, "a negro girl Charlotte, daughter of Charity." William Anthony Beaven (Billy) is listed in the 1880 Kentucky census as the sixteen-year old son of Marthy, mulatto, age 36, and Anthony, mulatto, age 35, Charlotte's son. When Malissa met Billy he was living in an intact, two parent black family. His mother and father had sustained a marital relationship from their early twenties and had passed onto their son a desire for education and a strong sense of self-confidence. Doted on by his teachers because he was so smart, Billy went as far as the eighth grade at St. Monica's, one of the earliest black Catholic schools in Kentucky, quite an accomplishment for a black man in the 1870s.

There is only one photograph of Malissa and Billy, an old tintype taken in 1885 shortly after their wedding day. They are standing on opposite sides of what looks like a part of a wooden gate, she on the right side with her hand on the post and he a few feet away with his right arm draped over the left side of the gate. She is tall and full-figured, light-skinned with long black hair, and her eyes set so deeply in her face that she looks ten years older than Billy, who is small and muscular. He is wearing a three-quarters length dress coat over a dark vest and a white dress shirt. She has on a form-fitting, floor-length, high-collar dark silk dress with a pearl brooch at the neck. The fact that they are not touching but looking soberly straight ahead at the camera seems in keeping with the no-nonsense Malissa I knew as my grandmother—but I also know from my mother how deeply and passionately she loved Billy. Maybe she didn't trust herself to turn and look.

To imagine what life was like for these newlyweds in the 1880s in Kentucky, you have to unmask words like "freedpeople" and "emancipation" which encourage us to slide over the facts. In some ways life after slavery was as bad as, or worse than, slavery. Whites were not prepared to accept black people as free and equal. Some even refused to give up their slaves and threatened those who dared to leave. The violence against the freedpeople was so great that when an official from the Freedmen's Bureau tried to determine what particular people were responsible for terrorizing them, an old man answered indignantly, "Tell me, Dear Sir, who is there in this locality that wouldn't kick a nigger if he had the chance?" Violence against the newly freedpeople was random, irrational, unmerited, and unpunished. The picture for Kentucky blacks after the war is a bleak one of people fleeing violence, going to cities where they often ended up homeless, or in dilapidated housing, starving and freezing, with disease rampant, death early, and no state funds for medical care. There were, of course, pockets of progress, and schools were popping up everywhere, supported by the donations, fund raising, and tuition that came mainly from black people themselves. Blacks were forming state conventions and meeting yearly to discuss the state and fate of Black America, but my grandparents were outside of all these circles, among neither the most destitute nor the most favored.

I am not sure how Malissa and Billy were affected by the dramatic events that took place between 1875 and 1895. All I know of their lives during these years is that they started farming, probably contracting for wages with a white landowner, and they began having children immediately. The first child, Charlie, was born in 1886; then Walter (who died at six months of diarrhea) in 1887; Bessie in 1889; Lawrence in 1891; Cora in 1893. Malissa told my mother that Billy was "a man who could see things ahead." He had plans for owning their own farm, for sending their children to school, eventually moving to Indianapolis where most of his family lived. He gave Malissa special gifts on each birthday—the first was a sewing machine, the kind with a foot treadle, which we kept until the 1960s and then foolishly threw out as junk. They may have had as many as eight years together before Billy contracted tuberculosis. He told Malissa he wanted her to get settled in Indianapolis before he died so that she would be near his relatives and in a city where she could get work. Malissa said that July 4, 1895, the day she left her mother and sister in Kentucky and traveled to Indianapolis with four small children and a dying husband, was the saddest day of her life. Whenever she retold the story of Billy's death, she always said the same thing: "Charlie cried so when his father died."

Of Malissa's life between the years 1895 and 1899 I have only one or two pieces of factual evidence: Elsie, her first child by her second husband Frank, was born in January 1899, which means that sometime between 1896 and 1898, she married Frank Dalton, a very proper, distinguished bachelor, who was boarding at the home of people who knew Malissa from church. Papa Dalton, as he was called by his four children, was a thirty-third degree Mason from Virginia, a Methodist (soon converted to Catholicism by Malissa), a night janitor at Union Station in downtown Indianapolis. He fell in love with the beautiful widow Malissa Beaven and accepted her children as his own. Together they produced four more—all girls—Elsie, Sarah, Helen, and my mother, Mary Catherine, born in 1906 when Malissa was forty. Was this a marriage of necessity? Frank and Malissa were married for nearly forty years until his death. I have no way of knowing what she felt for him. My mother said when I asked her about their marriage, "Mama was always the boss."

In the Indianapolis census of 1910, my grandmother is living at 1442 North Missouri Street (in a house and a neighborhood my mother grew to hate) with Frank and ten others, including their eight children and Malissa's mother and sister. Looking at this written record, this state information on clean white paper, with straight black lines keeping the information orderly, everything looks peaceful and undisturbed as though these lives might proceed in the same predictable pattern; but in the next seven years Malissa's life was in turmoil.

In 1915, just before she was to be married, her sister Bet was taken to the hospital for a routine operation and hemorrhaged to death. Sarah was inconsolable and within a year she also died. Two years later Malissa's oldest son, Charlie, died at thirty of tuberculosis and typhoid. Her second son, Lawrence, went to Europe to fight in World War I and came home moody and silent. The next three children—Bessie, Cora, and Elsie—left home, the latter two following dubious men. Frank eventually became a permanent invalid with crippling arthritis. Malissa had to convince a blue-eyed man in charge of Union Station that she could work as hard as a man, which she did, so that she was able to take over Frank's job cleaning at night with my mother's help. My mother's entire teenaged life was spent helping her mother scrub the long corridors of Union Station. By age fifty Malissa had experienced every kind of grief imaginable—the deaths of an infant, a young husband, her mother and sister, a thirty-year old son, and Frank in a wheelchair. My mother said that my grandmother was sad for so long that she had to consciously resist her mother's pessimistic outlook on life: "Mama, I am going to look on the bright side of things," she would say angrily. And there was a bright side.

Somewhere between 1920 and 1927 in Indianapolis, were the good years, the years that Toni Morrison says were spent "neither on our knees nor hanging from trees," those private times that never enter the archival record because they do not interest the historians, sociologists, or record keepers. In 1920 Malissa was fifty-three years old; Frank was fifty-five. They were established figures in the black community of Indianapolis, a handsome couple, doing fairly well for themselves. Papa Dalton had a good job at Union Station and Malissa was a real businesswoman (this is my mother's voice), trying her hand at everything that could bring in money. One year she collected coal from the railroad station and sold it. She made and sold ice cream. (She said it was hard to keep up that business because one of the kids, usually Elsie, was there trying to get a lick.) A white man let her sublet the house next door, and she and Frank divided the house into several suites and made a nice profit. When the man saw how well it was doing, he took it over himself.

Malissa entertained during these years. She belonged to a club called the Royal Fourteen and later to the Royal Art and Needlework Club. When she was appointed secretary and treasurer of these clubs she memorized everything, came home and recited the facts to one of her daughters who then wrote down all the information so that her friends never had any idea that she could neither read nor write. She was angry when Frank joined the Masonic Lodge because she didn't like the elitism of "society folks," but she went with him to all their parties and dances. My mother said they made a beautiful couple.

Up against this picture of Malissa and Frank dancing with the Masons, there is another which always interrupts, with a force and power to freeze the dancing couple into still life. Again there are two figures— mother and son, Malissa and Charlie. In these same years of dancing and entertaining and struggling to make ends meet, Charlie was constantly in trouble. I have never known exactly what he did, something about knife fights and sporting houses and refusing to be humiliated by the white police. He was in and out of jails. In that flat voice she uses when she is trying to cover up something she doesn't want me to write about, my mother said of Charlie and his troubles: "Women liked him."

I ask, "Did Charlie have any children, Ma?"

"He may have, but Mama never let him bring any of that in her house."

When he got into fights, Malissa would jump in the middle to stop him. He said she hit harder than the men. Once when someone tried to stop Malissa from hitting Charlie, he raised up in anger and said, "Leave my mother alone." He was proud of her fierceness and as loyal to her as she was to him. He looked a lot like Billy. One night when Charlie had his throat cut in a fight, my grandmother had to hold him while the doctor stitched his throat. When the police came to take Charlie to jail, he was so angry he tore the stitches out and Grandma had to ride with him in the police wagon while the doctor stitched him up again. I don't know how much of that story is the gospel truth. It changed over the years, but the core of the truth is there: Charlie kept Malissa embroiled in his wild life. Finally she began to pray for him to die—at home and not in the streets in a knife fight. When he was about thirty, he contracted tuberculosis and came home to die. One day on their way to church, my grandmother and mother stopped in Charlie's room where he was bedridden, and he turned to his mother and asked: "Mama, do you think I'll be lost?" My mother says she knows Malissa told him "the right thing." They found him that morning leaning out of bed as if he had been trying to call someone.

By 1925 nearly all of Malissa's children had left Indianapolis and had settled in Cleveland, Ohio. My mother, a quiet twenty-two year old, was desperate to follow them and full of excitement and hope over the prospect of a new life in the North, of leaving a town of hold-backs where once when she and Malissa were leaving the Union Station they walked straight into the middle of a Ku Klux Klan parade—men on horses in white robes and pointed hoods, parading in downtown Indianapolis as carefree as at a county rodeo. When I asked mother what attracted her to Cleveland, she said, "You were so closed in in Indianapolis. In Cleveland there were trees, parks—and the lake. And the beautiful old houses. It looked like here you could catch your breath."

The lake was Lake Erie, and those houses were the stately mansions on Euclid Avenue, known as Millionaire's Row. The houses on Euclid were owned by famous Clevelanders whose names are landmarks so familiar to Clevelanders we forget they were once simply someone's last name: Chisolm, Hanna, Wade, Hay, Carnegie, Severance, Mather, Warner, Swasey, and, of course, Rockefeller. Mansions set so far back from the road that even their deep lawns suggested the wide open promise of a better life—even to the servants. My mother and grand-mother may have been servants in those houses, but at least there were no "colored" sections at the movie theaters, or on the streetcars, or in the downtown department stores—none that you could see. In that young and still-growing Ohio city on the lake, a center of vigorous in-dustrial activity, a city founded by abolitionists, which in 1859 had mourned over the death of John Brown, where you could pay your five cents and sit anywhere on the streetcar or in the theater, my family felt at home, as though they were part of this lively experiment, a part of the promise. After the sweltering heat of Indianapolis, the cool breezes off of Lake Erie must have seemed like a gentle flag rippling in welcome.

In the snapshot taken shortly after they arrived in Cleveland, Malissa and my mother are standing in the backyard on either side of Frank, who is seated very majestically in a dining-room chair, concealing the fact that he is unable to stand or walk. Malissa looks solemn as she al-ways does, her hair still dark at sixty-two. She is heavier than in other pictures, but tall and stately and well-proportioned. What stands out are her hands which are so large they seem to be part of another, larger, more masculine body. Within months she has a job cleaning and cook-ing for wealthy whites. The three of them live on Amos Avenue in a house owned by Malissa's oldest daughter, Bessie, now married to Scott Riffe who owns a prosperous hardware store on Cedar Avenue. Aunt Bessie's impressive two-story house sits in the front facing Amos Av-enue, and my grandmother's little cottage sits in back facing Aunt Bessie's back porch in front and the alley in back. All of this property is in the downtown area of Cleveland set aside for migrating black people.

What I now know about racism in Cleveland I did not learn from my family. They said simply that there were prejudiced people in the world and that we should avoid them, but they did not want their chil-dren to feel burdened by the facts of race. There was much they could not have known, like how many jobs were not open to them. In an arti-cle written in 1930 for the Cleveland Chamber of Commerce, writer Charles Chesnutt set out to document that things in the Forest City were pretty bleak for black people. Blacks, he wrote, were kept out of all unions—electrical workers, plumbers, structural iron workers, and most railroad unions. All jobs as clerks and salespeople in department or chain stores were denied them. No blacks could be conductors or motormen on streetcars. They were not hired in any of the public utili-ties except in menial positions. The YMCA and YWCA did not admit black members except at the Cedar Branch which was in the black neighborhood. No blacks were received in the Cleveland Orphan Asylum or at the old folks home. There were no black firefighters. Out of 350 professional librarians in the city, about four were black. A light-skinned man, easily taken for white, Chesnutt concluded, "I do not know more than one place downtown where I could take for luncheon a dark colored man."

Despite the circumscriptions of black life, my grandmother's life did not seem limited to me. She took the streetcar three days a week to work. She came to our house to help take care of her eight grandchildren. And, several times a week, she traveled crosstown to the small black Catholic church, Our Lady of the Blessed Sacrament on 79th Street, to work and worship. Her youngest daughter and the Catholic Church were the twin anchors of her life. She carried a rosary with her and a prayer book thick with holy pictures, scapulars, and relics of the saints, a picture of Jesus as the Sacred Heart in a plastic oval, its edges crocheted in red thread. She went to daily Mass and Communion in the morning. In the evening she went to Novenas and Benediction. She kept track of all the apparitions of the Blessed Mother. These rituals were vivid, dramatic, and passionate, even more so at Blessed Sacrament where the deep rich sound of black southern voices singing "Tantum Ergo" and "Holy God We Praise Thy Name" completely revised Catholic rituals. Was it here at the altar that my grandmother imbibed the taste of hierarchy, of domination?

Certainly she dominated my mother's life. From the time my mother was born in 1906 until Malissa's death in 1960, they were never more than five minutes distance from each other. As I write this, thinking of these two lives, a picture gradually begins to emerge, silently, troubling. As a young woman my mother wanted to become a nun, but my grandmother couldn't bear such a separation. All of my rebellious aunts left home as soon as they were able, determined to get outside of their mother's control. Only my mother stayed, faithfully and dutifully devoted to her mother. I am convinced that my grandmother helped to engineer my mother's marriage, urging her to marry a man with a house and a steady job, to be safe, to take no chances. And when that marriage became cold and unloving, I know my grandmother, in alliance with the Church, was there with the lessons of female submission to the will of God.

For all of its hardships, my grandmother's life seems so much freer than my mother's. There was nothing in my mother's life to match the social whirl of parties and entertaining in my grandmother's life. I never once saw my mother get dressed up in the evening to go out with my father as my mother watched Malissa and Frank. When we were grown, my sisters and I gave the parties for my mother, decorated the house, invited the friends, sat by her side, and watched her enjoy herself. Despite the effects of slavery, poverty, illness, death, and racism, Malissa seemed somehow in charge, the architect of the limited resources of her life. Maybe because there were so few social structures in place, she had a kind of freedom to invent herself. There was no Cult of True Womanhood (none she was aware of) to tell her she was supposed to be genteel and passive and an appendage to her husband. She belonged to the black Catholic church which meant a community of spiritual support, not the church I knew in the 1950s which bludgeoned its members with guilt and humiliation. She was physically strong, almost never ill, and never once in a hospital. She had no formal education herself but she wanted her grandchildren to get as much as they could.

I am riding the Metro into D.C. this January morning to work in the American Studies office. In my hand, ready to be mailed, is a card to my friend, John Ford—Father John Ford—a priest in Cleveland who has been invited to be the celebrant at Mass the first Sunday of Black History Month at St. Aloysius Church, my current parish. I look at this envelope with its Black History Month stamp (James Weldon Johnson) and I am startled by the realization that this could so easily be Malissa riding into Dupont Circle, planning church events for Black History Month. I have the most uncanny feeling that I am acting out a story she wrote long ago with her own life. My mother used to tell Malissa that she should have been writing those Dorothy Dix columns in the paper because she had better ideas than Dix. Is Malissa the guiding force behind my writing? Unlike my mother, I like to entertain friends and throw parties, and do so with ease and pleasure. That's Malissa entertaining her Royal Fourteen. Like her I am deeply involved in the Catholic Church, although I doubt the Pope would recognize my style of Catholicism. Malissa may have been more faithful to the letter of the law, but she also confronted priests and bishops about their racism and stood her ground with them.

The more I write about Malissa the more I see connections between her life and mine, and I wonder how many women have this same feel-

ing, that they are unlike their mothers, that certain genes skip a generation, then return later, connecting them to their grandmothers in some
essential ways. Once when my mother came to visit me in Boston, I
took her to church with me. She was waiting impatiently for me after
Mass as I ran around with messages to other members about dates for
events and plans for new liturgies and lyrics to new music, and greeting those I hadn't seen in a while. When I finally got back to her she
was standing outside the door in the cold, leaning on her three-footed
aluminum cane, looking at me with a combination of exasperation,
anger, and respect, remembering, I suppose, the many times as a girl
she had waited after church for Malissa: "You're two of a kind," she
said. "Just like my mother."

One Village

Naomi Shihab Nye

IT IS FIFTEEN YEARS since I have seen my grandmother. I feel some guilt about this, but her face, when we meet in the village, betrays no slant of blame. She is glad to see me. She blesses me with whispered phrases, Mohammed this, Mohammed that, encircling my head with her silver ring. Later she will ask, "Why didn't you ever write a letter?" and the guilt will return, unabsolved by fact: *She can't read. Who would have thought she'd want a letter?* I had forgotten she is so small, barely reaching my shoulder as I hug her tightly, kissing both cheeks. I am stunned with luckiness; so much can happen in fifteen years.

The village smells familiar—a potent soup of smoke, sheep wool, water on stone. Again it is the nose retrieving memory as much as eyes or ears—I poke into courtyards, filled suddenly with lentil broth, orange blossom, olive oil soap. Whole scenes unfold like recent landscapes; a donkey who once entered the room where we were eating, a dusty boy weeping after a wayward kickball knocked him on the head. I was a teenager when last here, blind in the way of many teenagers; I wanted the world to be like me. Now there is nothing I would like less. I enter the world hoping for a journey out of self as much as in. I come back to this village remembering, but it is more like I have never been here before. This time I am awake.

"What do you do every day?" I ask my grandmother.

She replies in Arabic, "*Cad.* Every day I sit. What else would you want me to do?"

But I will find this is not quite true. Each morning she prays, rising at 4:30 to the first muezzin's call. It seems strange that the sun also rises this early. The days stretch out like gauze—we are pulled from sleep by too much brightness.

Each morning my grandmother walks across the road to *the cow*, singular, to carry home a teakettle of fresh warm milk. Take me with you, I say. And she will take me, laughing because I like this black-and-white cow enough to touch it on the head and thank it, *Shookrum, haleeb.* "She speaks to cows," my grandmother will say later, pointing at me. "This is a girl who speaks to cows."

Every day she lights the oven, fat stone mound heated by the dung of sheep and goats, *taboon* for bread cooked on the black rocks. She enters barefooted, her headdress drifting about her. "Could be dangerous," says my father, "I don't think she should light it anymore," but it is one of the ways she remains a vital part of her corner of the village, one of the things she does better than anyone else.

Her face is deeply mapped, her back slightly bent. Three years ago she made a pilgrimage to Mecca, became a *Hajji*. For a year afterward, she wore only white. Today she alters this slightly, wearing a long white dress embroidered with green over black-and-white pyjamas. It is cool here in the West Bank in late May; people think of the whole Middle East as a great hot desert, but here in this high, perched village the days feel light and breezy, the land a music of terraced hills.

Feelings crowd in on me; maybe this is what it means to be in your genetic home. That you will feel on fifty levels at once, the immediate as well as the level of blood, the level of uncles, of weeping in the pillow at night, weddings and graves, the babies who didn't make it, level of the secret and unseen. Maybe this is heritage, that deep well that gives us more than we deserve. Each time I write or walk or think, I drop a bucket in. Staring at my grandmother, my *Sitti*, as she sits on the low bed, rocking back and forth in time with conversation, tapping her fingertips on her knees, I think this is the nectar off which I will feed.

"Does he beat you?" she asks of my husband, back home in Texas. "No? Ah, good. Then he is a good man." It is simple to define things here. If God wills it, it happens. A bird poops on my head in the courtyard. "That means you will soon have a boy." Looking up, Sitti says, "It's an impolite mother who didn't put underpants on her baby." Conversation stops. My uncle slaps his head and laughs. "She's always saying things like that."

It's amazing what facts we have about each other. She knows I "write." What does that mean to someone who never did? I know her husband had three simultaneous wives, but my Sitti was in some way "favored." Her husband, my grandfather, died when I was five. We were living in St. Louis; my father lay in silence across his bed for a whole day. "Be kind to him," my mother whispered.

My grandmother had a daughter, Naomi, *Naimeh* in Arabic, then five or more babies who died, followed by two sons, of which my father was the last. Naimeh had two children, then died suddenly. My grandmother was having my father at the same time Naimeh birthed her second boy. My grandmother suckled her son and grandson together, one at each breast. I know these things, I grew up on them. But this trip I want to find out more: the large bird-like tattoo on her right hand, for example, from where?

"Many years ago, a Gypsy passed through. She was hungry and offered to tattoo someone in exchange for food. She poked pins in me and the blood poured out like water from a spring. Later the skin came off five times and I was left with this. Beautiful, no?" She turns her hand over and over, staring at it. It is beautiful. It is a hand prepared to fly away. I want to hold on to it.

Across the valley, a new Jewish settlement sits, white building blocks shearing off the graceful green hill. At night the lights make a bright outline. No people are visible from here—just buildings and lights. "What do you feel when you look at that?" I ask my grandmother. "Do you feel like those are your enemies?" In 1948 she lost her home in the Old City of Jerusalem to Israeli occupiers. She moved with her family back to this village. I've always heard that my father's best friend was killed in his presence. My grandmother is a refugee who never went to a camp. My father was a refugee who moved to the United States and married an American. What does Sitti think about all this now, in a region the Arabs will only refer to as the West Bank via Israel? Does she feel furious or scared?

She waves at the ugly cats lurking in every corner of the courtyard. Most have terrible fur and bitten-off ears. She pitches a loquat pit at a cat with one eye, and it runs. "See those cats? One night an Israeli jeep drove into this village and let them all out. Everyone saw it. What could we do? I think about that. And I think about the good ghosts we used to have in the big room, who floated in the corners up by the ceiling and sang songs late at night after we were asleep. I used to wake up and hear them. Happy friendly ghosts with warm honey voices, the ghosts of the ones under the ground who used to live here, you know? I tell you, they had parties every night. They were a soft yellow light that glowed. Then the Jews built that settlement across the valley and the ghosts were scared. They all went away. Now you wake up, you hear no singing. And I miss them."

My uncle, a stately Arab in a white headdress, functions as *mukhtar,* or mayor, of the village. He is proud of his new yellow-tiled bathroom. It has a toilet, sink, bathtub, and shower, as well as the traditional hole in the floor—for my grandmother. He is planning a new kitchen under the stairs.

His wife, a good-humored woman with square, manly eyeglasses, bore twenty children; eleven survived. Her dresses are a rich swirl of Palestinian embroidery—blue birds and twining leaves, up one side and down the other. Her two daughters remaining at home, Janan and Hanan, are the ones who can sew. Of herself, she says, "I never learned how."

Sitti lives with this family, our family, in one of the oldest homes in the village. My father estimates it as more than two hundred years. Stone walls and high arched ceilings grace the main room, where most of the visiting and eating take place. Sitti sleeps in her own smaller room off the courtyard. The rest of the family sleeps communally, parents on mattresses on the floor, guests on the beds. Everyone gets covered with weighty calico comforters stuffed with sheep's wool. I swear I have come back to something essential here, the immediate life, the life without refrigerated food.

"How did this rice pudding get so cool?" I ask dumbly one morning, and Hanan leads me to the stone cupboard where food is kept. It is sleek and dark, like the inside of a cave. She places my hand against the face of stone and smiles. Goat cheese floats in olive oil in a huge glass jar. A honey-dew melon tastes almost icy.

One afternoon a breathless red-faced woman appears in the doorway with a stack of freshly-picked grape leaves. She trades them with my aunt for a sack of *marimea* leaves, good for stomach ailments, brewed in tea. I can see by their easy joking this is something they do often. The woman motions to me that I am to walk home with her, but I'm not sure why. Her Arabic is too jazzy for my slow ear.

Down alleyways, between houses where children spin tops on the flattest stones—as children our father taught us to pare the tops off acorns to make quick spinners—up ancient stairs, past a mosque with its prayer rugs and mats spread out, waiting. Where is this woman taking me?

I stand in the courtyard of her home. Pigeons are nesting in rusted olive oil tins nailed to the wall. Their soft songs curl on the air. The woman comes back with her hands full of square cakes of olive oil soap. She presses it upon me, saying, "Take this to America. You need this in America." She says other things I can't understand. Then she reaches into a nest and pulls out a small bird. She makes the motion of chopping off its head and I protest. "Oh, no! Please! I am not hungry." She wants me to eat this teenaged pigeon today or tomorrow. I tell her I can't eat it tomorrow either. She looks sad. It was a big gift she was offering. "I will take the soap to America," I say. We kiss and stare at one another shyly. A line of children crouches on the next roof, watching us; they giggle behind their hands.

What is this need to give? It embarrasses me. I feel I have never learned how to be generous. In a Palestinian refugee camp in Jordan last week, I was overwhelmed by offers of coffee and Pepsi showered on me as I passed. Would I ever do that in the United States? Invite a stranger in off the street, simply because she passed my house?

Here in the village, the gifts I have brought seem foolish when I unpack them. Pantyhose in rainbow colors, two long seersucker nightgowns for the older women, potholders, perfume. What else could I have brought that would better fit this occasion? A lawn of grass? A kitchen table, swoop of formica, so the girls might pare their potatoes sitting up at something, rather than crouched on the floor? Bicycles with sizzling thin wheels, so we might coast together down past the shepherd's field, past the trees of unripe plums? But I unpack a tube of Ben-Gay for Sitti (someone told me she needed this), a plastic bottle of Ecotrin, and give her instructions, like a doctor. I want to make it very clear she should never take more than two pills at once. She nods gravely. She tucks these prizes into her bodice, the front panel of her dress left open at one side like a giant pocket.

"Is there anything else?" she asks. And I run back to my suitcase, unfold a gauzy white scarf bordered with yellow flowers—someone gave me this in Pakistan—I carry it toward her like a child carries a weed-flower tentatively home to mother.

Now she smiles broadly, rocks back on her heels. This strange slash of cloth is a pleaser. She and my aunt unfold one another's presents, touching them and murmuring. This is the worst moment of all. I didn't bring enough, I think. I gaze nervously toward my father, who is smiling shyly. He unpacked his own presents for everyone the day before I arrived. "It's fine," he whispers to me. "We'll go buy them chocolates too. They like chocolates."

In the corner of the room sits a large old wooden trunk painted green. It wears a padlock—this is where Sitti stores her gifts, opening the lock with a key from between her breasts. She places her small pile carefully on top of whatever else is in there, and pats it all down. Janan teases her, "Can we see your treasures?"

Sitti protests, locking the trunk hurriedly. "Not now," she says. "Not this minute." I think of the burglar alarms in America, the homes of old silver, furniture, shiny appliances, and remember the way I complain when somebody steals my trash can at night. And it seems very right that a Palestinian would have a trunk in the corner of the room, and lock it, and look at it often, just to make sure it is there.

In this village, which used to be famous for grapes, most of the grapes have died. A scourge came ten years ago, they say, and withered the crop. It has never recovered. Now the vines produce only leaves, if people are lucky. A few fields show traces of the old days: arbors where grapes once flourished, small rock shelters built so the people who gathered the grapes could rest in the shade. I want an agricultural expert like the ones we have in Texas to come and analyze this soil. I want a farming miracle, right now, to give this village back its favorite food.

The loquats in my uncle's patio hang yellow-ripe and ready. Sitti won't leave the house alone, for fear someone will steal them. One day we almost get her to go to the Turkish baths in Nablus, but she remembers the tree. "I can't leave a ripe tree," she insists. We peel the loquats with tiny knives; their slick seeds collect in an ashtray.

We go for luncheon at the home of Abu Mahmoud, an elderly man known for his militant rhetoric. "I'm bored with him," confides my uncle. But when we arrive, Abu Mahmoud is only interested in talking about gardening. He leads me inch by inch around his property, introducing me to eggplants, peppers, apricot trees, squash. The apple tree will produce for the first time this year. He stuffs my pockets with unripe fruit—I beg him to stop. He crushes herbs between his fingers and holds them under my nose. Then he stands me on a balcony with binoculars, so I can stare at the Jewish settlement across the valley.

"No people live there," he tells me. "Just buildings. Maybe there are guns in the buildings. I'm sure there are guns."

"Are you scared?"

"I'm tired of fighting," he says. "All my life, we've been fighting. I just want to be sure of one thing—that when I wake up in the morning, my fig trees will still be *my* fig trees. That's all."

This sounds reasonable enough.

Another day I'm walking with my father and two old men to Abu Mahmoud's house, to deliver some sweets as a thank-you gift, when an Israeli tank pulls up and trains its gun on us. "Why are you doing this?" I shout in English at the tank. And a soldier rises out of the top and stares at me curiously. I wave my fist as my father tries to quiet me. "What *right* do you have?"

Several years before the official beginning of the *Intifada*, I know firsthand why little boys throw stones.

The wedding picture of my parents hangs high on my uncle's wall. It's slightly crooked; I keep scouting for a ladder, to straighten it. One day I realize how long it has been hanging there. "Did you put that up in 1951?" I ask my grandmother, a woman unsure even of her own age. She says, "I put it up when I got it." My father looks serious in the picture, thin, darkly intense, in a white linen jacket hanging nearly to his knees. My mother, fair and hopeful at his side, already learning about pine nuts and tabooleh. In how many houses have they lived? And suddenly I want to leave the picture crooked, because it may be the single icon of our lives that has stayed in one place.

My father and I hike to the tomb of Sheikh Omar, high on a hill. We must overstep the lentil fields to get there. My father stoops to pluck a handful of fresh green lentils, saying, "Once you eat them raw, you never forget the taste." Sometimes I feel this way about my whole life. Who was Omar, when did he live? My father says he was a disciple of Mohammed. He lived a long time ago. The villagers know this is his tomb, so they have built a rugged mound of a mosque to honor him.

Inside, faded prayer rugs cover the floors. A ring of half-burnt candles stands in one corner. We take off our shoes and kneel. I don't really know how to pray like a Muslim, but I know there is something very affecting about people putting down shovels and brooms five times a day to do this. I like how life continues in the rooms where someone is praying. No one stops talking or stares; it is a part of life, the denominator. Everything else is dancing away.

My father wants to show me his land. He bought it in the 1960s, be-fore we came to Jerusalem to live for a year. Now he doesn't know what to do with it. Who can build here, knowing what shakiness sleeps in the ground? Yet people do. They do it every day. In recent years the Israelis have taken to surrounding villages with wire, calling them mil-itary zones, and ousting the villagers. The village of Latroun, near the monastery famous for wine, is flattened and gone. I remember it fifteen years ago as a bustling place. Its complete disappearance strikes me as horrendous and bizarre. This is only one erasure of many; in which camp or town do those villagers now reside?

My father's land is steep and terraced, planted with olive trees—five big ones, five small. When my aunt notices a broken branch, she stops to stroke it, asking, "Why? Why?" She tries to tie it up again with a stalk of wheat.

"I couldn't make a good house here," my father says wistfully. "It would make my mother very happy. It would make *your* mother very unhappy. Do you know my mother's one great hope is that her Ameri-can son will build a house and come back here to live? How could I ever do that?" I feel a sadness in my father which this land brings out, lays clean before us.

He asks why he is obsessed with property. In Dallas he scouts for condominiums, buys a block of duplexes, renovates it for resale. "Lots of people are that way these days," I tell him. "It's not just you."

"But you don't feel like that?"

My husband and I own our home and a swatch of Texas hillside. The only land that's ever interested me is the rolling piece of blank paper on my desk. Then again, I'm not a refugee. We've been robbed five, six times, and came the closest to imagining what a refugee might feel, but had insurance. A refugee has no insurance. A refugee feels violated in a way he might try the rest of his life to understand.

I tell my father I like his land.

We walk to a place called the Museum of Curiosity to see a woman who sells "souvenirs." She's big and ruddy, a recent widow, and wel-comes us with all kinds of exclamations and flourishes. Her shop offers a jumble of Bedouin coffeepots and amber beads.

I am intrigued by the massive clay pots lining her porch. At my grandmother's house, two of these stand in the courtyard, holding wa-ter. I know they were made in this village, which was once a well-known center for pottery. Why not today? My grandmother told me, "The clay went away."

I ask the lady if she sells her graceful pots or keeps them. She throws up her hands. "Oh, the Israelis love to buy these. Just today a man came and will return later with a truck to pick up a hundred. Maybe they use them for flowers, I don't know."

"Show me the hundred," I say.

She leads me up the hill to another small house and motions me in. A whole congregation of giant hundred-year-old pots sits gathered, some natural pink clay color, some marked with a blurred zigzag border or iron oxide lines, propped against one another, holding one another up. Their fat-lipped mouths are all wide open. I want to fall down into their darkness, hide there until I learn some secret perpetually eluding me. I want to belong to a quieter time, when these pots stayed living with the hands that made them. I am very sad these pots are going away.

She'll get more, she tells my father. She'll go to small villages and buy them up. It's hard times, she says, and people will sell what they have to keep going.

We eat dinner with Abu Akram, my first cousin, age fifty-five. This trip I have tried to clarify relationships. For the first time I met a beautiful olive-skinned second cousin named *Sabah,* morning, and we teased each other like sisters.

Abu Akram is at the moment a subject of controversy. He is building a three-story house that will be the tallest one in the village. No one likes it; they claim it blocks the sky. But he wants his whole family to live under one roof, and this is the only way they can have enough room. His sons went away to the Virgin Islands to make some money, but decided to come back. One tells me how lonely he was for his village. "If my sons and daughters do not know their *own real place,* what difference does money make?"

We eat stuffed grape leaves, *hummos,* and *frikke* soup, a delicate broth thickened with wheat. We peel oranges for dessert Over the table hangs a hand tinted portrait of a young man. I ask if this is another cousin

Abu Akram says no, this is a boy who was in school while he was still the principal. The boy was shot down last year by an Israeli soldier, near the post-office, after someone threw a stone at the tires of the soldier's jeep.

"*Someone* threw a stone? Did this boy throw a stone?"

Abu Akram shrugs. "It was never clear. He used to be very good in math. I put the picture up because we all liked him."

I ask my grandmother why things happen as they do, and she says God wants them to. I think of a poem by a Vietnamese refugee girl which ends, "God cannot be mean to me forever." I ask my grandmother if God can be mean. She looks at me for long time and her eyes seem to grow paler. I don't think she ever answers.

I ask my grandmother if I may see her hair and she shakes with laughter. "It is only as long as a finger," she says holding up a finger.

"I don't care. I want to see it." She keeps it so well-hidden under her scarves, it is hard to imagine.

"Then get up tomorrow morning at four o'clock before prayers," she says. "My hair will be visible at four in the morning."

I set my clock.

At four she is still asleep, on top of her covers. I poke her shoulder. "Where hair?" I ask. At 4 A.M. I have no verbs.

She bounds up laughing. "Here, here, here." She unpins her white overscarf and the satiny green and yellow one underneath. She unknots a quilted maroon cap that lives under the scarves and shakes out long strands of multicolored hair, gray, white, henna-red. I touch its waves. "Nice hair," I say. It is much longer than she said it was, rolling over her shoulders. And then she goes to pray.

Small things irritate me—why the Hebrew is larger than the Arabic on road signs, even in the West Bank. My cousin Mary refuses to eat packaged yogurt because the label is in Hebrew. We go to Ramallah one afternoon to find the daughters of a Palestinian writer famous early in this century. We knock on doors to find their house. My father is carrying a message to them from someone he met on the plane.

Gentle, intelligent women, they offer us fresh lemonade and an album of old photographs to look at. Neither has ever married. They have always lived together. What irritates them? They cannot have their telephones listed. If you are an Arab in the West Bank, you don't have directory privileges. "So how many people have we missed who might have visited us? You, you took the time to look. We are occupied people, but we do not wish to be invisible as well."

My father offers to take me to the Sea of Galilee, to Nazareth. He's described Galilee's crisp little fish to me since I was a child. Surely I must want to go taste them. But I don't want to go, not now. For now I want to soak up my grandmother's gravelly voice, her inflections; it's the way I make my own tatoo.

In the mornings Hanan and Janan wash clothes in a big pan in the courtyard, piece by piece. We hang them on the roof like flags. Our breakfast is fried white cheese, flat bread, rich yellow eggs. My grandmother wants everyone to eat cucumbers, which she peels slowly with a knife.

After lunch, I read and nap. I walk up and down the road. I follow the hillside path to the abandoned home of my Uncle Mohammed and stand on his porch, realizing how the poem I once wrote about him accurately imagined his view into the valley. It's strange to live lines you have already written. I could stay here. There are even shelves for books. Uncle Mohammed went to Mecca on pilgrimage and was struck down, hit-and-run, by a passing car. It took a month for the news to reach this village.

In the afternoons I prepare dinner with my cousins. We stuff squash, snip mint. One evening I show them how to make mashed potatoes, which inspires my grandmother to say, "Stay here, we'll let you cook all the time."

In the evenings we sit, visit. A generator comes on for three hours and pumps the houses full of light. A television emerges from hiding. All day it had a cloth over its face. We are watching an Egyptian soap opera in which each character does nothing but cry. By the third evening, I call this a comedy. My father switches the channel; there is *Dallas,* big and clear. He says the Arabic subtitles don't fit the actual dialogue at all. When J. R. says, "What a bitch," the Arabic says, "I am displeased at this moment."

Do they like this show? They shrug. Television doesn't seem to interest them very much. Maybe they liked it last year when it was new. The point is, what does it have to do with this life?

I try sleeping upstairs for one night, so I can leave a light on late to read. This newest room of the house has its own set of steep stairs down to the outside. At 2 A.M. comes a wild knocking on the door. It takes a while for it to filter through my dreams and rouse me.

Men's voices are shouting, "Open up!" in Arabic. I think, fire? Trouble in the Streets? I peek out a side window to see a group of Israeli soldiers, perhaps thirty with machine guns. I'll be damned if I'm going to open this door.

Suddenly a story returns: my young father in Jerusalem awakened by a similar knocking and the sound of gunfire.

"What shall we do?" wailed his terrified mother.

He said, "Just cover your head."

Tonight I do exactly that, cover my head, and the knocking goes on. I am grateful for these huge iron locks.

Then I hear the soldiers jogging around to try the main entrance. My uncle is roused and steps out, groggy, in his white nightshirt. They want him to come direct them to somebody's house. Reluctantly, he pulls his suitcoat over his pyjamas. As a *mukhtar*, he is obliged to act as counselor, mediator, guide.

We're all nerves now, everyone awake huddling together in the downstairs big room. Janan serves tea like a sleepwalker. I wonder how many times a day she makes coffee and tea. For every guest, for every meal, between meals, before bed, upon rising, and now, in the middle of the night. I worry about my uncle. When do you know which stories to believe?

Sitti starts humming to me. My father says it's a marriage song.

"But I've been married a long time!" I tease her.

"I know. But I missed the wedding." We talk about my husband. He'll come next year. We'll walk around the whole village, do all this again.

My uncle returns after an hour. He pointed out the house, the soldiers woke the family within, searched the rooms, dumped out every drawer, and smashed the toilet, then arrested the twenty-year-old son. He's been in Syria recently. Bad luck for him.

My uncle feels very upset. He hates giving directions.

"Why the toilet?" I ask.

"They like to smash toilets. Sinks and bathtubs too. It's one of their favorite things to do."

We will not hear of this arrested boy again before we leave. He's been sucked up by silence. For the rest of our stay, I sleep downstairs.

One day my father and I catch a bus into Jerusalem. He is going to show me the house his family lost in 1948. He saw it once from the rooftop of my school in the Old City in 1967, and he wept. I'm a little worried about trying to see it face-to-face today, especially after my father stops to uncork a nitroglycerin tablet from his pocket and pop it down without water. He says he hasn't taken a heart pill in two years, but today he's "having pain."

The Old City's hodgepodge self is a comfort, though punctuated by Israeli teenagers with artillery. An Israeli Jewish friend wrote me a letter describing the first time she ever walked through the Souk after the Six-Day War. "At first I felt victorious," she said, "but that feeling dissipated quickly, as I looked into the faces of the old Arab men in front of their shops. By the time I left through another gate, I felt like a trespasser." I buy one short broom for fifty cents from a toothless old man who sits weaving them, straw over straw. My father swears he's been there since his own childhood.

We pass a bright bouquet of T-shirts: Jewish schoolchildren with canteens and lunch pails, listening to their teacher. My father says he walked this road as a schoolboy too. We circle between massive stone walls and vendors with towers of sesame bread.

Once we cut through someone's private garden. "It didn't used to be here," he says. "This used to be a street." We pull back wires and step between.

In front of us, a flight of iron stairs ascends. "I cannot tell you," whispers my father, hand on the railing, "how many times I traveled up and down these stairs."

We seem to be standing in the middle of someone's construction. A pile of stones, a box of nails and tools.

I stare at the house where my father grew up, realizing it is not as I have pictured it. It is much larger, taller, with a view. An old-world stone, connected-to-other-houses house. I never pictured it connected.

A young Jew in a yarmulke approaches us.

"May I help you?" He picks up a hammer.

"We're just looking," whispers my father. "We just wanted to see something."

The man speaks cheerily. "We're renovating here. This will be one of the new dorms for rabbinical students. Ha—new—but can you believe it? This building is seven hundred years old."

He talks with such a Brooklyn accent I have to ask, "Are you from New York?"

"I am. But I've decided to be an Israeli." He speaks proudly, with emphasis. "I'm what's called a New Immigrant, under the new plan; have you heard of it? It's really fantastic being a settler—now I know how the pilgrims felt."

He's so enthusiastic, I can't help liking him. Anyone would. He's staring at my father, who's still staring at the house. "If you know the rabbi," he repeats, "he might let you see inside."

Now my father looks at him. The refugee and the settler. "I've already seen inside," he says. "I grew up on the inside. I'm an Arab. I used to live here. This used to be our house."

The man looks puzzled. "You mean you sold it to the rabbi?"

My father shakes his head. "We didn't sell it. We never sold it."

A silence in which the settler half opens his mouth and closes it again and the Arab takes his daughter's arm and steps quietly back.

"I'm sorry," the young man blurts. He looks shaken. He puts out his hand, which my father takes. "I'm really sorry."

And I really think he is.

Back in the village, my father reports, "We saw the house," and my grandmother sits up, interested.

"What did it look like?"

"It looked nice."

Once my father arrived from America to find my grandmother in a funeral procession, weeping and wailing for the deceased. He asked, "Who died?"

"I'm not sure," she confided, real tears on her face. "I just wanted to help them out."

No one will build a house west of the cemetery. It's bad luck, though the land appears particularly luxuriant there. My grandmother advises us that we are to give thirty pounds to the poor right before she dies and thirty pounds immediately afterwards. We tease her. "But how will we know? If you're not dead yet, how will we know you're going to die?" She is famous for her sudden revivals of health. We're to bury her with a pocket of air above her in the ground, so she'll be ready to sit up when the angels come to visit. She doesn't like to talk to people lying down. If someone reports the birth of a girl baby, she shakes her fist. I ask, "Why are you happier over boy babies?"

"It's obvious," she says. "A girl goes away with her husband and be-

longs to someone else. A boy sends money home and continues to belong to his own family."

"What about belonging to yourself?" I ask. "I'm married, I work, I'd
give my family money if they needed it. What about belonging to the
world?"

She tilts her head. "You're odd."

Three days before we leave, my grandmother starts mooning around
the courtyard. She plucks endless bits of invisible lint from her dress.
She mumbles to the lemon tree. I ask, "What's wrong? Are you tired?"

Her face trembles and falls into tears. "I'm only going to be tired after your go. Then I'm going to be very very tired."

When she cries, I cry.

Two days before we leave, the gifts start showering down. My aunt
gives me a red velvet prayer rug from Saudi Arabia. My uncle hands
over worry beads. "From *me!*" he says in English. He worked in Texas
once, in a produce house where everyone spoke Spanish. The souvenir
woman delivers a necklace of orange stones. Janan is stitching me a
small purse the size of my passport. Her face as she sews is weighty,
morose. Hanan produces a shiny-threaded scarf and takes to her bed,
claiming stomach trouble. "It's a ritual," says my father. "I refuse to get
caught up in this melancholy farewell ritual."

And Sitti, dear Sitti, comes to me with three trinkets from her treasure trunk in hand. A fat yellow bead, a heart-shaped locket carrying
the image of the holy mosque at Mecca, and a basketball medal. Two
players with out-stretched arms are pitching the ball through the hoop.
The incongruity of these items makes me want to laugh. "Where did
you get these?"

She swears the basketball medal came from Mecca along with the
locket.

"But do you know what this is?" my father points to the players.
"Do you know what these men are doing?"

She says, "Reaching for God?"

She tells us the yellow bead will guarantee a happy marriage. "It's
very old," she says. I notice it has a seam, as plastic things do, but I
don't mention it. My aunt brings a thread and attaches the trinkets to
my prayer beads. When will I ever see these people again? I wonder,
stricken with how far apart our lives have planted us. I think, maybe
never. I think, I will always be seeing them.

A circle of kids from across the street chants at me whenever I pass them. "How are you?" rolling the *r*, speaking the words as one word, musically. They learned it in school. They call out when they see me on the roof.

"I am fine!" I shout. "And how are you?"

Now they chirp, flutter, fly away from me. They are poor, shy kids, dressed in dust and forty colors. They have this new red Arab hair, springing out in curls, and what do they play with? Stones! Sticks! The cans that peas come in! And they are happy!

My favorite, a striking girl named Hendia, wears a yellow headband and a dazzling grin.

"Hendia!" I shout. "*Shu bitsewee?* What are you doing?" She leaps like a chicken being startled from behind. Yikes! I'm being spoken to! She runs and hides.

My uncle gets mad at the racket. He steps out and waves the kids away.

On this last day I look for Hendia. I have gum for her and candies for all the kids. She is gone, says her sister, to Ramallah to have her picture taken. "Tell her to find me when she gets back."

Later I hear her piping voice. "Naimeh! Howareyou?"

I run to the upper landing and drop her surprises down.

She swoops upon them, looking at me curiously.

In Arabic I tell her, "Tomorrow—good-bye."

She says in English. "Good-bye." She hides her face.

All the relatives file through the house to pay their respects. Sitti sits on the bed with her great-great grandson in her arms. I ask her if she knows the names of all her grandchildren. "Why should I?" she says. "I say, come here, little one—and they come."

I step out into the night, pulling on my sweater, to get one last sense of what we are leaving. One village, in a terribly troubled country full of cousins who should have been able to figure this out by now. What do we really know? And a shadow leaps on me, startling. It is Hendia. She has been waiting in the shadow of the loquat tree for me to emerge. No telling how long she has been here; it is the first time I've seen her enter the courtyard.

Into my hand she presses a packet of peanuts. "Good-bye!" she says again. And runs away so fast I have nothing to thank but the moon.

Two Grandmothers

Anneliese Wagner

THERE WERE NO GRANDFATHERS. Both died before I was born. Oma Emma and Oma Berta, the two grandmothers, both widows, were born about thirty years before the turn of the century. They retained the convention of hair parted in the middle, braid bunned at nape, and long skirts covered by a perennial apron.

In Oma Berta's house in Heinsheim, my father, his siblings, and I were born. The height of frivolity for the grandmothers was to don a blue-and-white polka-dot apron, the only exception they permitted themselves from widow's black. The hierarchy of aprons ran all the way from "rough" for picking potatoes in the garden to "good," a show apron of black sateen. God forbid even a hint that work was not in progress should be detected; except of course, on the Day of Rest, on holidays, on making a visit, and at bedtime. In my ear I still hear the command, "Put your apron on," as if a dirt-flecked dress would indicate an unclean character. Jobs like blacking shoes required two aprons, one to protect the other. Dirndl aprons, the folk version of this mystique, were at times, actually dispensed with for children. I have a photo of my two friends, my two cousins, and myself in our flowered dirndls, apronless sybarites in the garden, squinting into the sun.

Oma Emma, born in 1874 in a village of less than ten houses near Bayreuth, lived after marriage in a good-sized town. Her dowry had been lavish. She remained, however, a country woman, with the knack, even in the Bronx, of transforming flour, suet, and a few pears into a memorable main dish. In the asphalt, brick, and cement surroundings of the Bronx, she yearned for a bit of garden, a vine for grapes she could turn into Passover wine, for the chance, as she had had in Germany, to drop in on her neighbor, Frau Baierbach, who, besides running a grocery shop and tending twenty-one children—all of whom lived to adulthood—dispensed pharmacological aid to half the town. In America, Frau Baierbach's expertise with forest remedies for Oma was replaced by a refugee doctor's practice of blood-letting, by the basinfull, which I had to empty into the toilet. For her arthritic shoulder, Oma Emma had a stiff old cat's hide prescribed by Frau Baierbach which I tied on with ribbons, fur side in. It smelled of lilac powder, to my nose more curative than the odor of Ben-Gay.

My parents and I arrived in the States in 1937. My grandmother joined us in 1940, and she and I shared a bedroom. In that room, her feet on a low stool, the emotional spectrum ranged from hopeless black to cheerful yellow. Although "dear David" had died in 1904, she told me that she had "never looked at another man." At their engagement, Emma and David shook hands, and a year later, on their wedding night, the first kiss kindled their lips.

Oma Emma's escape from Germany began in an easterly direction to Prague and eventually, after ninth-hour papers arrived, continued westward. She boarded the last plane, along with the fleeing Czech president, Dr. Benes, to Amsterdam. For years she rehearsed this story for me: a woman who had hardly absorbed the switch from horse-drawn wagon to railroad car, she was tucked into a narrow seat on a rickety plane and transported into the sky. "I knew if I didn't die on the flight," she told me, "I might live forever." After Amsterdam, then what? How would she fare in a metal tub on so much water with submarines buzzing beneath her for two weeks?

She arrived in Hoboken. The New York skyline unscrolled before her eyes; eyes that never wore glasses, though she lived to be seventy-one.

Oma Emma's firm belief in the successful intercession of God to save her from Hitler equalled her worshipful attitude towards President Roosevelt. He was her earthly saviour. Her English vocabulary consisted of three words—God Bless America—which she had learned from Kate Smith. Once a week, when the Kate Smith Hour on the radio began with that rousing invocation, she laid her busy hands to rest and sang along, "God Bless America," in a delightful though wobbly soprano voice, the tremolo more from emotion than aging vocal cords.

I'm glad she died before the facts appeared: Roosevelt's and Churchill's flagrant lack of effort to rescue Jews and other endangered people. It might have brought on the despair she had not permitted herself after the catastrophes of her life.

Oma Emma ventured deep into the Bronx on a trolley car every few months to her other daughter, Lucie's, apartment. There she sat on a folding chair in front of Tante Lucie's and Oncle Max's candy store, with a smile for passing Italian Americans; a silent ambassador to the dark counters of Milky Ways, daily papers, and smelly black cigars. Her lap always held a pile of Tante Lucie's sewing. To sit there with "idle hands" would have been unthinkable.

Back at our apartment, which she seldom left, she cooked and sewed and looked out the window at a similar apartment house that might just as well have been a brick wall. (In my dreams, our apartment building comes back replete with windows, but no doors.) Due to the steep terrain of the area and the limits imposed by her "rheumatism," there was no park or ice-cream parlor to which I could take her. She refused to go to the movies with me on Saturday afternoons. Not what a pious Jewish woman does on the Sabbath. For me, Judaism fizzled away when I realized how mean God was to ignore our prayers and the appeals of relatives and friends in the camps.

In Oma's mind, if neighbors of forty years duration could do an about-face, could participate in tormenting Jews—beating people, carting them off to camps—and could simply avert their gaze when civil rights were denied, often in some publicly humiliating way, it could just as well happen in the States. It could happen on Nelson Avenue among the strangers with whom she had never exchanged a greeting. Although Oma Emma could read and write German, and read Hebrew, she was minimally educated. A concept such as democracy struck her as utopian. She had a soft spot for the Kaiser, whose moustache, she told me, was as fine as her dear David's.

After the Kaiser and the short years of the Weimar Republic, came the Depression. Then came the Nazis. It seemed to Oma just a matter of time before Hitler would sail into New York harbor. The size and strength of America and the success, eventually, of the Allies remained vague. Her experience, except for her flight through the sky and the crossing of the ocean, had been within the parameters of a village or a town. In the Bronx, it contracted to our apartment and visits to the North Bronx, to her seat in front of the candy store.

Without a German language paper or even a telephone for reports of the news, she had to depend on a young girl often distracted by the effort of becoming an American teenager. My parents worked on weekends and were too tired to discuss current events with Oma. Additionally, the indignity of not being able to contribute money to a threadbare household bothered her. It was not easy to dissuade her from habitual lamentation, a convention, I later realized, not simply a family trait on my mother's side but a common pastime among German Jewish women, a sort of communal mourning practiced with family and friends. Based partly on pity for those still suffering in Europe, it also contained a shudder from the cold draught expelled by a slammed door, one so nearby it raised the hairs on one's neck. To distract her I had only to say, "Oma tell me again about the time Mutti (mother) peed in the tent erected by the Baierbach boys," and off she'd go, telling the anecdote as if we were standing at her window looking down into the Baierbach's yard when the boys discovered the puddle. I didn't understand all her innuendoes, but a great deal of the country hi-jinks and town intrigue infected the flights of imagination that took us above the dull, anxious, constrained atmosphere of apartment 2A, and seemed to pitch us right through the roof of 1340 Nelson Avenue, into open air.

Oma Emma died in April 1945, within a week of Roosevelt's death of the same illness, a cerebral hemorrhage. At her funeral a relative, seeing my grieving face, said, "It's better that she's dead: who knows how she may have had to suffer." I wanted to hit her. How could it be better for Oma to be gone? I'd lost my best friend, my roommate, the fingers that dried my tears when my parents threatened, during their tireless spats, to break up their marriage. Oma Emma provided a bridge to the freedom I'd lost years back, the rural child's paradoxical world of delicious rambles and potential dangers.

For example, during my German summers I'd walk barefoot with my friends Hilde and Elisabeth across fields and along forest paths, the three of us singing or making up stories about Gypsies. How we hoped they *would* steal us; if not, we'd join them the next time we saw their wagons leave. The wander mystique from my storybooks was as powerful for me as the story of Pocohantas, the pure Native girl, is for an American girl. In the Bronx, my early idyllic existence sunk into forbidden memory. Any yearnings for *drausen*, the other side, were discouraged. It led to horrible confusion. House, yard, chicks, walnut tree, river, berry-picking, any nostalgic look back was considered destructive, even immoral. We'd been *kicked out* and tender feelings for anything German, except favorite dishes, were discouraged.

But Oma Emma, in the privacy of our apartment, permitted the old world secret entrée. She'd tell me stories of adventures and betrayals, love matches and pious acts; some that took place years before the turn of the century. In turn, during long hot summers in the confines of our apartment, I'd tell her the plots of books I carried home by the armful from the library. My proficiency in English, useful for the family, was regarded as an inborn trait, much like the ability to wriggle one's ears. I had unlimited freedom to read anything the library permitted me to borrow, as long as I finished my chores first. Same with homework. Reluctance to sweep the carpet daily was tantamount to committing a sin. Reading, since it required no physical activity other than moving the eyes, smacked of laziness, of amusement before work. Actually, the radio had higher value, since one could unstring beans or hem a skirt while listening.

The simple, old ways were best. Every nail, every stray jar top, was re-cycled or stored. Peasant frugality required the practice of ecology, long before it became fashionable or necessary. My parents' six day a week, ten-to twelve-hour workdays barely covered rent, food, and the gas and electric bill. Oma Emma baked bread, re-soled shoes from the inside with cardboard, converted my mother's skirt into a dress for me, and instructed me how to iron my middy blouse with our antique iron: detachable cast-iron slabs heated on the gas stove, one heating while the other was in use, the sizzling one then hooked on to the wooden handle. The entire operation was much more chancy than with a shiny electric model with a temperature dial.

Even before her forced exile, a part of Oma Emma had been permanently shattered by early loss of her mother (age ten), early responsibility of running her father's estate, which included meals and amenities for two brothers and numerous farmhands (age eleven), and young widowhood (age thirty). David had died at age thirty-two, of pneumonia. His wine business required frequent descents into a chilly cellar; re-emergence in hot weather caused a chill, then fever. Antibiotics were still unknown. Oma, learning to live with, or perhaps despite, perpetual sorrow, suddenly had Manfred age five, Lucie age three, and my mother, Minna, age three months, to raise.

Every Friday evening before attending synagogue, Oma Emma's father-in-law appeared at the door with his silver-handled cane, and as a father substitute for his David, he caned Manfred on the buttocks ten times and the girls five times each on the palm, not as punishment but to prevent naughty conduct in the week to come. Oma Emma approved of this prophylaxis, but I think it damaged my uncle: he had a quizzical look on his face for the rest of his life.

Oma Emma, smiling by the window as I looked up on my way home from school, appeared to be the only person who understood me. I came home in tears one day. The teacher had given me a D on my composition.

"Why?" Oma asked.

"She said I didn't write it." When I mispronounced aluminium as alumINium the teacher had insisted I hadn't written it, but perhaps my father or mother had. My father couldn't speak, much less write English, and my mother wouldn't have performed a task assigned to me— that would have been bad upbringing.

"Forget about it," Oma said. "She is a stupid woman. Someone just like her lived next door to me one time. I said, 'Good Morning' and 'Good Evening' and that's all. Be polite to your teacher. Next year a new one will see you don't need help from anyone to write about AlumINium."

I lived in Heinsheim, with Oma Berta as my daily companion, for the first eight years of my life. In America Oma Emma replaced her through my early adolescence. At times, conflating them into one, into Grandmother, feels natural. Not one shred of memory remains of Oma Berta. I know how she looked only from the face pasted on the inside of a small, otherwise empty album she gave me as a parting gift. An expression of equanimity and strength emanates from classically even features. She knew when she gave me the little album and inscribed it in ornate Gothic script: *July, 1937, for remembrance, on emigration, of your grandmother Ottenheimer,* that we'd never see each other again. The album, which I filled one rainy day while still in high school, is entitled— with what I now think of as endearing innocence—*The Evolution of a Refugee.* It begins with an age three months, bare-bottom photograph and concludes with a picture of me, age seventeen, kissing a sailor, my boyfriend Kurt, under the George Washington Bridge.

Some of the pictures break my heart: the contrast between two, especially. The first, taken the day before the emigration, the *Auswanderung,* the fiendishly ironic *wandering out,* shows my parents and me in our new clothes on cobblestone streets surrounded by of medieval buildings. The site was, obviously and naively, chosen by my parents to lend traditional grandeur. Despite the revocation of citizenship, the pograms, the difficult restrictions placed on the daily life of Jews, my parents felt themselves to be deeply German. My father had been in the First World War for four years and my mother frequently sang nationalistic songs while accompanying herself on the lute as she'd done with schoolmates all her life.

My parents knew we had to leave, that it was final, more final than my uncle Manfred's emigration in the twenties. He had been sent to America, probably by his cane-wielding grandfather, because he was having an affair with a married woman.

Our possessions had been sent on months ahead. To obscure the fact of our departure my parents and I spent an odd day here and there for numerous weeks, walking (we didn't own a car) to neighboring villages and towns as if we were enthusiastic holiday-makers, my mother carrying only her purse, and I with a shoulder bag, which on the actual day of leave-taking enclosed Oma Berta's blank album, its cover of nubbly taupe fabric laced with green-and-brown threads. The charade of dressing up and leaving the village, then casually returning, was thought a necessary precaution because beatings and unexplained disappearances had occurred in other places when departure seemed imminent. I remember asking my mother why, what had we done. Nothing. No Jew had done anything wrong. It was simply the last chance for bullies to vent their rage on Jews. There was nothing to stop them. The year after we left it became more than official policy: it became a nightmare of shattered glass, burning synagogues, brutal clubbings, and internments in Dachau.

The second picture, taken about a year later, shows my parents and myself posing on the tar-lined roof of a Bronx apartment building. My father is almost unrecognizable. He had lost more than thirty pounds. With unemployment high that year, and as foreigners with no skills, no English, and cursory grade school educations, my parents took any jobs they could get. In that year my father had lost his first job of builder's helper—carrying sections of iron for fire escapes—because he fainted after five days. Finally, after weeks spent searching for a job— on foot to save a subway nickel—he found work as a dishwasher in a seedy "Bar & Grill" on 34th Street in Manhattan, a twelve-hour a day job he welcomed with glee, at least so it appears in the photograph.

My mother, after switching from cleaning woman to garment

worker—once her entire week's pay check, seven dollars, had to be spent on a pair of arches to put into my shoes—seems to be caught, in that photograph, in transports of the same glee as my father. Her hand is braced on my upper arm as I stand in front of them. Is she signaling me with a quick squeeze to give my best smile? We were desperately trying to exude a sense of well-being, which makes me think the picture was staged for Oma Berta, a copy sent to relieve her anxiety about us.

I'll never know if Oma Berta saw that picture. When the SS came to get her in October 1942, they gave her one hour to pack. The contents of the house, some of it dating back eighty years or more, disappeared. I have no idea who owns her old armchair, copper pudding basins, lace-trimmed, strategically split ladies' drawers, or what became of her hand-sewn shroud, a series of white garments that were designed to cover the corpse from head to toe except for the face.

Recently, during my latest visit to Heinsheim, I asked my hostess, my childhood friend Elizabeth, if the removal of my grandmother from her house had been noticed by her family, since they lived across the street. Yes, she said, they saw her taken out. At the time, with only a quarter of a stomach after a radical operation, Oma must have looked more frail than she generally did. What could this bewildered old woman have had the presence of mind to pack after the certainty, suddenly demolished, that *they* wouldn't take her, that she was no threat. Her fields had been sold, she had no trove of valuables, she had been a good citizen and neighbor. What could they want of her? She wanted only to stay in Heinsheim near the grave of Abraham and, when the time came, to be laid in her plot beside him.

"Where did they take her?" I asked my friend.

"To the town hall." That small structure, which houses proof of Ottenheimers as residents of Heinsheim from the inception of public records, is three houses and the breadth of a tiny common from Oma's house.

"They kept her there until the trucks came next morning." After a moment, Elisabeth, her eyes misting over, said, "On a hard wooden bench. My mother wanted to bring her a blanket but we didn't dare approach the guards."

Some onlookers, like Elisabeth and her mother and sister, were deeply troubled. But others, Elisabeth candidly told me, some of them still alive, whooped with joy. They had been waiting for the day when the Jews would be thrown out. Now a good house in a prime spot on the main street was available to a *real* German. These honest, hard-working, pious people who had lived in amity with my family for generations sincerely believed that Jews had been the cause of their misfortunes and that the proximity of Jewish blood, indelibly tainted, was a potential menace.

Heinsheimers, all peasant stock except the Baron and his family, had not lost their Protestant or Catholic faith despite Hitler's anti-religious pronouncements. They looked to their priest or pastor for direction, but the men of the cloth did not care or dare to object to the round-up of Jews. Everybody knew several nuns had been taken away. And the Jews had killed Christ, hadn't they? To this day Elisabeth worries about the answer to this question. It had not arisen in public school. "It's what we learned in Sunday School," she said. "We had no idea, what it was leading to, no idea," she added.

Elisabeth is a generous, exceptionally kind person. For me she embodies the last whisper of my early life, as well as a window I keep trying to look through, an aperture on an existence of which I have no memory. In my little album there are several pictures of a hay harvest, of Elisabeth's mother carrying a colossal forkful of hay she's about to pitch onto a hay wagon already filled to a tower's height. On the very top stands her father ready to tamp it down. Little Elisabeth holds a giant weed she's just pulled; her sister Hilde, reins in hand, keeps the horses steady. Even though I'm not in the picture, I know what I'm doing. I'm jumping up and down in excited anticipation of the approaching moment when we children will climb up to the hay top for the smells and rolling thrills and heat of the ride home.

The grandmothers, so much alike in background, did not arrive at similar deaths.

Oma Emma died in the bed mext to mine and is buried in New Jersey near her children.

Oma Berta has no grave. She was shipped to Gurs, a camp in the Pyrenees, a sizable trip from southwestern Germany, made to seem even longer since no destination was given. For two years she lived in a freezing barrack with five dozen people, all slept on pallets covered by verminous blankets, fed on rations of gray water called soup, and suffered frequent illness. Via the Red Cross, she managed to send us two postcards. "Thinking of you with much love. . . " She knew that to say more would activate the censor's black marker.

My father's eldest brother in London had money stashed in Switzerland and managed to arrange huge bribes to have Oma released. Just before the rescue could take place, Oma Berta slipped on icy mud and broke her hip. Some nuns tended her in a convent. Almost eighty years old and limping, she was shoved into a cattletruck, pitched out into the hippodrome in Drancy among masses of people pressed together in unspeakable conditions, and then, several days later, stuffed into a cattlecar to Auschwitz. I doubt that, after days and nights penned in that hellhole, she was among the ones still breathing when the train arrived.

Nevertheless, the Auschwitz ledger records Berta Ottenheimer, resident of Heinsheim, wife of Abraham . . .

What sort of person was Oma Berta? I have two sources: my mother and a Heinsheim-born great-cousin who recently died in Berlin.

My mother hated her mother-in-law, hated her with an ugly passion that lost none of its rancor through time. In her eighty-eighth year she said, "Your Oma Berta deserved the death Hitler gave her."

What had Oma done? According to my mother, Oma Berta ruled the house autocratically, required my father to give his first allegiance to her before his wife, and used my mother as a *slave*, despite the availability of a servant. My mother came from a town where young wives of good family were not required to lug large baskets of wet linen sheets and tablecloths to the clothesline, beyond the garden, after scrubbing and boiling them; they were not expected to churn butter and then forgo the pleasure of eating some. "She locked it in the cupboard," my mother used to tell me, the bitter taste of her deprivation acrid in her tone of voice. In her mind the absence of butter on her bread held as much weight as the lack of a father had meant in her emotional life. I think she resented her own mother for striking the bargain for her marriage, one that had exiled her to a backward village. She never dared bring the resultant anger to consciousness.

"Oma Emma," she explained in defense of her mother, "lost most of her savings during the Depression and when it came to a dowry for me, couldn't afford the price asked by the family of the man I loved." She sighed, "And so I had to marry Papa." I wanted her to be happy to have married Papa, but she never was.

Great-cousin Nellie had a different view of Oma Berta. Nellie had retired to Berlin after many years in Israel. When I visited her there she told me that Oma Berta had been popular in Heinsheim, an exemplary woman. "And generous," Nellie said. "She always had an apple or a bonbon in her pocket for a passing child. It broke her heart to lose you forever."

My mother had told me Oma Berta favored my cousins over me. "No, no," Nellie said, "you were the apple of your Oma's eye."

She loved me, yes, but did she torment my mother? I'll never know. Perhaps earlier, coming as a young bride to Heinsheim and living in great-grandmother Adelheit's house, she had been the brunt of her mother-in-law's dissatisfactions. If Oma Berta really did treat my mother cruelly, it changes nothing. All that heartache, the age-old rivalry of mother and daughter-in-law, is blown away; a quaint practice now in light of the powerful wind that buffeted one Oma west and one east, saved one but lost the other.

All I know is that both of them knew the old way of spreading their long skirts across open knees to make a commodious lap for their granddaughter.

During the Reign of Queen Anna

Marguerite Guzman Bouvard

MY REAL CHILDHOOD began when I was ten years old and my grandmother entered my life. Before that, poverty and the War made me grow up before I could make sense of what was happening around me. Poverty meant that my mother who worked all day could not afford to have someone take care of me afternoons after school. Once the door of our New York City apartment closed behind me, I knew I was in mortal danger, for our building overlooked an empty lot filled with broken glass where gangs congregated. I could see them from the back window and I was certain that those distant knots of boys would climb up the fire escape and crawl into our apartment to get me. All I could do was squeeze myself into the space against the front door and sob until my mother came home. But I did learn how to take care of myself and often I was put in charge of an older sister who had difficulties I couldn't fathom.

The War meant mysterious letters from Trieste, the city where I was born and where my large family remained. My mother locked herself in her room to read them, emerging with a strained tearful face I dreaded. The War was a film she brought me to one afternoon, where I witnessed booted soldiers dragging a white haired man off to prison and felt as if I was with him as he pounded against the doors of his cell. The War was a group of friends and me in the park and the friends taunting two girls called Lisel and Trudy for being German until they cried and I turned to water inside.

Then my mother won a fashion design contest sponsored by the *Chicago Tribune* and my family took the train to Chicago where she began a job that changed our lives. My sister and I spent a year in a Catholic boarding school while my mother settled into her work and found us a house in the suburb of Wilmette. Heady with freedom from rules and with green expanses to explore, my new life seemed magical. And one morning my grandmother appeared, yet another sudden and wonderful change in my circumstances. I was out on the front lawn when a cab pulled up in front of our house and Nana stepped out, tall, straight backed, just as fresh as if she had come from the next town instead of across the ocean from Trieste, Italy. When I entered the house tentatively not knowing what to expect—for I barely remembered this elegant woman—she smiled at me and presented me with a diamond ring! I was nonplussed by such a sumptuous gift, but my mother told me she had had them made for my sister and me from a set of pendants her husband gave her when they were newly married.

From the time she came to live with my family, my grandmother brought an entire world with her and wove me into her ways. Our once quiet house was filled with her comings and goings, and her firm authoritative steps. My mother worked long days and the only sounds my sister and I made when we weren't quarreling, were those of the pages rustling in our books. Now there was the clatter of dishes in the kitchen because Nana loved to bake, one of the only household chores she would consider, and she and my mother's voices resonated from downstairs long after I had gone to bed. I couldn't make out their words but their tonal differences lulled me to sleep.

Nana carried herself like royalty and claimed space at a time when women were supposed to stay at home, like my friends' mothers who played cards and talked about nothing all day. She wore diamond earrings set in delicate tracery when she went out and a silver filigree bracelet with corals and a matching ring most days. She sat for long periods to keep that already ramrod back straight, as she had learned in school, staring at the foliage outside her window because "Green is good for the eyes." When she went to run errands, she strode through Wilmette as if everyone owed her homage. I had never seen a queen before, but I knew that was who she was; walking down the streets, her head held high, transforming our dull midwestern town.

She entered a new landscape, and what must have seemed like strange customs as if she had lived there all her life. I saw her as a conquering heroine, for I was keenly aware that I was a foreigner at a time when they were not welcome and when prejudice was raw and blatant. I was dressed differently from my friends in school and I preferred coming right home after classes rather than joining them in their games. When my classmates used slurs against anyone who was unlike them, I was particularly uncomfortable because I felt that I too didn't belong. Nobody else I knew spoke foreign languages at home, so I stopped speaking Italian and when my teacher asked me to speak French to the class, I purposely pronounced it with a horrible American accent for fear of being teased afterwards.

But Nana was used to being taken seriously and with her unquenchable self-confidence she plunged into her new surroundings with gusto. She cut tea bags open to take out the tea and was astonished by Jell-O and marshmallows on salad. "What are those white things that keep opening when you chew them?" she asked me. Evenings she watched television to get a feeling for English, laughing at the Westerns which thundered across the screen. She also attended English classes. Coming from a multilingual society she spoke German, Italian, Slovene, French, and even a little Hungarian so that she seemed to pick up English and acquire friends in what she considered "the right circles" very quickly. Before many months passed, I saw shiny Cadillacs pulling up and Nana stepping in, all dressed up for afternoon visits.

At home, the languages swirled around me as Nana and my mother spoke German when they didn't want my sister and me to understand, although that inspired me to pick up vocabulary rather quickly. My mother preferred speaking in Italian, for she was a staunch supporter of the Italian Republic and a democrat. My grandmother longed for the pageantry and elegance of the Austro-Hungarian Empire. "Ils étaient si beaux dans leurs uniformes blancs" (they were so handsome in their white uniforms), she described the Emperor's guards. She and I spoke French, the language of her education during a time when speaking French was a sign that one was cultivated. Because of her, I grew up believing that it was normal to have a multilingual family and relished the different modes of being and intonations that were an inextricable part of the crisscross of words. I learned about places like the resort of Porto Rose on the Adriatic, seaside Istrian villages, the city of Bled in Slovenia, and shifting borders: landscapes that took root inside me and ultimately made me feel like a citizen of the world.

Nana swept me into her life through her stories, a terrain that soon became mine and where I learned about our family who remained in Trieste, Rimini, Innsbruck, and parts of Slovenia. Our house throbbed with their presence. Afternoons when I came home from school, grimy and tousled, I stepped out of one world and entered another. Nana was waiting for me, smiling and gracious and while I sat down in the kitchen over a snack she had prepared, the tales unfolded.

She met my grandfather when her brother brought home a classmate from the University of Vienna to spend the holidays. She happened to be in the kitchen when he arrived, not helping, for her family had servants, but just sampling the dessert for the evening meal. She was licking a spoon that had chocolate on it, an uncharacteristically undignified pose, when he caught sight of her asking "C'était bon, Madmoiselle?" (Was it good, Miss?) They hadn't even been properly introduced and she wasn't dressed for the occasion. I could see her standing in the doorway, her black hair swept up, blushing at being discovered in such a private gesture and overcome with embarrassment.

Only a year later she married him at the age of nineteen. I imagined she already knew who she was and that she was ready, having spent most of her years in a Catholic boarding school in Sion, Switzerland. There she learned social graces as well as history and literature, discovering Jane Austen, a love we shared later in life. She spoke of friends from Brazil, France, and Egypt, all of whom were "très gentilles" (very well brought up).

Nana's grandfather sent her to the Sisters at Sion because her mother had died shortly after she was born, even though her grandmother moved in to help her father run his household. "She wore gray silk in the afternoon and black silk in the evening," Nana told me with gravity, and I assumed with childlike innocence that somehow this was a sign of her importance. I still have a photograph of her standing behind her grandchildren, with my grandmother holding my mother on her lap and her husband looking fondly at them. Nana was so young and radiant and she looked just like her own grandmother, although in retrospect, she had a gentleness emanating from her that contrasted with Nana's imperious ways.

My grandmother was not even thirty when my grandfather died while serving in World War I. Ironically, he died shortly before Armistice was declared, not on the battlefield, but of the Spanish Influenza which raged through the troops at the time. In the photographs Nana treasured, he was so handsome with the dark hair and fine features of his

Spanish forbears. I learned that he designed the reconstruction of the harbor and the Canale Grande in Trieste and that he was a friend of the Emperor Franz Josef. Nana spoke of her husband so often that I began to understand that even though she had many admirers, no one could measure up to the husband she had loved so much.

It seemed at times as if my more interesting life took place in the Austro-Hungarian Empire. While my friends were playing baseball or crowding in booths around lime sodas at Walgreens, I ran through the tall grass in Nana's stories as she described the family estate with its fields, its smoke house, and its chapel. Nana's father had a brewery there in Sennosechia (now Senosecic in Slovenia) and the family would leave the city to spend the summers in rare freedom. Tante Meyer, the aunt who lived there year-round, wore no underwear under her white linen dresses and allowed the younger children to run around naked summers because she believed they should be unencumbered. I tried to imagine everyone piling into a coach and four for a day's journey to Sennosechia that might now take a few hours at most. Nana still had the tiger-skin blanket that kept her warm when she rode at night, and she still corresponded with her coachman's daughter who had become a doctor.

Nana brought the presence of history to my life in a town that seemed frozen in the present like a smooth and shallow pond unruffled by weather or change. We studied the War Between the States and memorized state capitals in my class, but that world seemed to stop at the borders of my school and its playground. At home, I learned Nana's versions of World War I and World War II before I ever took a course in European history, for she was not only a storyteller but a wonderful mime, playing the maid who ran off with the partisans after World War I and returned chastened and hungry. Nana also mimed the German officer trying to requisition her apartment on Via Cavana during World War II, as she stood before me barking his questions in a threatening voice and then replying with great dignity in her perfect German that the officer was at the wrong address. She told me how she would wait until just before the first light to dump her garbage in front of Nazi headquarters, as if she were performing the simplest task. She never mentioned the fear or the hunger and deprivation I would witness when I visited Nana's sister Cornelia in Trieste as a teenager and saw how she continued to hoard food as if it were gold. Nana never complained about those terrible times or about the period of occupation by the Yugoslav army after the Germans retreated. My cousins later told me that the Yugoslav soldiers surpassed the Nazis in their brutality: that many people had "disappeared." When Nana recounted her escapades, she seemed so brave to me. As I grew older I understood that she was letting me know that a person always has a choice, no matter how difficult the situation, a lesson that would accompany me throughout my life.

Nana didn't seem to mind having lost so much during war, though she mourned the family members who died. The family property was only the setting where they gathered, and she knew how to travel lightly. The letters still came pouring in from her sister, her nieces and nephews, and their children. Rather than feeling bitterness at the destruction and partial dismemberment of Trieste, I remember her as joyful and optimistic, always ready for a new discovery. And while she was dignity itself, with her lorgnettes and her queenly bearing, she was also secretly proud of my unruly nature.

In fact she was my staunchest ally, managing my difficulties at school with ease and equanimity. When I was in trouble, which was often—once I locked some boys in the janitor's enclosure on the school yard during recess—she would arrive at school like Queen Elizabeth paying calls. She, who could take on the German and Yugoslav Occupation Forces, turned my stern-faced teachers into beaming creatures. No more sitting in the principal's office for me, staring at his white buckskin shoes while filtering out his angry words. I never knew what she said; I only remember her sailing through the school doors with a charming smile and utter self-confidence. She was royalty itself while I was a rebel, yet I sensed that we were kindred spirits.

Before Nana came to live with us, my mother took me to mass, but she didn't fool me about her religious feelings, for she kept on her sunglasses so she could sleep during the homily. Then Nana took over the task of shepherding me to church. When everyone had seated themselves according to the Catholic ritual, she stood up, following her prayer book and her own timetable. I noticed that she murmured her prayers in Latin even though services were now conducted in English. Once, while the priest was intoning the homily, she got up and began adjusting the windows to let in fresh air. She performed this task slowly and with noisy deliberation as if somehow she were in charge rather than the priest. I still remember the squeak of the handle resonating in the congregation's stunned silence as the window swung open.

Yet the Catholic faith was the cornerstone of her life, and prayers were an inextricable part of her day. She kept a statue of the Virgin Mary in her room and a sepia-tinted portrait of Saint Anthony over her bed. One prayed to him for lost objects, but I noticed that if he didn't deliver, she withheld her prayers and that she recited them as commands rather than as supplications. She always uttered them in a well-organized manner, counting off plenary indulgences. My year in boarding school and my early years with the Sisters of the Sacred Heart in New York City had turned me against religion. I thought of the clergy as tyrants, but Nana never commented on my defiant attitude or tried to impose her views on me.

Catholicism in the United States was imbued with puritanical attitudes then, but Nana was both devout and fun loving. She loved going out to parties. Sometimes she and my mother went together, Nana wearing her diamond earrings and a black lace décolleté dress revealing the tops of her abundant breasts while my thin flat-chested mother wore a suit. Once I overheard them quarreling after a gathering because my mother had discovered Nana and their host kissing passionately under the stairwell.

She also had gentlemen callers. They were European and seemed very stiff and formal to me, especially Signor Sergardi, whom I fantasized wore a corset to maintain that strange stiff-backed shape. Once my older sister confided to me that she had seen Nana and him necking in the car ahead while she was out on a date. However, Nana was not interested in getting married again, and she always made it clear that her many admirers would never intrude upon her life, a stand that was very much at odds with the times, and which made a profound impression on me.

She carried a gold-tooled leather-bound book which included various messages of homage and love from her friends, and which spanned the pre-World War I years to the present. One man had painted delicate watercolors on a page, another included some bars of music he had composed for her. There were also lines from Schiller crossing the page in fine tracery, and, as usual, messages in German, Italian, French, and then in English as she acquired American friends. My favorite was a delicate drawing by her husband in red and black ink of an extremely elegant lady with a flamboyant hat, lifting up her skirts and crying "Dio, up toro!" (Heavens, a bull!) in front of a tiny barking dog rolling his eyes ferociously.

Nana was out a lot with her friends and even took a course on bandaging from the Red Cross. She practiced on me and I didn't mind being swathed in gauze because we had such a good time together. Meanwhile, I too was trying to forge a path for myself, doing well at school, which was the best way to become unpopular, and rejecting the narrow spaces that young women were supposed to squeeze themselves into like the girdles that were standard then. At the time, I little suspected that it was Nana's example that helped me through the turmoil of trying to discover who I really was, for I rebelled against her belief in class distinctions and her imperious ways.

In high school I discovered not only that I was passionate about learning, but that I wanted to change the world. When a man showed up during one of our study halls with a film about the Off the Street Club for children in Chicago's Skid Row, I decided I wanted to volunteer there, and before long I was on the elevated train headed for one of the worst sections in the city. My mother and grandmother were horrified, but Nana made it a point never to interfere in my life and didn't try to dissuade me.

I remember looking at the cavernous and grimy hall where the children were supposed to play and deciding it needed more cheerful colors. When the director told me there was neither money nor manpower for such a project, I headed for the neighborhood hardware and supply stores. I canvassed store after store, telling the salespeople that I had no money to buy paint but that the children needed better surroundings. I finally found a store manager who reluctantly handed me the cans of paint I asked for, and I headed back through the streets. I was so pleased that I was not even afraid of the drunks sprawled out on the streets or the group of boys that chased me and whom I eluded by slipping into a drugstore until I saw them pass by. I made it back to the Club with my treasure, three cans of bright red paint which I applied myself, none too neatly. I can still hear the director's howl of dismay when he saw the color, but the children loved it.

Later, following my own path meant fending off boyfriends who wanted marriage and attending graduate school where I completed a masters degree and eventually my doctorate. Nana was thrilled when I wrote her that I was learning German as part of the requirement for my Ph.D. She replied, "Meine süsse liebe (my sweet darling), Guiguitte," in her rush of joy that we might someday converse in her favorite language.

I continued to take risks and plunge into uncharted territory, while Nana greeted my achievements as if she were not at all surprised. I visited her frequently until marriage, a full time job, and two children made traveling impossible; but the letters flew back and forth between us.

She surprised me with a week's visit before Mother's Day, when our son was five years old and our daughter was only a year but a torrent of energy and determination. Nana was delighted with my house and tried to help me dry the dishes even though it was too much for her. She told me she wanted to take my daughter outside with her, and with some trepidation I settled the two of them on a blanket in our back-yard, watching from the window in case my daughter should tear off. Instead, I saw her sitting still for once, calmly and beatifically smiling up at her great-grandmother with a sense of recognition.

I had no idea I would see Nana only a few times after that. She went to live in a residence near my mother's home office in Peoria, Illinois when she became too frail to stay alone during the day. It was run by Catholic sisters, and although the new circumstances must have been a very difficult adjustment, Nana made a circle of friends, devoting her-self to her usual morning prayers and her version of Catholicism. Her handwriting had become shaky by now, but she sent me photographs of herself, still elegant and beautifully turned out in a royal blue suit with a silk scarf.

Nana and I spoke over the telephone periodically, but the very last time we talked, she asked when she would see me in a tone she had never used before. I will never forget the vulnerability in her voice, and then the terrible silence when I couldn't bring myself to tell her it was impossible, and when I realized that she understood. Even her reply telling me it was all right had a shaky bravado that haunted me for years afterwards.

A few months later she entered the hospital and my mother told me over the telephone that she had been asking for her favorite dress. I thought that boded well, and Nana soon returned to the home. But only days later, I received a phone call from the director late at night telling me that Nana had died. I was stunned: the voice speaking from the telephone seemed to be coming from another planet. I just couldn't believe I had lost her as I made hasty arrangements to leave for Peoria and help my mother through a very difficult passage.

I felt as if I were invading Nana's very being as I opened her draw-ers at the home and started the wrenching task of sorting and packing. I was surprised to find a book of poems by Rabindranath Tagore besides her ubiquitous Bible. Inside the poetry book were the usual holy pictures, but also a death announcement for a man in the home whom she apparently loved, along with the prayer by Saint Francis of Assisi begging God to help him accept what cannot be changed. I was touched by this very private vulnerability. I also found an envelope with a detailed account of the family history just in case I might have forgotten her stories. The red velvet slippers I had sent for her return from the hospital sat unopened in their box and echoed my desolation.

Her will stated that she wanted to donate her body to science, a decision that shocked my mother and me, but was in keeping with her independent nature even though it violated the practices of the Catholic Church. It took me some years to understand that she knew she would never return to Trieste, and that she was confident of her immediate ascension to heaven on the ladder of her daily prayers.

For years, I was inconsolable, for I thought I had lost her. I now realize that I have been walking in Nana's wake all my life. Looking in the mirror I see her and her grandmother's features tracing the bones of my face. And I am discovering, just as Nana did, that charting one's own path is the work of a lifetime. When I was struck with a disabling illness, she was there as I reinvented my life, for she showed me how to face events head on. The optimism she radiated took root in my soul and I hold fast to the lesson she taught me: when constricted by a trying situation, it is always possible to mine the inexhaustible treasures of the inner self.

Among those treasures are the stories I carry with me, which have become a world that is forever alive, and a sense of belonging that is as strong as it is invisible. Her tale is nested within the stories she told me so often they became the music of my childhood. Now, when people ask me where I grew up, I answer, "In the Austro-Hungarian Empire," for Nana taught me that one can never lose the people one loves so deeply. Their voices continue to speak within us, ebbing and flowing within our veins.

Memories of My Grandmothers

Florence Cawthorne Ladd

I SUMMON THE MEMORIES of my grandmothers, Ella Taylor Cawthorne and Florence Wood Willis, and my names for them, Mama Cawthorne and Mama Willis.

Mama Cawthorne, my city grandmother, and Mama Willis, the
small town grandmother, had in common the experience of living in
the South during the latter part of the nineteenth century. Both were
daughters of former slaves.

Mama Cawthorne was born in rural Virginia. In her late teens, she
followed an older sister to Washington, D.C. in search of a better life in
domestic service—in the kitchens, nurseries, and laundry rooms of
white families. After three or four years, she was rescued from domestic
service by marrying my grandfather, a printer's assistant at the U.S.
Government Printing Office, who provided her with three stepchildren
and a house to maintain. (Some rescue!) In 1900, their first child—my father, William Cawthorne, Jr.—was born. Four other children followed.

Mama Willis, born in New Bern, North Carolina, and named Florence for the city in South Carolina, had a son when she married Henry
Willis. They had two daughters: Nettie and Eleanor, who is my mother.
They lived in a house on Jones Street with a parlor, dining room, and
kitchen; upstairs, via a narrow, creaking staircase, were three bedrooms
with tin pitchers of water and basins in each room. They used the
house with sense of great pride; for it was built by my grandfather who
was a carpenter. He had built the outhouse too.

My father met my mother at the funeral of Hattie Cawthorne Martin, my father's half-sister, who had married my mother's cousin, William Martin, while he was in medical school at Howard University. My parents married in 1930. The marriage afforded my mother passage from the nosy small town of New Bern to an indifferent Washington. Soon after my birth in 1932, my parents moved from an apartment in the northeast area to a townhouse in northwest Washington, on the same street—although nine blocks apart from—where Pop and Mama Cawthorne lived. Their house was within walking distance of ours.

Proximity and family routines made for frequent visits to my grandparents' house, which we called the "big house."

Mama Cawthorne

Among the special occasions at Mama Cawthorne's were an annual supper to benefit the Second Baptist Church, the pre-Christmas gathering of women who baked fruitcakes, and the Sunday dinners when the entire family—the families of my grandparents' seven offspring—gathered at their house. The festive mood that surrounded those events fascinated me. Mama Cawthorne delighted in the preparation of a table for special occasions.

And there were the not-so-special occasions when my sister, Ethel, my cousins, and I were in the company of Mama Cawthorne in her role as baby-sitter or after-school caretaker. She always seemed busy—making beds, cooking, sewing, dusting, and washing clothes in giant metal tubs. And she always enlisted our help: "Fetch the clothes pins," "Dust the radiators," "Sweep the front steps." Constantly occupied with household tasks, she distributed the lesser chores among us to reduce her burden and expose us to housewifely duties.

I frequently accompanied Mama Cawthorne on Saturday shopping expeditions. Starched dresses, patent leather shoes, and white gloves— our Sunday clothes—were the required attire for shopping trips. We went downtown to the department stores on 7th Street—Hecht's, Landsburg's, and Kahn's—where she searched for sale items and bargain prices on clothing, linens, and other household items. The ritual of going from store to store to compare the prices of similar goods was very time consuming. Always certain that she would not make a purchase until she was assured that it was worth the price, I watched her examine and reexamine blouses, underwear, and socks with a keen eye for flawed goods. A flaw or irregularity, when brought to the attention of store managers—men readily identified by carnations in their lapels—sometimes reduced the price of an item. Success! My frugal grandmother went home and reported proudly another commercial victory.

Every Sunday morning, Mama Cawthorne arrived early at Second Baptist Church, for the eleven o'clock Sunday service. She arrived by car, driven by my father or an uncle. She always wore a hat, not an outlandish platter of a hat with a brim bedecked with flowers, but a modest hat—navy or black straw in spring and summer, felt for fall and winter. And she wore gloves, even on the warmest of days. A deaconess of the church, she sometimes wore a white uniform—a dress that buttoned down the front—very much like a nurse's uniform. In the uniform, her hat, and gloves, she marched down the aisle before the service began with half a dozen other women similarly dressed. They sat in the pews at the front of the church. Some bowed their heads in prayer or lifted their eyes solemnly to the stained glass windows and beams supporting the vaulted ceiling. Others scanned the congregation, nodding their greetings.

Twice during the service, before and after the sermon, the deaconesses were called upon to walk along the aisles passing the collection plates. When the nickels, dimes, and a few dollars of the congregation had been deposited in the plate, the deaconesses assembled at the front of the church before the altar, where the minister blessed the audience and thanked God for the generosity of those who had given and for the services of the good sisters who had accepted their donations. That my grandmother was one of the good sisters made me feel that heavenly rays beamed on me.

After the lengthy service of hymns and spirituals, prayers and preaching, communion and collections, we clustered outside the church and waited for my father and uncles to drive up in their polished Fords and take us away to the "big house."

Even from a more affluent and adult perspective, Pop and Mama Cawthorne's house was commodious: a brick house with a living room, dining room, kitchen, pantry, and back porch; upstairs there were five bedrooms. When their children and grandchildren visited on Sunday afternoons, my father and uncles, drinking beer and smoking cigars, occupied the living room. My grandfather, Pop, who did not drink, sat apart in a seat of honor—a large overstuffed chair by the window which afforded him a view of the street. Mama Cawthorne, my aunts, and my mother were in the kitchen and aproned for the preparation of Sunday dinner. My cousins and I played hide-and-seek, checkers, or merely watched the rituals of the visit unfold.

Out of that kitchen seeped the aroma of chicken simmering on a cast-iron wood stove. Aunt Lucinda's corn bread baked in the oven. Aunt Hattie stood at the stove seasoning a pot of collard greens; Aunt Mary sat at one end of the table mashing potatoes; and, at the other end, my mother and I snapped the stems off green beans. Mama Cawthorne, with floured hands, shaped dough into two dozen spheres, and dropped them one-by-one into the hot bubbly broth surrounding the chicken in a four-quart black cauldron. Something miraculous occurred in that cauldron: those dough balls were transformed into dumplings!

Dumplings—luscious, soft gobs—were cooked in the broth to which Mama Cawthorne added flour. She stirred in the flour and soon had made gravy—another miracle of her cauldron. When the chicken, dumplings, and gravy were "done," she transferred them to a tureen and marched proudly to the dining room. The other foods were brought to the table: greens, green beans, buttered mashed potatoes, and corn bread. My five cousins and I, seated at the children's table, were served first. I said "no, thank you" to everything except chicken and dumplings smothered in gravy.

The grown-ups took their places at the table. My grandmother, standing at the foot of the table, served each a portion of chicken and dumplings. Bowls of greens, beans, and potatoes were passed around. Uncle Sylvester stretched across the table for a piece of corn bread, and someone remarked about his "boardinghouse reach." At the head of the table, Pop cleared his throat and reverently thanked God for food and family. Then the clatter of dining and occasional conversation began.

I ate only the dumplings. Munching warm morsels, I ate in silence, maneuvering the pasty substance around in my mouth until I felt it slip beyond my palate and inside me. The dumplings' taste and texture were soothing. A few lumps of stewed dough, prepared and served by my father's mother, were satisfying and sufficient.

After dinner, Mama Cawthorne entertained the family with stories. We all gathered in the living room where she sat on the sofa surrounded by sons, daughters, and grandchildren eager to hear tales from her childhood of rural mysteries. There were always ghosts in her stories: ghosts in the woods, in church, and in the graveyard. She told stories about deserving kin, visited by the ghosts, and then cured if they were ill, or blessed with abundant crops if they were poor. And there were accounts of evil or ill-willed kin whose lives were cut short. They dropped dead or were literally frightened to death by ghostly intervention. Her stories had a purpose, always a moral.

Mama Cawthorne's bountiful table, her energetic, entertaining presence, the company of caring kin, and the assurance that we would gather the next Sunday and the next, in celebration and thanksgiving, is now a memory recalled by one word: dumplings. Mama Cawthorne was a dumpling of a grandmother: soft, round, soothing, satisfying, and sufficient.

A dumpling of a tumor grew in her throat. I was thirteen years old when she died, at sixty-three years of age. After her death, the family ceased gathering for Sunday dinner. Pop gave up his chair with a view of the street and moved to the home of his youngest daughter. The special occasions that drew us to the big house became special memories.

Mama Willis

Throughout my childhood, my parents, my sister, Ethel, and I went south to North Carolina every summer. We spent a week or more at the home of Papa Willis and Mama Willis. Tall and dignified, she wore long skirts which enhanced her grace. She seemed aloof and austere. A woman of few words, I remember her silences better than her voice. I recall observing her more than interacting with her. I watched her strip ears of July corn from stalks and feed the flock of clucking chickens, before selecting a few for dinner. I saw her wring the necks of chickens, deftly behead them, and then, in steaming water, pluck them and prepare them for frying. I was awed by her deliberate actions that ended the existence of chickens that hours earlier were alive and clucking; and I was amazed by her turning them into the most delicious fried chicken I have known.

Over a wood-burning stove in the heat of summer, she cooked the chickens until they were crisp and golden brown. We came to the table in the dining room with appetites sharpened by the fragrance of chicken frying, corn steaming, and biscuits baking. After saying grace, Mama Willis surveyed the table to see that everyone was well served. And while we ate—I had a notorious capacity for her chicken—she returned to the kitchen to produce more of everything.

When she was not bent over her own stove, she was cooking for the Catholic priests of New Bern. She worked at the parish house of the white Catholic Church in town, where she cooked and cleaned. It was not her religion—she was Methodist—it was a job. I am sure she was paid poorly for her service; but I also know it was one of the few opportunities available to her.

There was a rocking chair on the front porch of the house in New Bern. I believe I saw Mama Willis sit and rock in that chair only once. She had little time to sit and observe the procession of neighbors who came to the pump in front of her house for water, or the children at play on the street. Instead, she steadily moved from one task to the next with a formality and quiet dignity that I witnessed and tried to emulate.

My three cousins living in New Bern had a much closer relationship to Mama Willis than I. They saw her daily. In her presence, they were not reserved and respectful of her silence as I was; instead they chattered playfully, entertaining each other with gossip and games. I envied their unself-consciousness, their playfulness, their comfort with her company. I wanted to feel closer to her, to know her better; after all, I was named for her.

When I was ten years old, Mama Willis died of a heart attack on Mother's Day, in her sixty-sixth year. We were told that she had not appeared ill. In fact, she had a day of routine chores before she quietly died. She was gone before I had a sense of who she was, before I had established a meaningful connection to her.

Their Legacy

In shaping my identity, I concluded that, as the namesake of Mama Willis, I resembled her temperamentally. Conscientious, deliberate, purposeful, and often silent, in adolescence I imagined my spirit as an extension of hers. Proud of being tall, I tried to walk with Mama Willis's dignified grace. Although nobody ever suggested that I was like Mama Willis, I assumed we had much in common.

As a friend read these profiles of my grandmothers, she exclaimed that I was just like Mama Cawthorne, causing me to review my memories and characterizations of both grandmothers. Perhaps I owe Mama

Cawthorne thanks for the pleasure I derive from the creation of festive events, the capacity to convene relatives and friends for a moment made special by their presence, and for my fascination with the art of storytelling.

Episodes from everyday life are memory's material. I now wonder what my unborn grandchildren will find memorable in their hours with me? Indeed, how will a grandmother spend her time with children born in the twenty-first century?

The Grandmother Speaks

SPIRITS OF PLACE

Padma Hejmadi

Spirit of place. Place of spirit. Many places in one spirit.
Many spirits in one place. Many spirits in one spirit, many places
in one place. . . .

OH, ROLL THE PHRASES and implications around your tongue as much as you like, there it'll stand, the place that is especially significant to you. Mine is where the two coasts of our subcontinent go slanting toward each other to meet at a point by the ocean. No, not on the seashore. Show me the map. Here, see? Inland, a few degrees north of the equator, where the hills of the east and the mountains of the west also taper together. Some of the peaks can get pretty high: seven thousand, eight thousand. But lower down is what I'm talking about. Below all the tidy glistening mounds of tea and coffee plantations until you get to the foothills. Here you sometimes find great feathery up-curving sprays of bamboo; sometimes red ant hills steepled together like praying hands, higher than a person. But mainly jungle; some thick, some thin. Teak, simal, silk cotton, Beautea frondosa, Flame of the Forest. Lots of rain. Waterfalls.

For years, people sick in mind have been trundled along the muddy roads between the tree roots to be bathed back to health beneath those waterfalls. The most spectacular of the falls has a little stone temple

217

next to it: very holy, built in the seventh century, just where the deafening torrent from the waterfall curves into a river running more sedately down the slopes. Pilgrims as well as ill people have been flocking there ever since. Yes, thirteen hundred years.

One day, in the ninth century, a woman poet took this pilgrimage and sat down to rest by the roadside. Framed under the branches of a very old tree, she saw the waterfall and the temple and the curve of the river; and she wrote a poem describing the place, its spirit, and her spirit in it. From that day to this, her seeing has been kept intact. No one down the centuries has built anything to impede that view; as soon as one old tree shows signs of dying, another is planted in time to replace it. We can still walk into her poem, into her mind and eyes a thousand years ago. At least, so far . . . With as much stupidity as spirit in this world, who knows for how much longer? But my own grandmother saw that tree too, and told me about it as I am telling you, my granddaughter.

"What was it like?" I asked my grandmother.

"Old," she said. "Old, so old its leaves forgot to fold themselves at night."

When I saw that tree it was a jackfruit, whose leaves are large and don't close. Maybe they planted a different tree each time? Maybe she was thinking of some other tree somewhere else? Does it matter? Her words stay in my mind, so her tree stays in my mind, vivid as the poem that first woman handed down to us.

See that dot? That's the nearest town where all the bus routes and train tracks came to an end—still do—and they say it keeps getting bigger and dirtier all the time. People used to sing lewd street songs about the place in Tamil. "They're selling guavas in that town, uncle. Go pawn your only loin cloth and get me some, uncle."

Oh well, it doesn't translate. But we got spanked by a visiting elder for singing that. He came and spanked and went, but it kept him busy. There were eight of us cousins, all shapes and sizes, spending that summer under the umbrella of an uncle very different from the one in the song, and an aunt we all fought to sit next to. Technically her husband, our uncle, headed various governmental projects—famine relief, flood control, community development, housing for textile workers—but his passion to help, to be of use, went beyond projects. Even we knew that. So each summer, between the first and second rice crops, he was invited on an inspection tour around the district by the *Zamindar*. Zamindars were local landowners, little maharajahs, like playing card kings, and often ruthless extortionists. Not this man. However pernicious the "zamindari" system, his passion to be of help almost outdid Uncle's. Also, unlike Uncle, he was happily mad. Doubtless he bathed under the healing waterfalls, but he stayed mad.

That was a time of definitions for me. What is "mad?" What is "sleep?" What is "rainbow?" Not what is it made of; what is it like, really? People too. Whenever they crossed our path, we noticed them with a child's acute but fragmentary apprehension of its surroundings. Yet, for me, this was where their resonances began to happen.

How old was I? Let me think. Seven, eight, thereabouts. Four of us girls, between the ages of roughly six to fourteen, were sandwiched between four boys: a couple of younger ones and a couple older, but not by much. Most days they were out playing cricket, with three straggly chalked lines drawn for wickets on a broken-down old compound wall, a gaggle of village kids rounded up for their team, a borrowed ball, and a bat inherited from somebody. Ramu, the eldest, was always seasoning it with a discarded golf ball put into an old sock soaked in linseed oil, which he thwacked steadily up and down the surface of the wood. Thunk thunk thunk. It was easy to have secrets from him; you could hear him coming a mile off if you didn't already smell the oil. Thunk thunk thunk.

As boys and the oldest, Ramu and Shamu could also range farthest afield and bring back snippets of exotica. Once it was the persistent rumor that a real live sheikh was coming all the way from the Sahara to bathe in our falls.

The rest of us were made to sleep every afternoon. No, we didn't mind. Perhaps because of the way Aunt arranged it. A whole lot of mats and pillows put together in the middle of the floor, and the lot of us lying on them in a tangle of arms and legs. Of course we chattered and played and quarreled, but she never more than merely looked in to give us a cursory "ssshh!" now and then.

That time I mentioned, when I was trying to define sleep, I had disentangled my legs from under my smaller cousins and my arms from under the bigger ones. Then I crossed one leg over the other, like so, and stared and stared at this mole on my shin, as a concentration point on which to keep myself awake enough to recognize sleep—know it—at the e-x-a-c-t moment it came.

Aunt looked in just then. None of this close-your-eyes-and-go-to-sleep stuff with her. She gave me a kind of enquiring grin, one spy to another, and only asked me about it afterwards. She wasn't just indulgently watching a child's game either. She really wanted to know what happened.

What do you think happened? You do your sleep research with labs and electronics, I did mine with the mole on my leg. Other children must do it other ways. It's a matter of boundaries, isn't it? Between how much you can and cannot know. The measure of places you can't measure. Aunt was with me in that place. I sometimes think she walks between our worlds, yours and mine, a loving conspirator. How can I say this right? There are some of us women who walk these boundaries with each other, even in small ways. Dead or alive, we're with you.

The house Uncle rented that summer provided another kind of companionship for us, boys and girls alike. It was built square and white and simple in a clearing between the forests above and the fields below. The jungle came down thick as an animal's pelt to the very bottom of the hill behind us; the rice fields stretched away in front, slaking your thirsty eyes with their intense, life-giving green, all the way across to where the heat of the plains began. Everyone called our place Tiger House because the hill behind us was Tiger Hill.

Silly, of course no tigers are that far south! No need to be so literal. Panthers occasionally, because of the proximity to the jungle. Once, after the rains began, we found a clear spoor tracked across the wet earth behind the kitchen, and got very excited. Bhatta, who cooked, was frightened and climbed the table, but none of us caught sight of a single one of the graceful creatures. Not for want of trying . . . staying up as quiet and late as we could. No electricity in that house, just hurricane lanterns; and the one big room downstairs held the flaring white hiss of a petromax lamp—what you call a Coleman lantern—which brought moths banging against the screen door. At night, through the open windows, we could hear the laughter of hyenas.

So many presences, seen and unseen. Ghosts too, how not? Beyond us, by the long road into town, there was an outcropping of rocks crowned by a ramshackle old building that looked so much like a haunted house that it couldn't possibly be one, but was. Or so we convinced ourselves, scaring each other with one story more blood-curdling than the last every time we passed the place. Sagging roof, once red, now brown; blistered windowsills, once green, now black; broken panes, topsy-turvy verandas with pillars and railings fallen drunkenly askew; and always the wind moaning around because it stood so high and exposed.

My next oldest cousin Sumitra and I once saw something there—no, wait. It was actually what we didn't see. We'd been combing our hair at an upstairs window and chanced to look out upon the nearest, most dazzling and tangible rainbow we'd ever seen: one end arched solidly over the haunted house, the other dipping down right into the road to town, close enough to touch. We dropped our combs, held hands—so as not to lose that touch, you know?—and ran, ran, ran over the rocks toward it. Of course, the closer we got the farther it receded. You too? What happened? No, nothing so lucky with us. We could see one end on the road to our right, and the other just beyond the dilapidated house to our left, but nothing overhead. Maybe we were right underneath where the light was being refracted? Oh, alright. Spare me your scientific theories. But I was never to know what it was really like. Sumitra, always inventive, finally said: "Maybe the ghosts ate the top of the rainbow." So we left it at that.

Across the rocks, as we returned, something strange was going on at Tiger House. Noise: from the big room downstairs where the petromax lamp would be lit and screen doors closed at dusk. Now they stood open. It was as if two armies had been drawn up. Uncle and Aunt on one side, a crowd of angry men on the other, all yelling together about setting a bad example, until Uncle finally held up his hand.

"You refuse then?" one of the men shouted.

"I refuse," Aunt said without fuss.

The crowd made a concerted movement aimed at Uncle.

"I agree with my wife," Uncle said, just as unfussed.

That brought on a wave of derisive sniggering. "Listens to his wife," somebody commented, and somebody else taunted him with the Tamil phrase for "henpecked." Uncle didn't respond. The man who had shouted raised his fist—like this. No one said anything after that. The silence grew louder than the noise. It was like another version of the rainbow. What was there? What was not there? Then they all turned and left. Uncle and Aunt waited until the last of them had disappeared across the clearing on to the road into town.

At the bottom of the waterfall a couple of boulders stand like that, the torrent rushing every which way around them until it slows down at the curve by the temple. But they say water wears down stone.

"Don't be frightened," Aunt said, seeing us at the door.

"Who were those people? What did they want?"

"A deputation of orthodox elders from town, angry because I invited the Zamindar's wife to lunch tomorrow."

I didn't tell you about the Zamindar's wife, did I? She belonged to what used to be called the dancing girl caste—trained artists dedicated ostensibly to the temple, actually to corrupt priests and men who paid. Yes, I know, we've talked our throats dry about the evils of the system, and that other tradition of the geisha in Japan, which had its own autonomy. Our women were considered the disreputable ones of course— victim turned culprit, as you say—not the men they serviced. In my mother's generation dancing still had a bad name, though some women had started to break ground; and by the time you've come along things are a lot better. I'm told parents even pull strings now for the first public performance of their daughters' debut, the *arangetram*. You're right, it's not really better at all, only perhaps in terms of women who dance.

Do you remember those nights during the riots in Bombay a few years ago, when the city was burning and we were hiding our Muslim neighbors? For the first time you were ashamed of being a Hindu, so furious you were crying—what was it you said? That the very notion of a fundamentalist Hindu was an oxymoron. True, but look at it, child. Look where it all began, with that age-old split in our culture between religious tenets and social codes. On the one hand so transcendently wise and peaceful: live and let live, no holy wars, no crusades, no holier-than-thou conversions, no killing and maiming in the name of religion. On the other hand, a culture that has survived for over five thousand years with one-half of its population never touching the other. That very word "untouchability" is indictment enough. The caste system may have begun simply enough as a matter of trade guilds . . . bartering skills in kind while empires rose and fell overhead. But look at the bigotries and divisions it ossified into, from all that way back. It's not just a vein, it's a mine of sanctioned inhumanity, available for anyone stupid or cruel or corrupt enough to dip into, no questions asked. My own place of spirits also had this split in it, it wasn't just pretty or primordial. The same people who venerated the ninth century poet spat on the Zamindar's wife.

Aunt sat us down that afternoon and talked about this. She never tried to hide facts in the name of bringing us up properly, another reason we loved being with her. She told us the Zamindar's wife Kamala was barely out of her teens, just a few years older than Ramu over here thwacking his cricket bat. Trained all her life to be a superb dancer, she didn't particularly like to dance. Married to the Zamindar, she didn't have to; he tried to make everything as easy and gentle for her as possible.

"But I've seen the Zamindar," cousin Leela said. "He's supposed to be mad, and he's easily as old as Uncle." She herself was the oldest of us girls, always making objections we somehow liked her for—she seemed to have a certain kind of brains for the rest of us. You know, in some ways we were far more protected than your generation, than our grandmothers' too, who were child brides, remember. So though we didn't know what this age thing was with grown-ups, when they were all so old anyway, we dutifully parroted them and cried out, "Oh, poor lady," about the Zamindar's wife.

The smile in Aunt's eyes didn't quite reach her mouth. "That's not your business," she said. "Your business as hosts in this household is to make them both feel welcome, and to do it yourselves. You can all help serve the meal. The little ones set out bowls and platters, and you bigger boys bring in the dishes for Bhatta. He's still frightened of the panther." The rickety wooden-roofed walkway from kitchen to dining room was open to wind and weather and wild animals. You could cover the dishes against exposure, but you couldn't cover more than your own head.

At noon the next day, the Zamindar's car drove in from town. The driver stepped out and opened the rear door. First the Zamindar emerged. He looked—what? Bulbous. In that heat and sun he wore a tailored English suit, dress shoes, a hat, a tie, a scarlet cummerbund, and seven overcoats. Afterwards we teased Uncle that we didn't know he was an invisible dancer, but that was the effect. He seemed to move around the Zamindar without actually moving, the way Aunt sometimes did around us; and slowly, one after the other, one a little larger than the next, each overcoat came off. Somewhere along the way the tie and the cummerbund did too; he removed his hat, and wiped his face and neck and hands. Suddenly he looked a lot thinner, and got comfortable.

Ah, but the Zamindar's wife! She was like the flash of a bird's wing, a butterfly skimming the air—almost not whole, but part of something that showed you the whole more perfectly than you'd ever see it in your life. We were all mesmerized, watching her open-mouthed, her slaves forever. Any cliché you want, help yourself. You know, it wasn't just that she was beautiful. She was happy. Incomparably happy. Which was against everything we knew: her mad old husband, her terrible cruel unjust life. Nobody could take her away from herself, the way she stood by that loving man, so proud of her in all his overcoats, in that sun, in that clearing, by the jungle behind Tiger House.

Leela, of course, muttered, "For how long?" but we didn't care. Yet we were almost afraid to touch her, brush by her, lest she break. And she seemed almost as entranced with herself as we were with her. There weren't many mirrors in Tiger House, but one hung in an old wooden frame on the corner wall outside the dining room. Patting her blue-black hair she'd glance fleetingly into it, or tilt her head on one side to catch the light glinting on her amethyst ring. Oh, we adored her: her amethysts, her butterfly glances.

If her husband wore overcoats, she wore silk. Not simple summer cottons like Aunt's, but heavy, heavy glowing South Indian shot-silk, all rose and aubergine and gold. Going out for an appointment, Aunt would absentmindedly stick a wristwatch on her left forearm and thrust the traditional bangles on her right. Kamala had gold, pearl, and enameled bracelets from each wrist to elbow, and a diamond watch peeped between them. Fascinated, I looked from her to her husband. He had taken off his overcoats by then and pushed back his shirtsleeves to eat better, but on each wrist he still wore seven watches, with manly leather straps.

At lunch he also glanced at these embellishments, his own as well as his wife's—but only in connection with drought and floods and plans to return most of his inherited land to his tenants. "I'll have to sell these things or we won't be able to manage. I've already waived the taxes, and will give back everything except the Home Fields. But nothing is any use without a good harvest. And since the floods, you see, rebuilding isn't the problem, it's relocation. These orthodox Brahmin fellows make trouble if the farmers' villages come too close. That at least I can deal with. How am I to fight the clouds and the sun and the rain?" He had been speaking with his mouth full, and when he paused to swallow we could hear all seven wristwatches ticking.

On our next trip to the waterfalls we passed their house. Not the Zamindar's ancestral home which sprawled on the eastern outskirts of town, but the place he had built for Kamala as a marriage gift, where they lived with her mother. Quite soon after that lunch, Aunt and I paid her a courtesy call since she didn't go out much. She sat like a little mountain on the biggest chair in the house, set right by the front door where she could see everything—a jolly lady with her face so plentifully daubed with powder that it caked in the crease on her neck. "You stop dancing, suddenly, you get fat," she'd said, not sounding very sorry about it. Then she smiled at her daughter and became beautiful. "Not like my Kamala," she said. "Not like my Kamala." The house itself was not whitewashed but pinkwashed, with a pink compound wall to match; ("Gaudy," cousin Leela said), lacy balconies, Moorish arches, and a garden crammed with cannas and marigolds. It stood in a direct line between Tiger House and the waterfalls. We could see it bright as a toy from the town road, all the way until we turned off toward the temple.

We'd all piled three-deep into Uncle's protesting old car that day—even Bhatta having been persuaded to join us. As we scrambled out, there near where the poet had once sat to write her poem, we ran bang into Ramu and Shamu's fabled sheikh from the Sahara.

At any rate, this was a man dressed in full Arab regalia, bowing to each direction of the compass: making four Meccas of his own. When he noticed us he started to speak: not in Tamil but in the Hindi of the north, with a wonderful accent at once guttural and mellifluous, like Persian poetry. "I have been to Shiraz," he said. "I have been to Tabriz. Now I finally reach Teheran, and they put me in jail. Is this just? Only Allah can help."

The sun glinted on his prison bars and vaporized them as we breathed. Two attendants, who came hurrying up to guide him toward the waterfall, became no more than gnats to be brushed away, while he resumed the direction of his prayers: north, south, east, west. . . . And our everyday South Indian trees spread out resplendent against the sky like the Persian Empire in all the blues and greens and golds of an illuminated manuscript. For quite awhile after Independence, until hell surfaced everywhere, our ambassadors from Iran were always poets, did you know?

That afternoon the path to the falls was very crowded. A neighboring Ayurvedic hospital sent its patients twice daily—the schedule never precisely fixed, but they always got first preference. So we waited until they went by, their heads pungent with medicinal oils, to the broad and rather slippery stone ledge cut into the rocks, its double railings giving them a handhold to clutch while they stood in a safe row beneath the pounding of the waterfall. At that moment somebody called out,

"Look! LOOK!!" A question mark of smoke was rising above the trees from the direction of Tiger House. Oh God, child, to have Uncle and Aunt and Bhatta right there within sight was the definition of "relief," the eye of the storm inside all the surrounding chaos and panic. People were shouting and running toward the smoke, fire engines came blaring and jangling in from town. Somewhere in the stampede the sheikh and his attendants disappeared. I never knew what became of them.

Tiger House, mercifully empty, hadn't been harmed—perhaps the venom against Uncle and Aunt didn't run deep enough. At Kamala's place the fire had been so carefully engineered that though the structure was of brick and not wood, by the time we could get anywhere near it, all that remained of the gaudy pink through the choking stench and dust and smoke was blackened rubble and broken archways.

Her mother had been pulled out, chair and all, as she drowsed by the front door. She was crying in the middle of the road, berserk, refusing to let Aunt take her home. "Why couldn't it have been me, why couldn't it have been me? Why couldn't it have been me? My child, my beautiful child, what harm did you ever do to anyone?"

Kamala had gone upstairs earlier than usual for her afternoon nap. The Zamindar, coming home, rushed in, and needed immediate rescuing himself, so terribly burned that he had to be hospitalized for the rest of the year.

They said: only a madman would have rushed in like that. They said: only a madman would have started giving his land to his tenants before the government asked him to. They said: if this is madness, it is so big and so kind, how can anyone put a name on it? He better not die.

He didn't. He scarcely lived, but long enough to complete the distribution of his property.

Nobody said anything about Kamala. Nobody could.

Our days and nights at Tiger House were a part of it all, though we could say nothing to the grown-ups, and—now I know—they could say nothing of it to us beyond what we all knew. Tiger Hill was part of it too, the invisible leopard, the cruelty everywhere, everywhere.

For months afterwards Uncle was in the thick of the trial. Definitions of another kind: "arson," "conspiracy," "murder." None of them bringing her back.

We went to the falls one last time that summer, to say goodbye to the poet—for some of us her place of pilgrimage now became part of our own stumbling journeys to knowledge.

Sumitra and I stood hand-in-hand as usual, hesitating at the entrance to the bathing ledge. Sunlight on the outer spray kept dazzling our eyes with a hundred small rainbows. We knew we'd see a million far more incandescent and exhilarating once we actually got underneath, but we continued to hesitate. Then someone pushed us in, and the first pounding of the waterfall came down like a fist on our back, sucking our breath away.

Contributors

Paula Gunn Allen is professor of English, American Indian studies, and creative writing at the University of California, Los Angeles. She is the author of a novel, several collection of poetry, a collections of essays, a collection of traditional and contemporary American Indian myths she "rendered," and one collection of critical essays. Her recent publications include *The Song of the Turtle: American Indian Literature 1974–1995; Life Is a Fatal Disease: Collected Poems 1968–1995;* and, with Patricia Clark Smith, *As Long as the Rivers Flow: The Stories of Nine Native Americans,* all released in 1996. Her work has been translated into Italian, French, Dutch, and German.

Marilou Awiakta is the author of poetry books, a children's book, *Rising Fawn and the Fire Mystery,* and of *Selu: Seeking the Corn Mother's Wisdom.* She is also a widely published essayist, the recipient of many awards including the Distinguished Tennessee Writer Award, the National Organization of Women's Person of Quality Award, and the National Conference of Christians and Jews Leadership Award. She is a cofounder of the Far Away Cherokee Association of Memphis.

Robin Becker is the prizewinning author of the poetry book *All American Girl,* and of short stories. Her previous books include *Back Talk* and *Giacometti's Dog.* She received a fellowship in poetry from the National Endowment for the Humanities and was a fellow at the Bunting Institute of Radcliffe College. She is the poetry editor of the *Women's Review of Books* and an associate professor at the University of Pennsylvania.

Marguerite Guzman Bouvard is the author of numerous books in the fields of psychology, women's studies, and politics. She has also written four books of poetry, including the prizewinning *Journeys Over Water*, edited a collection of poetry and short stories of exiled writers, *Landscape and Exile*, and her poetry has been widely anthologized. Her more recent books include *The Path Through Grief: A Compassionate Guide* and *Women Reshaping Human Rights: How Extraordinary Women are Changing the World.* She is currently a resident scholar with the Women's Studies Program at Brandeis University.

Laurence B. Calver is an actress, translator, and editor who lives in London. She has written a play on the life of Anaïs Nin and was the female lead in the original cast of *The Buddy Holly Show* and in the Israeli film, *The Flying Camel.* She has been a reciter with the British Symphony Orchestra at the Royal Albert Hall and has been featured in numerous television productions.

Christina Chiu is the author of *Lives of Famous Asian Americans: Literature and Education* and *The Teen Guide to Staying Sober.* Her short stories have appeared in an anthology, *Not the Only One,* and in the *Asian Pacific American Journal.* She is currently working on a novel. She is a founder and former trustee of the Asian American Writers' Workshop in New York City.

Michelle Cloonan has published numerous books and articles on the preservation of cultural heritage and the history of publishing and the book trade. She has received several grants and awards, including grants from the National Endowment for the Humanities and a Robert Vosper Fellowship of the International Federation of Library Associations. She is an associate professor and department chair of Library and Information Science in the graduate school of Education and Information Studies at the University of California, Los Angeles.

Martha Collins is the author of three prizewinning books of poetry, *The Arrangement of Space, A Catastrophe of Rainbows, and A History of Small Life on a Windy Planet,* as well as a number of essays. She has translated the poetry of Nguyen Quang Thieu, *The Women Carry River Water,* for the University of Massachusetts Press. She is the director of the Creative Writing Program at Oberlin College where she also teaches poetry.

Jean Gould is the author of the novel *Divorcing Your Grandmother* and editor of *Season of Adventure: Traveling Tales and Outdoor Journeys of Women Over Fifty.* She is currently editing a new collection of essays, *Dutiful Daughters.* Her essays and short stories have been widely anthologized. She has been a teacher of fiction and writing workshops for many years.

Padma Hejmadi is the author of *Birthday, Deathday, and Other Stories.* Her books of fiction and nonfiction have also been published under the name of Padma Perera. Her shorter work has appeared in the *New Yorker Magazine* and *Parabola,* she has been anthologized by India's National Academy of Literature, and included in a number of collections of international and contemporary women's writing. In 1997 her work was represented in the *Vintage Book of Indian Writing,* edited by Salman Rushdie. Her books *Views from a Portable Tradition* (a reader of fiction, nonfiction, poetry, and photography) and *Sumi Spaces* (a work of creative nonfiction) will appear in 1998 with Capra Press and the University of California. Ms. Hajmadi is also a widely exhibited collage artist and photographer.

Anna Kimmage and her parents fled to Czechoslovakia via Mexico during the McCarthy Era, and they also spent a year in China after the Slansky Trials. She returned to the United States when she was twenty-one and attended graduate school at the University of Chicago. She is the author of *An un-American Childhood* and of numerous articles. She teaches interdisciplinary courses in the humanities as well as Russian at the State University of New York in Plattsburgh.

Florence Ladd is the former director of the Mary Ingraham Bunting Institute of Radcliffe College and the author of the prizewinning *Sarah's Psalm,* as well as articles in the field of environmental psychology. For many years she has studied gender and social issues and housing and urban development as it influences the status of black women in the United States and abroad. She lives in Vermont, where she is affiliated with the School for International Training, and she is currently working on her second novel, *Isaac's Seasons.*

Monty S. Leitch is a native of Virginia and has been a columnist for the *Roanoke Times* for the past twenty years. She is the author of short stories and essays which have been published in *Shenandoah, Union Street*

Review, the *Writers' Digest* and other literary magazines. Her awards include *Shenandoah*'s 1992 Thomas H. Carter Prize for the best published essay, the Hollins Critics Prize for Short Fiction, and a fellowship from the National Endowment for the Humanities.

Aimee Liu is the author of *Cloud Mountain,* 1997 which has been translated in several languages, and *Face* (1994), as well as of *Solitaire,* a highly acclaimed account of anorexia nervosa. She edited business and trade publications, worked in television and was an associate producer for NBC's *Today* show before turning to full-time writing. She has coauthored seven nonfiction books and written numerous articles on medical and psychological topics.

Beryl Minkle, LICSW is a psychotherapist at Tapestry: A Counseling and Educational Center, a mediator, and Coordinator of Counseling Services at the Episcopal Divinity School in Cambridge, Massachusetts. A community activist, she cofounded and directed Harbor Me, a support and advocacy nonprofit organization for battered women and their children in the Boston area, and she provides training and consultation to schools, businesses, and community organizations on diversity, conflict resolution, and organizational development. She is a former newspaper reporter and has published articles in sociological journals.

Naomi Shihab Nye is the prizewinning author of four collections of poetry including *The Red Suitcase* and *Words Under the Words: Selected Poems.* She has also written a collection of essays, *Never in a Hurry: Essays on People and Places,* has edited *This Same Sky,* an award winning anthology of international poetry, and *The Tree Is Older Than You Are,* a bilingual collection from Mexico named a Best Book of 1995 by the American Library Association. The author of numerous children's books, her first novel for teenagers, *Habibi,* and a new picture book, *Lullabye Raft,* is forthcoming. She was featured by Bill Moyers on the television series, *The Language of Life,* as well as on NPR's *All Things Considered.*

Patrica Traxler has published three volumes of poetry and has completed a novel, *Houses,* and a collection of short stories, *The Eternity Bird.* She has been a Bunting Institute Fellow in Poetry and has also won Radcliffe's Presidential Discretionary Award, as well as the Open Voice Award for Short Fiction from the Writer's Voice of New York City.

Her poetry and fiction have appeared in numerous magazines and literary journals and one of her poems was selected for inclusion in *The Best American Poetry* (1994).

Ana Alomá Velilla is author of a book of short stories, *Una luz en el camino,* and of poetry, *Versos claros como el agua.* Her stories have appeared in numerous anthologies, most recently in *Cubans of the Diaspora,* edited by Julio E. Hernánez Miyares. She has been a professor of Spanish literature at Boston University and Regis College.

Annelise Wagner is the author of four books of poetry, including *Hand Work,* a winner of the Eileen W. Barnes Award, and of *The Phoebe,* a Journal of Literary Arts Short Story Award winner. Her work has been anthologized and most recently appeared in *The Crimson Edge: Older Women Writing,* edited by Sondra Zedenstein.

Mary Helen Washington is a professor of English literature at the University of Maryland and editor of *Black-Eyed Susans, Midnight Birds,* and *Invented Lives: The Tracing of African-American Literary Traditions.* She is currently working on a memoir about growing up black, female, and Catholic in a working class family.